W9-CZU-432

INTRODUCTION TO LIBRARY TECHNICAL SERVICES

INTRODUCTION TO

LIBRARY

TECHNICAL

SERVICES

BY
FRANCES
SIMONSEN
BERNHARDT

Acquisitions Librarian
Northern Virginia Community College
Annandale, Virginia

1979   THE H.W. WILSON COMPANY   NEW YORK

Copyright © 1979
By Frances Simonsen Bernhardt

All rights reserved. No part of this work may be reproduced or copied in any form or by any means, including but not restricted to graphic, electronic, and mechanical—for example, photocopying, recording, taping, or information and retrieval systems—without the express written permission of the publisher, except that a reviewer may quote and a magazine or newspaper may print brief passages as part of a review written specifically for inclusion in that magazine or newspaper.

Printed in the United States of America

Library of Congress Cataloging in Publication Data

Bernhardt, Frances Simonsen.
  Introduction to library technical services.

  Bibliography: p.
  Includes index.
  1. Processing (Libraries) I. Title.
Z688.5.B47 025'.02   79-12630
ISBN 0-8242-0637-1

Acknowledgments

Grateful acknowledgment is made for permission to reprint the following material:

Classification schedules: reprinted from the 10th Abridged Edition of *Dewey Decimal Classification and Relative Index* by permission of Forest Press Division, Lake Placid Education Foundation, owner of copyright.

Title pages and Cataloging in Publication Data: from *The United States Congressional Directories, 1789-1840*. Copyright © 1973 Columbia University Press. Reprinted by permission of the publisher; from *Chinese Family Law and Social Change*, edited by David C. Buxbaum. Copyright © 1978 by the University of Washington Press; from *Medieval Music*, by Richard H. Hoppin. Copyright © 1978 by W. W. Norton & Company, Inc.

Excerpts from *Cutter-Sanborn Three-Figure Author Table, Swanson-Swift Revision*. Copyright © 1979 by Richard A. Cutter. Courtesy of Richard A. Cutter per his agent, Esther M. Swift. Distributed by Libraries Unlimited, Inc.

Catalog cards: Baker & Taylor cards, copyright by The Baker & Taylor Company; Harper & Row card for Library of Congress, courtesy of Harper & Row, Publishers; LJ cards, copyright by LJ Cards (Xerox BiblioGraphics); METRO catalog card, courtesy of Metro Litho Company; Modern Learning Aids card for Library of Congress, courtesy of Ward's Natural Science Establishment, Inc.

Excerpts from *ALA Rules for Filing Catalog Cards*, Second Edition, Abridged. Copyright © 1968 by the American Library Association. Reprinted by permission of the American Library Association.

Library forms: reproduced by permission of Clayton Junior College, P.O. Box 285, Morrow, GA 30260.

Contents

Preface

THE READERS for whom this book is intended are those who want to learn how books and other materials are acquired and organized for use by libraries. Thus, this book is a general introduction to technical services, for the following categories of people:

1. those presently employed in a library
2. those enrolled in a course of study leading to a library career
3. those who desire to know more about library technical services before making a career decision

With this readership in mind, the book includes discussions of both theory and practice. Although it is not basically a procedures manual or a book of helpful hints, it does include some instruction in basic technical services procedures and some suggestions that may prove useful to practicing technical services personnel.

This book was written more specifically as a textbook for a course in technical services in a two-year library/media technology program. The best textbook for such a course is not necessarily one that is directly addressed to prospective library/media technical assistants, but may instead be a book presenting technical services from a more general viewpoint, which can be related by the instructor to the particular needs of his students.

The principal objective has been to give readers a general understanding of various phases of technical services work and an interest in further study of the subject. The scope of the book is broad. It not only covers the acquiring, cataloging, and processing of all types of library materials but offers a comprehensive presentation in a manner relevant to libraries of all sizes and to technical services personnel at all levels from clerk to professional librarian. An attempt has been made to stimulate interest and provoke discussion by describing both sides of controversial issues and occasionally presenting a particular point of view, as in the chapter on library subject headings.

One of the objectives of this book is to provide an introduction to the study of cataloging. It should be noted that detailed rules adhere to AACR 1967, which has been the code generally followed by most libraries. With the publication of AACR 2 in late 1978, many rules were changed. Variations contained in the new rules and a discussion of the rules are included in the Appendix.

FRANCES SIMONSEN BERNHARDT

CHAPTER 1

Library Technical Services: What They Are

DEFINITION.

ONE WAY to divide the work performed in libraries is to say that it consists of public services and technical services. Answering reference questions, reading stories to children, and charging out books to patrons are examples of public services (also called user services). Typing book orders, cataloging books, and pasting in book pockets are examples of technical services.

Public services are readily observable by the library user. Frequently, librarians and library assistants with widely varying duties are dismayed to discover that their friends and relatives believe that their work consists chiefly of circulating books, since this is one of the most visible of library functions. Few people who have not worked in a library are aware of the many different types of activities that must be performed to help a library, especially a large library, serve its public.

Technical services are usually performed behind the scenes. In many libraries, staff time spent on technical services equals or exceeds time spent on public services. Although work in technical services usually involves little or no direct contact with the library's users, lack of public contact is not the sole criterion for defining technical services. Certain nonpublic functions, such as shelving books and typing overdue notices, which are closely connected with the circulation of books, are not normally considered part of technical services. Technical services are usually considered to be the operations involved in acquiring the library's materials and organizing them for use. The two major areas of technical services are acquisitions and cataloging. Technical services also include the physical preparation of materials for shelving and often the related routine of book repair. Since technical services need not be limited by type of material, they usually include the ordering, receiving, and cataloging of audiovisual materials, serials, and other materials as well as books.

VARIATIONS FROM LIBRARY TO LIBRARY.

Libraries are like people. No two people are exactly alike and no two libraries are exactly alike. However, we sometimes find it useful to group people into categories, such as children and adults, men and women, or students and workers. Likewise in discussing libraries we may differentiate between public libraries and private libraries, school media centers and university libraries, or small libraries and large libraries.

It is seldom safe to assume that because a particular library operation is satisfactorily performed in one way in a particular library, it is performed or should be performed the same way in other libraries, even other libraries of similar size and type. The existing standards for different types of libraries, cataloging codes, schedules of classification, and textbooks on library operations have not brought uniformity to the ways in which different libraries meet their objectives.

Many books have been written about the administration of different types of libraries. Many books have also been written about cataloging and classification, which are an important part of technical services. Some books have also been written about acquisitions and a few about the area of technical services in general. However, people who have worked in technical services for many years will never find their experiences exactly reflected in any book and will probably disagree with certain portions of any book that covers their areas of interest and proficiency. Likewise, in visiting libraries other than their own, they will often be surprised to observe new ways of performing the basic library operations, some of which they will admire, but others of which they will disapprove. Beginning workers in technical services should be particularly wary about generalizing from their experiences in particular libraries to how similar work is performed in other libraries.

Library systems and individual libraries organize technical services in many different ways. In municipal or regional public library systems, one main library may do the ordering and cataloging for all libraries in the system. In public school systems, a service center or central office may do the ordering, cataloging, and processing for all schools. It is also possible for independent libraries to join together to establish a central processing center to meet many of their technical service needs. Even in a library system served by a central processing unit, certain functions usually considered to be in the realm of technical services will probably be performed by the individual libraries—for example, receipt of magazines and other serials may be recorded, cards filed in card catalogs, gifts received and processed, and books repaired as the need arises. Moreover, it is useful for personnel working in such libraries to have a basic understanding of acquisition and cataloging problems, so that they will not unduly blame their service centers for what appear to be delays, errors, or inconsistencies.

In libraries that are responsible for their own technical services, the functions may be organized in a variety of ways. Some libraries are divided into public services and technical services divisions. In these libraries, the public services division usually includes reference and circulation, and the technical services division includes acquisitions and cataloging. However, in most elementary and high school libraries and many other small libraries, there is no organizational separation of technical services from public services. The librarian and staff (if there is a staff) work on whatever needs to be done, in many cases using time not required by active service to the public to perform the necessary technical service functions.

In large libraries, whether university libraries or public, a single two-part split into public services and technical services is unusual. Such libraries are usually organized into many departments, including circulation, reference, acquisitions, cataloging, serials, documents, gifts and exchange, newspapers, archives, rare books, audiovisuals, humanities, social sciences, science and technology, and other functional, subject, and form-of-material departments. Although there may be an advantage to coordinating the technical service functions of acquisitions and cataloging by placing them under the authority of one person, large libraries often do not find this expedient.

It is chiefly in medium-sized libraries, such as junior college learning resource centers, small college libraries, and medium-sized public libraries, that the two part division into public services and technical services takes place. An advantage of placing acquisitions and cataloging together in one department is that they cover closely related types of work. Acquisitions personnel search to verify information given on book requests before books are ordered; cataloging personnel search to verify correct forms of names and other information as part of the cataloging process. Acquisitions personnel record receipt of serials, and cataloging personnel catalog them. One of the possible unfortunate results of separating acquisitions from cataloging is that sometimes an attitude of competition rather than cooperation develops, with each department blaming the other for errors and delays. Regardless of how acquisitions and cataloging are organized, the process of acquiring and cataloging books and other materials should be considered in totality so that the entire technical service function can be performed smoothly and efficiently.

WORKERS IN TECHNICAL SERVICES

Library personnel can be separated into a number of different job levels, such as: librarians, school media specialists, library assistants, library media technical assistants, library clerks, library aides, and library pages. Although there is considerable variation among libraries in the use of these terms, certain generalizations can be made.

The term *librarian*—sometimes called "professional librarian"—is commonly reserved for personnel with a master's degree in library science. At the elementary and high school levels, the term *library* has often been replaced by the term *media center*, to indicate that all types of materials are included, not just books. Along with this change in terminology the title *school librarian* has frequently been changed to *school media specialist*. A bachelor's degree, a teaching credential, and a specific number of hours of library science (or media) courses are usually required. Persons educated or certified as librarians or media specialists are considered professionals.

The term *library assistant* is sometimes used to refer to a staff member with a bachelor's degree and responsibilities just below the professional level, but it may also be used as a general term covering all nonprofessional staff. In college and university libraries, students often work part-time as library assistants.

A *library media technical assistant* is a semiprofessional library worker who is a high school graduate and probably has either several years of library work experience or has graduated from a two-year library technology program. A *library clerk* often has clerical or secretarial training, but probably no specific education in library procedures.

At the bottom of the career ladder are the student *library aide* (usually unpaid), who works in a school library, and the part-time *library page*, who locates and shelves books and other materials, as well as performing other simple tasks.

Because technical services include many duties that do not require the knowledge or skills gained by acquiring a master's degree in library science, in many libraries there are two or three times as many library assistants or clerks as there are librarians working in the area of technical services. Professional librarians working in this area are often responsible for such duties as managing the acquisitions budget, determining policies and work procedures, assigning duties to other staff, resolving difficult bibliographic problems, and cataloging materials for which cataloging copy is not available. Paraprofessional (semiprofessional) and nonprofessional assistants have such duties as assisting with verification of book requests, preliminary cataloging, comparing books with catalog cards, preparing books for circulation, and various typing and filing assignments.

Whether technical services personnel are working at the professional, paraprofessional, or nonprofessional level, it is advantageous for them to know as much as possible about all technical services assignments. For example, it is useful for the librarian in charge of technical services to understand the advantages and disadvantages of various ways of labeling book spines with call numbers even though labeling book spines will almost certainly not be one of the librarian's duties. As another example, clerks or library assistants working in acquisitions may perform better if they understand how the materials budget is allocated and how books and other materials are selected.

Four occupational descriptions taken from the U.S. Employment Service's *Occupations in Library Science* (Washington, DC, Govt. Print. Off., 1973) are shown in Figures 1 through 4. The descriptions in Figures 1 and 2 are for the professional positions of acquisitions librarian and

ACQUISITIONS LIBRARIAN
(library) 100.288-010

OCCUPATIONAL DESCRIPTION

Directs technical processes connected with purchase of books, periodicals, and other library materials and may select or participate in selection of materials: If involved in selection, reviews publishers' catalogs and announcements 'and compiles lists of publications to be purchased or recommended for purchase. Compares selections with card catalog and orders in process to avoid duplication or supervises workers who perform this work. Selects vendors on the basis of such factors as discount allowances and delivery dates. Compiles statistics on purchases, prepares necessary reports, and may maintain book budget records and receipt records for book and money gifts. Supervises clerical personnel concerned with the clerical aspects of ordering and receiving library materials. May recommend acquisition of materials from individuals or organizations or exchange with other libraries. In academic situations may work in cooperation with teaching faculty to select materials. May circulate selection lists to branches and/or departments for comment.

EDUCATION, TRAINING, AND EXPERIENCE

Master's degree in library science, with emphasis on publishing and bibliography. One or more foreign languages frequently required. May require similar experience, with demonstrated organizational and supervisory ability.

WORKER TRAITS
Aptitudes

Verbal aptitude required to supervise workers and to deal with vendors and professional library staff.
Numerical aptitude necessary to prepare reports, compile statistics, and maintain budget records.
Clerical perception needed to compile information, prepare reports, and review the work of others.

Interests

A preference for activities involving business contact with people and for activities of a concrete, organized nature.

Figure 1. From *Occupations in Library Science*

(continued on following page)

Temperaments

Adjustment to situations involving a variety of duties and adaptability to assuming responsibility for the direction, control, and plannng of an entire activity.

Physical Demands and Environmental Conditions

The work is sedentary, is performed indoors, and requires reaching and handling, talking and hearing, and seeing. Clerical perception necessary to maintain library materials, to keep records, and to conduct library routine.

Figure 1. (continued)

CATALOGER

(library) 100.388-010

cataloger–classifier; descriptive cataloger; subject cataloger; catalog librarian; classifier

OCCUPATIONAL DESCRIPTION

Classifies library materials, such as books, films, periodicals, recordings, maps, and serials, according to subject matter and compiles catalog cards to identify materials and integrate information into library catalog: Reviews materials to be classified and cataloged, using wide knowledge of subjects, vocabulary, and historical and current events. Searches information sources, such as book reviews, encyclopedias, and technical publications, to locate more subject information to assist in classifying. Selects and assigns classification numbers and descriptive headings according to Dewey Decimal, Library of Congress, or other library classification system. Composes annotations (explanatory summaries) of material content. Compiles cataloging information, including title, author, classification number, publishing data, and bibliographic and other information for clerical preparation of catalog cards. Insures that related activities, such as tabulating number of cards and requisitioning additional cards, are performed. Usually supervises workers who copy classification numbers into library materials and file catalog cards.

In smaller libraries may, in addition, perform many of the duties listed under LIBRARIAN. In larger or specialized libraries catalogers may

Figure 2. From *Occupations in Library Science*
(continued on following page)

specialize in particular materials, such as journals or foreign language publications. May supervise staff, including LIBRARY TECHNICAL ASSISTANT and LIBRARY CLERKS. (The CATALOGER usually does only original classifying and cataloging—on materials not previously classified by the Library of Congress or other major contributor to *National Union Catalog*. Cataloging-classifying which consists of editing Library of Congress or similar copy is usually performed by semi-professional or senior clerical personnel.) Descriptive cataloging and classifying may be separate functions in some libraries.

EDUCATION, TRAINING, AND EXPERIENCE

Master's degree in library science. Further training is on the job and may last from 1 to 4 years, depending on the nature of assignment. Some jobs may require languages in addition to English.

WORKER TRAITS

Aptitudes

Verbal aptitude and clerical perception needed to catalog and classify library materials.

Interests

A preference for activities of concrete and organized nature and for situations that are primarily nonsocial in nature.

Temperaments

Adaptability to situations involving repetitive work that is carried on according to set procedures and sequences and to situations involving the control and planning of an entire activity.

Physical Demands and Environmental Conditions

The work is sedentary, is performed indoors, and requires reaching and handling and seeing.

Figure 2. (continued)

cataloger. The description in Figure 3 is for a semiprofessional position of library technical assistant. The description in Figure 4 is for the nonprofessional position of library clerk. Since the descriptions of library technical assistant and library clerk include public services as well as technical services, the technical service duties have been underlined.

The occupational descriptions in *Occupations in Library Science* are generalized and do not describe specific jobs in particular institutions. Some idea of actual technical service jobs available may be gleaned from the following job descriptions and requirements taken from advertisements in journals and newspapers:

TECHNICAL SERVICES HEAD for medium-sized public library. Coordinates acquisitions and cataloging operations for central library and three branches with materials budget exceeding $100,000 annually. Supervises three clerical assistants. Qualifications: M.L.S. from an A.L.A. school plus two years acquisitions and/or cataloging experience preferred.

ASSISTANT SERIALS CATALOGER. Duties include full cataloging of serials in LC classification and daily revision of public catalog files under direction of serials cataloger. Master's in library science from A.L.A. accredited program is required and working knowledge of at least one foreign language is essential.

ASSISTANT CATALOGER. Preprofessional position in cataloging and indexing using both traditional and computerized methods. Qualifications: good typing, ability with detailed work.

LIBRARY ASSISTANT. Prefer previous library experience and foreign language ability. Requires 40 WPM accurate typing. Will be using SOLINET terminal.

LIBRARY TECHNICAL ASSISTANT

(library) 109.368-012

library technician; library assistant

OCCUPATIONAL DESCRIPTION

The LIBRARY TECHNICAL ASSISTANT is a semiprofessional library worker who performs any of the following duties in a library: Provides information service, such as answering questions regarding card catalogs, and assists the public in the use of bibliographic tools, such as the Library of Congress catalog. Does simple descriptive cataloging, such as fiction and children's literature. Files cards in catalog drawers according to the system used. Answers inquiries of a nonprofessional nature on telephone and in person and refers persons requiring professional assistance to LIBRARIAN. Verifies bibliographic information on order requests. Supervises workers in a section of a department or division, such as ordering or receiving sections of an acquisitions department, card preparation activities in a catalog department, limited loan or reserve desk operations of a circulation department, or maintenance of stacks. Performs more difficult clerical tasks as assigned.

EDUCATION, TRAINING, AND EXPERIENCE

High school graduation. May require library clerical experience of 2 to 3 years or may require graduation from a junior college program for LIBRARY TECHNICAL ASSISTANT. On-the-job training is customary.

WORKER TRAITS

Aptitudes

Verbal aptitude required to assist the public, do cataloging, and direct the work of other workers.
Numerical aptitude and clerical perception required to do recordkeeping and perform many clerical tasks.

Interests

A preference for activities of a routine, concrete, organized nature, involving business contact with people.

Temperaments

Adaptability to variety and change and to dealing with people beyond giving and receiving instructions.

Physical Demands and Environmental Conditions

The work is light, is performed indoors, and requires reaching and handling, talking and hearing, and seeing.

Figure 3. From *Occupations in Library Science*

LIBRARY CLERK

(library) 249.368-050

OCCUPATIONAL DESCRIPTION

Performs a variety of duties in a library: Examines shelves to determine that books and other library materials are correctly located according to identifying markings. Sorts books and publications according to classification code and returns them to shelves, files, or storage area. Types information on catalog and shelf list cards and files cards. Types orders, files order record material, and retrieves order records for received materials. Verifies correctness of bibliographic information on order requests. Maintains serial and periodical check-in files. Locates books and publications for patrons and searches for requested materials not readily accounted for. Charges books to patrons, recording identifying data and due date by hand or using photographic equipment. Receives returned books from patrons, inspecting books for damage, verifying due date, and computing and receiving overdue fines. Prepares bills for lost or overdue materials. Issues identification cards to borrowers according to established procedure. Repairs books and other materials, using mending tape, paste, and brush. Depending on type and size of library, may perform receptionist or stenographic duties.

EDUCATION, TRAINING, AND EXPERIENCE

High school graduation. On-the-job training is customary.

WORKER TRAITS

Aptitudes   Verbal aptitude required to assist patrons.
Numerical aptitude needed to make arithmetic computations.
Clerical perception required to perform a great variety of filing, typing, copying, examining, and sorting activities.

Interests   A preference for activities dealing with things and objects and involving business contact with people.
A preference for activities of a routine, concrete, organized nature.

Temper—aments   Adaptability to working under specific instructions and according to set procedures and sequences.
Adaptability to dealing with people in actual job duties beyond receiving instructions.

Physical Demands and Environmental Conditions

The work is light, is performed indoors, and requires reaching and handling, talking and hearing, and seeing.

Figure 4.   From *Occupations in Library Science*

Law Library. Position available for individual with accurate typing skills with minimum 1 year clerical experience. Responsibilities include processing of books, bibliographic searching.

Library. Paraprofessional, circulation and acquisitions position. Full-time. Library exp. and some arts history background req.

Technical Services: A Satisfying Career.

Job descriptions of library technical services do not reveal why it is such an interesting and satisfying career. Some jobs appear exciting when one hears about them but can be repetitious and full of frustrations for many people employed in them. Technical services positions, on the other hand, often surprise people by being much more challenging and interesting than expected. Among library positions, jobs in reference work are probably the most prestigious, with highest appeal to people considering a library career, but if you talk to people who have worked in libraries for many years, you will find many who prefer cataloging or other technical services work to reference. Some will perhaps tell you that they began their library careers wanting to work in reference but now prefer behind-the-scenes work in building and organizing the library collection.

Technical services personnel are builders. They build the library collection. Construction workers may well enjoy looking at huge buildings that they have helped to build. It is just as satisfying for library employees to walk through their libraries' collections and recognize books that they have helped select, purchase, or catalog. If it is a small collection, they may have had a principal part in creating a collection that meets the needs of the library's users and is frequently admired by visitors. If it is a large collection, their contributions will be interspersed with those of many other people, but they may derive special pleasure when they watch as a library patron finally finds just what is needed, right where it was supposed to be, and know that the book would not have been there if it had not been for their efforts.

Another reason why work in library technical services can be satisfying is that it gives staff members a chance to use knowledge and skills acquired through many years of education, but which are in little demand in most occupations. In college and university libraries and other libraries containing foreign language books, foreign language ability is an asset for anyone working in acquisitions or cataloging. Knowledge of almost any subject, from sports to nuclear physics, will also aid the cataloger or bibliographer and may even be the basis for a special assignment in that area.

It is not true, as some believe, that the people best suited for work in library technical services are those who do not like to work with people. As with many other careers, the ability to work harmoniously with other people is one of the principal requirements for success in library technical services. Not only is it important that everyone in technical services work together as a team, but also that operations and policies be coordinated with other divisions of the library. However, it may be true that people who prefer intellectual problems to "people" problems have a particular affinity for technical services, because it is an intellectually challenging area of work and does not usually involve direct contact with the public.

At both the professional and nonprofessional levels, the principal difference between technical services work in large libraries and small libraries is that in large libraries each staff member is usually assigned to one particular area, while in small libraries each staff member performs many different technical service functions. It is somewhat like a choice between being a little fish in a big pond or a big fish in a little pond. Fortunately, some people derive their greatest satisfaction from being a master of one particular skill, such as cataloging rare books or handling serials efficiently, while others like to work at a variety of activities.

Why You Should Know about Technical Services even if Your Career Lies Elsewhere.

Knowing about technical services is useful even for people who do not plan to make it their career. Library administrators should be well informed about acquisitions and cataloging so that they can make appropriate decisions. For example, an administrator who does not understand all of the cataloging operations may be unrealistic in an estimate of the extent to which cataloging costs can be cut by simplification or automation of work routines.

Public service personnel cannot adequately assist the public in using the library's catalog if they do not understand it themselves. A knowledge of cataloging principles and rules of library filing will help them interpret the catalog to those whom they are assisting. Understanding how the materials in the library collection have been acquired and organized will also help them answer patron questions about the holdings of the library and the location of particular items.

Workers in small libraries may not feel that they need to know all of the intricacies of cataloging and other technical service routines, since simplified procedures are used in their libraries. However, knowledge of policies and procedures used in large libraries will be useful to them if they are involved in interlibrary loan or if they use large libraries for their own personal research. The more one knows about library technical services, the more one can benefit from the vast resources in the libraries of our country.

CHAPTER 2

Libraries, Authors, and Publishers

PROBLEMS IN ACQUISITIONS AND CATALOGING.

WITHOUT UNDERSTANDING the variety of materials contained in libraries and the many sources from which these materials come, it would be difficult to appreciate the problems that may be met in acquiring and cataloging them. Aren't there reference books that list all the possible books that libraries may wish to acquire? Isn't it true that library materials fall into definite groups—such as books, phonograph records, and magazines—each of which may be acquired from a particular source? Isn't all of the necessary information for cataloging a book given on the title page or other standard location in the book? Since books, audiovisual materials, and other library materials are produced by companies that would like to sell them to libraries, aren't the materials produced in formats easily usable by libraries? To understand why these assumptions are not true we must consider the types of materials that libraries have chosen to collect and the motivations and methods of the people who produce them.

WHAT LIBRARIES CONTAIN.

The history of libraries goes back even further than the history of the printed book. By 2700 B.C. Sumerians had established libraries of clay tablets. In ancient Egypt libraries held large collections of papyrus rolls, and in medieval Europe manuscripts were collected and organized into libraries. It was not until the middle of the fifteenth century that Gutenberg invented the printing press and the printed book became an important medium of intellectual communication. Since libraries have always collected the records of civilization in whatever form they appear, it should not be seen as revolutionary that libraries of today contain many other materials in addition to books.

Diversity of materials collected is not limited to one type of library. In many elementary and high school libraries, audiovisual materials are a basic part of the collection. The motion pictures, phonograph records, filmstrips, tape cassettes, slides, and other audiovisuals are presented by teachers to their classes and used directly by students. Public libraries also frequently have collections of motion pictures, phonograph records, and art prints for use of their patrons. A few public libraries even circulate more unusual items, such as garden tools to adults and educational games to children. In university and research libraries, audiovisual collections are less important, but collections of periodicals, newspapers, documents, technical reports, maps, and microforms frequently rival book collections in importance. It is not unusual for such libraries to spend at least as much on periodical subscriptions as they do on books.

All library materials have one thing in common: their origin lies in the creative and intellectual capacity of the human mind and in the need to communicate with others. A novelist tells what he has learned about life through his stories, a composer creates music that is recorded on tape or disc, and a scientist writes a journal article communicating the results of his research. Any medium, whether print or nonprint, that is used to communicate human thought and creativity is an item of possible interest to libraries.

To publish means to bring before the public, to issue, or to offer for sale. Publishers are intermediaries between authors and the public. Books and other materials that libraries may choose to acquire are produced and distributed in many different places by many types of publishers. Some of them will be described in this chapter.

TRADE BOOK PUBLISHERS.

Trade books are books such as novels and popular nonfiction that appeal to large numbers of people and are sold to individual purchasers through the book trade—i.e., bookstores. Because of their wide audience, these are the books that usually sell the most copies per title and are likely to appear on the best-seller lists. If you wrote a novel, a biography, or other book on a subject of current interest, you would probably submit it to a trade book publisher. Unfortunately, unless you have had previous books published or are a very famous person, your chances of having your manuscript accepted would be slim, because most publishers are able to publish very few if any of the many unsolicited manuscripts they receive. Publishers more seriously consider books by known authors, books by experienced writers on popular subjects, and books by experts in their field. Sometimes the idea for a book originates with the publisher, who then commissions an author to write the book.

Selecting manuscripts for publication is one function of a publisher's editorial staff. Editors also help prepare manuscripts for publication, many times working closely with the authors. Authors sometimes attribute the success of their works partly to the excellent guidance their editors have given them. Another function of the publisher is arranging for the physical production of the book, although the actual typesetting, printing, and binding are usually done by independent manufacturers. The final important function of the publisher is the marketing and distributing of the book. Publishers sell to wholesalers and jobbers, who in turn sell to bookstores and libraries. Most publishers also sell directly to bookstores and libraries, or even individual customers.

The publishing of trade books is an important industry in our country, not only because of the dollar amount of total sales, but also because of its contribution to the spread of knowledge and the enjoyment of literature. In recent years trade books, including both adult and juvenile books, have accounted for over half a billion dollars in sales. Almost all libraries except specialized research libraries buy large numbers of trade books. Fortunately, current trade books are usually well advertised, listed in *Books in Print* and other bibliographical tools (these tools will be discussed in Chapter 4), and can be obtained easily by libraries either from wholesalers or directly from the publishers. They are also the books on which libraries can expect to receive the largest discount from the publisher. The number of acquisition and cataloging problems caused by trade books is usually small when compared with the total number of trade books received by a library.

SPECIALIZED PUBLISHERS.

The line between trade and specialized publishers is not a distinct one. In fact, many trade book publishers also publish books in one or more specific areas, such as reference books, religious books, or school and college textbooks. Specialized publishers, however, can probably be identified by the fact that instead of trying to sell their books to a wide general audience through the book trade, they concentrate their efforts on one type of book and one particular audience or market. Some types of publishing specialization follow:

1. Technical and scientific books
2. Medical, nursing, and related fields
3. Business and management publications
4. Religious books (including Bibles)
5. Legal books
6. Music and books about music
7. Juvenile literature and nonfiction
8. Bibliographies, indexes, and books on library science
9. Reprint publications

10. Encyclopedias, dictionaries, atlases
11. Elementary and secondary school textbooks
12. College textbooks

This list is intended merely to suggest possible specializations. Some publishers would not fit into any of the above categories, either because their particular specialization is not listed or because they publish in several of these areas. A few very large firms publish in virtually all these fields.

The first seven types of specialized publications listed above are of particular interest to particular types of libraries, given in the same order below:

1. Science libraries
2. Medical and hospital libraries
3. Business libraries
4. Church and other religious libraries
5. Law libraries
6. Music libraries
7. Elementary school libraries and children's sections of public libraries.

However, books in these seven areas are also acquired by other libraries. Categories 8, 9, and 10—reference books and reprints—are of particular interest to many types of libraries.

Elementary and secondary school textbooks, on the other hand, are not purchased by most libraries. College textbooks are sometimes purchased by academic or public libraries, chiefly because they may serve as basic books on specialized subjects. At the advanced level, books used as textbooks for one course may also be used as supplementary reading for other courses, or for information by anyone interested in the particular subject.

Specialized publishers range in size from very large to very small. Books from the major specialized publishers are as easy to obtain as trade books, but the price discount, if any, is usually less. On the other hand, some small specialized publishers have their market so well identified that they do little advertising, do not list their works in bibliographic tools, and do not use library book wholesalers. Their books frequently present problems to acquisitions personnel.

University Presses.

University presses are nonprofit, are owned by or connected with universities, and specialize in publishing scholarly books and journals. Almost every state in our country has at least one university press.

College and university libraries buy many university press books, because these books are characteristically well researched and authoritative. University presses often include among their titles books about the state or region in which they are located. These books, as well as some of the other more general books, are frequently purchased by public or high school libraries as well as college libraries.

Books from university presses can usually be obtained from library book jobbers or directly from the publishers without any special problems.

Subsidy Publishers.

If an author is not able to have his book published by a regular publisher, but feels strongly that what he has written should be published and will sell well once it is published, he may deal with a subsidy publisher. In this case the author pays to have his book published, hoping to get the money back in royalties later. Subsidy publishers are sometimes called "vanity presses," but this term is misleading, since it is often not vanity, but a need to communicate, that moves an author to take this route; he feels he has something important to say and has no other forum in which to say it. Unfortunately for the hopeful author, most books published by subsidy publishers sell few copies and are seldom read, because they have a reputation for poor quality and are not likely to be reviewed in the major review media.

Libraries rarely purchase these books but often receive them as gifts of the author.

AUTHORS AS PUBLISHERS.

Another route that an author who is eager to see his work in print can take is to hire a printer himself. He can then handle the sales through friends, local stores, or direct mail advertising. Histories of counties or towns are often published in this manner since they are chiefly of local interest. With certain types of books, the author may even be able to sell many copies and make a large profit. An example would be a book on how to be successful financially, socially, or sexually written by an author knowledgeable in advertising and marketing techniques and advertised widely in appropriate newspapers and magazines or by direct mail.

Many libraries do from time to time need to buy self-published books, such as those on local history or scientific treatises, and when they do they often face problems. Bibliographic citations for these books and even the books themselves seldom indicate the name and address from which they can be obtained. Moreover, it is not always the author of the book who pays the printer and handles the sales; it may be a friend or relative. As far as library acquisition is concerned, these books may be considered the opposite of trade books; their numbers are few, but the percentage of problems is high.

ASSOCIATIONS AND INSTITUTIONS AS PUBLISHERS.

Almost every large national association publishes materials in its area of interest. Examples are the American Library Association, the American Dental Association, and the American Mathematical Society. Smaller, more specialized, organizations and local and state societies also frequently issue books, pamphlets, and journals, although their publishing operation may not be so well organized. In addition, institutions such as schools, libraries, and museums produce and distribute a wide variety of print and nonprint materials. It should not be assumed that because a university has a university press, all publications of the university can be obtained from this press. Various departments and divisions of many universities sell their own publications in operations entirely separate from that of the university press.

Since most associations and institutions have a special area of interest, their publishing is in some ways similar to that of the specialized publishers mentioned earlier. However, there are two differences, both of which tend to make their publications more difficult for libraries to obtain. They are nonprofit, so they have less incentive to sell their publications. Also, they are not in the business of publishing but usually publish chiefly to serve the interests of their members, so they may not feel any particular need to sell their materials to a wider audience of libraries. Library wholesalers sometimes supply the publications of major organizations, but many must be ordered directly from the issuing institution.

GOVERNMENT PUBLICATIONS.

The United States Government, in the course of fulfilling its constitutional duties issues well over 10,000 publications a year, far more than any commercial publisher. These range from leaflets to heavy bound volumes.

State and city governments are also prolific producers of printed materials, many of which are substantial enough to be counted as books. The United Nations and other international organizations also produce books, pamphlets, and journals.

The United States Government Printing Office requires prepayment and requests libraries to use special forms for ordering its materials. Therefore, methods of ordering them differ from usual acquisitions procedures. Documents from state and local governments are frequently free to libraries, but if not they must be ordered directly.

FOREIGN PUBLISHERS.

According to UNESCO figures the United States accounts for about one seventh of total world book output. The types of publishers discussed so far also flourish in many other countries. Not only English-speaking countries such as Great Britain, Canada, and Australia but also countries such as the Netherlands, Denmark, and West Germany, produce English-language books and journals, particularly in the area of scientific communication. University and research libraries in the United States acquire materials in many other languages as well as English; so the total world book production, not just the English language portion, is a field of possible selection for them.

Acquiring and cataloging foreign materials is a challenging area of technical services work in libraries that obtain large numbers of publications from abroad.

NONBOOK MATERIALS AND PUBLISHING DIVERSIFICATION.

Two of the major types of nonbook materials, serials and audiovisual materials, will be discussed in later chapters. A chapter will also be devoted to miscellaneous materials such as pamphlets, documents, maps, and music scores. In regard to the publication of nonbook materials, it is useful to realize that, although they may be produced by firms specializing in a single medium,—say, microfilm or phonograph records—they are also frequently issued by the same commercial publishers, nonprofit organizations, and governmental organizations that publish books.

For instance, Harper & Row, the publisher of such best-selling novels as *Love Story*, also publishes a very specialized journal, *Journal of Obstetric, Gynecologic and Neonatal Nursing*, and a set of filmstrips on the metric system. Publishers of magazines such as *American Heri-*

tage, Reader's Digest, Newsweek, and *Time* may also publish books and audiovisual materials.

PROBLEMS CAUSED BY PUBLISHERS.

Individual publishers and certain categories of publishers create specific problems for libraries in the areas of acquisitions, cataloging, and physical preparation of volumes. Also, the sheer quantity and lack of systematic organization of total world publishing activity make the work of technical services personnel as well as other library workers more difficult.

Advertising methods of publishers can lead to problems for acquisitions personnel. When a book is advertised without a date of publication being given, it is easy to assume it is a recently published book. However, it may be merely a new printing of an old book, not a new edition as the person selecting the book supposes. On the other hand, it may be a book that the publisher plans to publish in the near future, but if publication is delayed, libraries may be left with unprocessed requests or open orders. Book advertising may also mislead by not giving complete or accurate information on the authorship of books.

Book publishers who make certain that all of their books are listed in bibliographic tools, such as *Cumulative Book Index* and *Books in Print*, make it easier for libraries to order their books. On the other hand, publishers who do not list their books, do not work with library book jobbers, and require advance payment are not likely to achieve maximum library sales.

Catalogers are chiefly concerned with the book itself rather than the advertising or bibliographic listing. Since the title page is the basic source for descriptive cataloging, publishers create problems for catalogers when they give either too little information, too much information, or misleading information on title pages. Suzanne Massonneau in "Bibliographic Control and Cataloging Cost Control: Interlocking Problems" (*Library Journal*, June 15, 1973, pp. 1890-93) gives some interesting illustrations of these three types of title page problems and makes a plea for standardization of bibliographic data by publishers.

Books that are poorly constructed or cheaply made add to processing and book repair problems. Margins may be so narrow that a book cannot be rebound. Occasionally a book available only in a cheap edition will have the index printed on the inside back cover, a chart or pictures on the inside front cover, and will not contain a blank page on which a library book pocket can be pasted. As a rule of thumb it may be stated that any publisher who issues his books in spiral bindings, especially with narrow margins, does not have the library market in mind, since these books do not hold up under library usage and may be difficult to rebind.

Are too many books published? The work of librarians, as well as bookstore managers, would be easier if fewer books were published, because they could then acquire a higher percentage of total book output and encounter fewer situations in which they could not supply books requested by patrons. However, from the viewpoint of a beginning novelist or poet, or a university professor who wants to advance his career by publication, it might seem that not enough books are published. They would like to see at least one more book published, namely their own. It would probably be to almost eveyone's advantage if fewer books of poor quality and for which there is little demand were published, but it is hard to see how such limits could be arrived at that did not abridge the right of people to express themselves.

THE SOURCE OF TECHNICAL SERVICE PROBLEMS: ANOTHER VIEWPOINT.

Perhaps it is not with the publishers that technical services problems begin, but with the libraries themselves. The 1978–1979 *Books in Print* lists about 500,000 titles available from 6,900 American publishers; so do libraries really need to obtain books from the minor publishers and obscure associations that are not included? Many publishers publish high quality, nicely printed, well-bound books with all of the information needed for cataloging clearly stated; so why do libraries insist upon buying flimsy books, printed and distributed in haphazard fashion? Looking at the problem from this viewpoint, it can be seen that the multitude of books and other materials produced throughout the world do not become of concern to technical services personnel until someone decides that particular ones should be acquired by their libraries. The next chapter will discuss how books and other materials are selected for purchase by libraries.

CHAPTER 3

How Books Get into Libraries:
Step 1, Book Selection

BOOK SELECTION sets in motion the technical services processes of ordering books and organizing them into a usable collection. Much of what will be said in this chapter about book selection and in the following chapters about the acquisition and cataloging of books is equally applicable to serials, audiovisual materials, and other library materials, but there are also special problems and procedures associated with nonbook materials, and they will be discussed in later chapters.

Although technical services personnel do not necessarily participate in book selection, their work is affected by selection policies and procedures. The books selected may be easy to acquire and catalog, or they may present many ordering and cataloging problems. Selection may be performed in a systematic manner with all necessary information indicated on selection requests, or selectors may leave the work of locating ordering information to the technical services staff. If you are working with the ordering, receiving, or cataloging of books and do not understand the basic principles and problems of book selection, you may well be puzzled by the reasons for adding certain books to the library collection.

This chapter will discuss who participates in book selection, what reference and reviewing tools they use, and some criteria for book selection. These subjects will be discussed, not as an attempt to teach book selection, but with the goal of giving an understanding of how books get into libraries.

PARTICIPANTS IN BOOK SELECTION.

The participants in book selection may be divided into two groups, members of the library staff and other selectors. In public libraries, most of the selection is done by librarians. In small and medium-sized public libraries the entire professional staff may participate, possibly with subject areas or certain selection tools assigned to particular librarians. In large public libraries and library systems there may be a special book selection committee or staff.

In school, college, and university libraries selection responsibility is shared by librarians and teaching faculty. Faculty members request books in their subject areas. Librarians often request books that cross subject lines, books for recreational reading and independent study, and reference books. Faculty are specialists in particular subjects, and they also know what topics they will be covering in their courses and what their assignments to students will be. Librarians, on the other hand, are in a better position to observe what books are actually used and to understand the objectives, needs, and resources of the library.

Librarians in special libraries—libraries maintained by or for users with special interests or needs—usually have some selection responsibility, but in most cases the clientele of the library also generate requests.

Among librarians, both technical services and public services librarians participate in book selection. Nonprofessional workers may also initiate requests, but these may need the approval of a professional librarian. There are three distinct types of participation in book selection:

1. Making suggestions. Anyone who works in a library or uses a library is usually welcome to suggest

books for consideration by the persons responsible for selection.

2. Submitting book requests. This responsibility is usually given to librarians, teachers, or other professionals associated with the library or the institution of which it is a part. The requests may need to be approved by a book selection committee or a departmental chairman.

3. Coordinating selection and final approval of requests. The head librarian or library director is accountable for the judicious spending of the library book budget. If available funds are not enough to cover all requests, a decision must be made on priority and allocation of funds. In large libraries responsibility for functions such as encouraging book selection in all appropriate areas, allocating funds among subject areas and/or types of materials, and assigning priorities to requests may be delegated by the library director to other librarians. If the library has a separate acquisitions department, this department will probably have at least some responsibility for coordination of book selection. University libraries frequently have subject bibliographers who oversee selection in particular subject areas. If they are not part of the acquisitions department, they work closely with it.

BOOK SELECTION OBJECTIVES.

When members of a teaching faculty submit book requests to the library, they frequently have one or more of these objectives in mind:

1. To read or use the books themselves.
2. To assign the books to their students.
3. To suggest the books to their students as supplemental reading.

4. To provide material that their students can use when writing term papers or doing research projects.
5. To improve their library collection by recommending well-reviewed or good basic books in their teaching areas or subject specialities.

At the university level the first reason alone would be sufficient for buying a book, because university libraries usually try to support faculty research needs. At lower educational levels, libraries often do not buy books that only meet the personal needs of one faculty member; so a book might not be ordered unless one of the other objectives also applies. Notice that only the first two objectives assure that the book will actually be used. In most academic situations, there is nothing unusual about a faculty member suggesting a book for library purchase but not charging it out when it arrives.

When librarians select books for purchase, they may have in mind one or more of the following objectives:

1. To add to their collection books for which they have had, or expect to have, many requests.
2. To provide information on subjects about which they have little or no information or not enough to meet patron demand.
3. To acquire books by authors who are popular with users of the library.
4. To fulfill the library's obligation to support the curriculum (or programs) of the institution of which it is a part.
5. To add to the worth of their collection by acquiring books of lasting value, such as books of literary merit and basic books on important subjects.
6. To obtain reference books that will supply information needed by the users of the library.

It can be seen that these considerations are based on predictions of patron demand, the intrinsic merit of particular books, and the objectives of the library. In order to determine whether a book will be popular and whether it is a book of literary, artistic, or educational value, librarians and other book selectors read reviews and consult book selection tools.

AIDS TO BOOK SELECTION.

There are two principal types of book selection, retrospective and current. The most exciting type of retrospective selection is the choosing of books for a new library. Perhaps it has been decided that the library of a new community college should open with a collection of 10,000 books, and some periodicals and other nonbook materials. The books will, of course, be selected from all books presently available, not just from those currently being published.

Even in existing libraries there is often need to fill gaps in the collection. A library user may point out to the librarian at a public library that the library has no books about swimming. If the librarian agrees that the library should have some books on this subject, then instead of waiting until a new book on swimming is published and reviewed, he may seek information on those books presently available.

Of the many bibliographies and reference works that can give guidance to the book selector who is choosing the collection for a new library or adding books on certain subjects to an old collection, only a few of the best known will be mentioned here.

Public Library Catalog. 6th ed. (New York, Wilson, 1973) An annotated list of 8,765 nonfiction titles selected by practicing librarians, designed for use in public, college, and university libraries. It is arranged by Dewey Decimal Classification with an index of authors, titles, and subjects and has annual supplements. The H. W. Wilson Co. Standard Catalog Series also includes *Children's Catalog, Junior High School Library Catalog, Senior High School Library Catalog,* and *Fiction Catalog.*

Opening Day Collection. 3rd ed. (Middletown, Conn., Choice, 1974) Intended as a list of books that should be on the shelves of every junior or four-year college library the day it is opened. This is a short, highly selective list containing only 32 pages of book listings.

Books for College Libraries. 2d ed. (Chicago, American Library Association, 1975) A six-volume work listing books for a core collection of 40,000 titles. It is arranged by the Library of Congress Classification with author, title, and subject indexes.

Also useful in retrospective book selection is the *Subject Guide to Books in Print* (New York, Bowker, 1978), which lists about 450,000 books available from American publishers under 62,000 subject headings. This annual list is inclusive rather than selective, but it is useful when other tools list few if any books about a subject. *Book Review Digest*, which annually lists reviews for about 6,000 books, (New York, Wilson, annual) can be used when evaluations of particular books are needed.

Although there is sometimes a need to buy older books, a high percentage of books acquired by most libraries are recently published books. Reviews of new books are published in many periodicals and newspapers. Faculty members frequently select books on the basis of reviews in the specialized journals that they read. Reviewing media such as *The New York Times Book Review* and the *New York Review of Books* are intended for the general reading public but are also used by librarians.

The following are some of the best-known journals that carry book reviews especially for librarians:

Booklist is published by the American Library Association as a current guide to materials worthy of consideration by small and medium-sized public libraries, school media centers, and community college libraries. It includes children's books. About 4,500 books a year are reviewed.

Library Journal, in addition to carrying articles on library subjects, reviews about 6,000 adult books each year.

School Library Journal reviews about 2,500 books for children and young adults each year.

Choice reviews books that may be considered for purchase by college libraries. It is published eleven times a year and reviews from 600 to 700 books in each issue. The reviews can also be purchased on three-by-five-inch cards.

A more inclusive, but nonevaluative, listing of new books is provided by *Weekly Record*, formerly published as part of *Publishers Weekly*, but now issued separately. About 35,000 new American books are listed each year. It is used by some large libraries to keep current with what is being published; books of certain interest to the library because of subject, author, or publisher may be selected from it.

VALUE AND DEMAND.

There are two approaches to book selection that sometimes come into conflict. One approach is to try to select the "best" books. The other is to try to meet as many as possible of the demands of the library's patrons. Unfortunately, library users do not always choose to read only those books considered to be books of literary or educational value. Regardless of how good a book might be, few libraries would add it to the collection if they knew it would never be used. In actual practice, however, demand is seldom the sole criterion for book selection. Most libraries prefer well-reviewed books that promise quality over poorly reviewed books that because of the notoriety of the author or similar reasons may receive considerable demand.

Demand for books is not a simple, easy-to-measure concept. When projecting demand, the following considerations must be taken into account:

1. Some books, such as best-sellers, will be in great demand, but only for a short period of time. Other books, such as great works of literature, may receive occasional use over a long period of time.

2. Demand can be manipulated. The appearance of an author on a television talk show creates demand for a book, as does any other kind of media exposure. On the other hand, librarians can also create demand for particular books with displays, book talks, and other publicity.
3. Demand and need are not always the same. A patron may think he wants a book, but upon examining it may find it boring or useless. At the same time, the librarian may refer him to a book which actually meets his need.
4. At the time of book selection, demand can only be predicted, not measured. If after several years a book has not circulated, it may be recognized as a selection error, but this may be a case of hindsight being better than foresight.
5. The types of books already in a collection may influence demand. If a library has a reputation for providing chiefly recreational reading, it may not be used by people looking for information on specialized subjects, and thus there will appear to be little demand for informational books on such subjects.

Because of these considerations, selecting books on the basis of projected demand is not always a simple task. However, using the alternative criterion of value is even more difficult. Judging which books are the best books must first of all be based on the objectives of the library. A book that does not fall within the scope of a library is not a good book for that library. The content of the book must then be judged on the basis of its contribution to the store of information contained in the library or by its cultural or recreational value. Some of the other factors used in judging books are recency, accuracy, style of writing, and physical format.

Different types of libraries have different problems with conflict between value and demand. In a children's library, the problem may be whether to purchase books in series such as the Nancy Drew mysteries, which are frequently read but not generally regarded as among the best of children's literature. In a public library, the question may arise as to how much of the budget should be spent in buying multiple copies of best-sellers. In a college library, should money be diverted from the purchase of scholarly books that are used infrequently to the purchase of additional copies of books that circulate frequently?

As a first generalization about library book selection practices, it can be stated that both value and demand are frequently considered, and that when they come into conflict, the usual result is compromise.

OTHER GENERALIZATIONS ABOUT BOOK SELECTION.

Wide participation in book selection is usually encouraged. In addition to taking advantage of the expertise and interests of all associated with the library, it dilutes the personal biases and preferences of individual selectors.

Censorship is resisted in most libraries. In accordance with the Library Bill of Rights of the American Library Association, books are chosen because of positive values, not rejected because of possible partisan or doctrinal disapproval.

Examination of the books themselves is desirable, but not often possible. Book selection decisions are often based upon the reading of reviews. Publishers' advertisements are viewed with caution, because they do not present an impartial viewpoint. Visiting sales representatives are treated courteously, but purchasing decisions are not based upon how often publishers' representatives visit or how friendly they are.

Different libraries have different needs. There is not one group of best books for all libraries of a particular size and type, such as small public libraries. Even for libraries within a particular library system, it is usually advantageous for certain libraries to acquire some books unique to the system for the following reasons:

1. The present collections are probably not the same, so some libraries may have gaps in their collections that others do not.
2. The communities served may differ, so that different demands are made upon the libraries.
3. The total number of titles owned by the system will be greater if all libraries do not acquire exactly the same titles.

The acquisition of duplicate copies of books in great demand and replacements for lost or damaged books can be as important as the selection of new titles. Weeding of titles no longer needed also helps to keep the collection attractive and useful.

A final generalization is that written book selection policies are beneficial. They are useful, not only when complaints arise, but also as a guide to the participants in book selection.

COST OF BOOKS AS A FACTOR IN BOOK SELECTION.

In recent years there has been a tendency for book prices to rise at a faster rate than library book budgets. Few libraries can ignore the prices of individual books when making their selections for purchase. *The Bowker Annual of Library and Book Trade Information* (New York, Bowker) reported in the 1978 edition the following average prices of books published in the United States:

	1967-69	1976
Hardcover books	$8.77	$17.39
Mass market paperbacks	.79	1.60
Trade and higher priced paperbacks	3.24	5.63

The average price for all hardcover books does not reveal the whole story. In 1976, juvenile hardcover books averaged only $6.01, works of fiction averaged $9.96, but both the scientific and medical categories had an average price of over $24.00 per book. Book selectors for a children's library might consider a $12.00 book expensive, but medical librarians would not.

The judgment as to whether or not a particular book is overpriced cannot be based solely on consideration of the book as a physical object consisting of a certain number of pages, illustrations in black and white or color, or a hard or soft cover. Just as the wheat in a loaf of bread affects only a small part of the final retail price, likewise the cost of the paper in a book makes only a small contribution to the final price. The editorial and many of the production costs of publishing a title vary little with the total number of copies produced. Therefore, one large factor in the pricing of books is the number of copies expected to be sold. A highly specialized scientific title that will sell only a few thousand copies must be priced higher than an introductory textbook that will sell many times as many copies.

If cost is to be considered in book selection, list prices should not be the sole basis of consideration. If a novel has a list price of $7.00, but the library receives a 35% discount, the actual cost is $4.55. On the other hand, the library may order a $2.50 paperbound work directly from the publisher, be charged $.75 for postage and handling, and receive no discount. If, in addition, the library spends $2.00 to have the book bound, the total cost is $5.25. Therefore, it is possible for a book with a list price of $2.50 to cost the library more than a book with a list price of $7.00.

Technical services personnel are in a better position than other members of the library staff to observe the true costs of books to the library. Not only do they notice the discounts and added charges, but they quickly become aware that expenditures in staff time are much greater for some types of books than for others. Books that can be routinely ordered from a book jobber require less time than those that must be ordered directly, one book per order, from various associations and institutions. Publications not likely to be acquired or cataloged by the Library of Congress may require additional time in searching and original cataloging. (This will be more fully explained in later chapters.) Ordering and cataloging foreign and out-of-print books is more time-consuming than ordering and cataloging recent works of American publishers.

The size of the budget and the number of books acquired are not the only influences on the amount of technical services work to be done in a library; the type of materials selected is also relevant. Much of the challenge and satisfaction of technical services work is derived from acquiring and integrating into the collection books that are not easy to obtain or catalog, but that have been selected for purchase because of their value to the library. If libraries were to avoid the selection of problem books, technical services work would be less interesting, some searchers and catalogers might lose their jobs, and library collections would have important gaps in their holdings. The fact that certain types of materials require more acquisitions and cataloging staff time should not stop a library from buying them, but since the cost of books is a relevant factor in purchase decisions, processing costs should also be considered.

CHAPTER 4

How Books Get into Libraries: Step 2, from Book Request to Book in Hand

What Is Acquisitions?

The word *acquisition*, which means "the act of acquiring," is frequently used by libraries to refer to the process by which books and other materials that have been selected are obtained. *Acquisitions* is not merely a highbrow substitute for the word *ordering*. It is broader in scope because it includes not only the acquiring of materials by gift or exchange but also processes not normally suggested by the word *ordering*, such as locating information about materials to be ordered and the receiving of materials. Large libraries often have separate acquisitions departments. In medium-sized libraries, the acquisitions responsibilities may be delegated to a technical services division or may be kept under the direct control of the library director. In small libraries, such as school libraries, acquisitions work is performed, along with many other duties, by the librarian or staff.

The Request Card.

Library acquisitions procedures start with the arrival of requests for purchase of books and other materials. Many libraries encourage participants in book selection to record their suggestions on three-by-five-inch request slips or cards. Commercial library supply-houses sell book request cards, but some libraries design their own cards or slips to meet particular local needs. A locally designed book request slip is illustrated in Figure 5.

Library Use Only	CLAYTON JUNIOR COLLEGE Learning Resources Center		
Date Received	Author (Surname first)		
PC	Title		
O			
H			
BIP	Publisher		Year
BPR	List Price	Edition or Series	Vols.
CBI			
PTLA	Requested by:		Priority
FB			1 2 3
NUC	Additional purchasing information or comments:		
Other			
LC Card No.			

Figure 5.   Book request slip

The use of book request cards or slips has a number of benefits, some of which would be applicable in almost any library, even a very small one.

1. Participation in book selection can be encouraged by distribution of the forms. For example, teachers may be reminded to suggest books for the school library when they are given a new supply of forms.
2. The items listed on the form will hopefully encourage participants in book selection to give the information necessary for ordering, such as publisher and price. Notice that the form illustrated in Figure 5 is designed to elicit an expression of priority, which is useful in some situations.
3. Requests can be more easily prepared for ordering if they are in standard format. It is easier to alphabetize and handle a bundle of three-by-five-inch request forms than a miscellaneous group of memorandums and publishers' advertisements.

4. The results of acquisitions checking and verification can be recorded on the forms in a systematic manner.
5. Typing orders is easier if the information needed is given in a standard format.
6. The forms can be used in various files, such as a file of books to be ordered when funds permit. They can later be returned to the requester to indicate that the book has been received and is ready for use.

Although request cards are useful, they are not always used for all items selected. Many libraries are more interested in encouraging book selection than in simplifying acquisitions work. Selectors may be permitted to submit requests by initialing publishers' advertisements, dealers' catalogs, or book reviews. Acquisitions staff members sometimes fill out book request slips for these items, but in other cases lists or catalogs are checked directly against the library's catalog and order files to eliminate the need for writing slips for items already in the library or on order. If requests are submitted on three-by-five-inch cards or slips other than the official request forms, such as Library of Congress proof slips, cards purchased from *Choice*, or advertisement cards distributed by some publishers, it is seldom necessary to copy the information onto request slips.

AVOIDING UNNECESSARY DUPLICATION:
IS THE BOOK ALREADY IN THE LIBRARY OR ON ORDER?

Book selectors are not usually held responsible for ascertaining whether or not books they select are already in the library. In a large library, determining whether or not the library owns or has on order a particular book is not always simple. Even if the selector states that the book is not in the library, the acquisitions staff will probably do its own checking.

A first step in checking is often to compare book requests

against the library's catalog. In a library that has had problems with unnecessary duplication of books, acquisitions staff may wish to check the requests under both author and title. In many libraries, checkers use symbols to indicate whether or not the book is listed in the catalog, perhaps an "o" for not found, and a "√" for found. If the book is found, the call number is also recorded. If the library has a different edition of the book, the variations in edition are noted. Some libraries expect their checkers to indicate whether the author's name is located in the catalog and to correct the name given on the request, if necessary, to agree with the form used in the catalog.

Next the requests will probably be checked against the file or files maintained by the library for books currently on order and books received but not yet cataloged. Requests for books already owned by the library or on order are returned to the requesters.

What Is Bibliographic Verification and Why Is It Necessary?

Bibliographic verification is also called acquisitions searching or preorder searching. It is one of the more esoteric of library routines. If you are employed as a "searcher," it may be difficult to explain to your friends what you do and why it is so interesting. Bibliographic verification and searching have little importance in small libraries that order principally recent American books, and these mostly on the basis of reviews in the standard reviewing media. University and large research libraries, however, that acquire many foreign books, older books, and books from small, little-known publishers and associations often receive scant information from requesters and therefore have the most need for employees skilled in bibliographic verification. College libraries and other medium-sized libraries also do a considerable amount of acquisitions searching. Even small libraries, such as school libraries, do occasionally need to verify the existence of a book or find more information about it.

The purpose of bibliographic verification is to ensure that the information given on book requests is complete and accurate. Complete, accurate information is necessary in order to avoid unnecessary duplication of titles and to provide a basis for efficient ordering of books. If the author or title is given incorrectly on a request, a check of the catalog and files may not reveal that the library already owns the book or has it on order. Incorrect or missing information about the edition or series may also cause unintentional duplication. A book thought to be a new edition may only be a later printing; or the library may have a standing order for a series of which the book is a part.

To order books efficiently it is usually necessary or advisable to know whether they are in print (still available from the publishers), the prices, and the names of publishers. It is also necessary to locate the publishers' addresses, if books are to be ordered directly from the publishers, instead of from a wholesaler.

In many libraries, bibliographic verification also fulfills another function: locating information, such as the Library of Congress card order numbers and the correct form of the authors' names, that will be useful later on in cataloging the books. However, these services should be considered a byproduct of acquisitions searching, not a main purpose.

After requests have been checked in the catalog and order files, they are examined to determine whether verification is needed. If books have been selected on the basis of reviews in current issues of journals such as *Library Journal*, *Booklist*, *Choice*, or *Weekly Record*, little verification may be necessary. (If a series is given for a book, the searcher will want to ascertain whether his library already subscribes to the series.) Many other requests, however, will be missing crucial pieces of information or contain unreliable information and so will need to be verified.

If verification can be thought of as a game, the purpose of the game is not to locate as many titles as possible as quickly as possible, but rather to correctly fill in particular pieces of needed information. The searcher will use various bibliographic tools that give varying types of information with variable reliability. He needs to know not only which tools will be most likely to list particular books, but also what types of information they give and whether they can be trusted.

Books in Print (BIP) is often a starting point for bibliographic searching, not only because of the huge number of books included, but also because it attempts to list all in-print books that are published or exclusively distributed in the United States, regardless of date of publication. It is, therefore, a convenient source when the searcher has requests with many publication dates and some for which the date of publication is unknown. If a book is listed in BIP, no matter how old it is, it is usually still available from the publisher. A drawback of BIP as a verification tool is that it does not always list authors' names uniformly. The name of a particular author may be given in different ways because listings are taken directly from information supplied by publishers, who may use varying name forms. Thus, you will find the BIP listings for Twain, Mark, and Clemens, Samuel, and the many variant forms for Dostoevski. Because of the uncertainty as to how an author's name will be listed, it is advisable to check the title index when a book is not found under the name of its author. If neither author nor title can be located in BIP, further searching will be needed to determine which of the following possibilities applies:

1. The book is out of print (no longer available from the publisher).
2. The book was published too recently to be listed or is not yet published.
3. It was published by a minor publisher who does not list his books in BIP.

4. It is not a book published or distributed in the United States.
5. Both the author and title given on the request are misspelled or incorrect.
6. It is a government document, pamphlet, or possibly even nonprint material, such as a filmstrip or cassette tape (occasionally requesters neglect to indicate such information on their requests).

Forthcoming Books (FB) is a source to check when it is suspected that a book has only recently been published or has not yet been published. Like BIP, it is published by R. R. Bowker Company, and it gives approximately the same information about books listed.

American Book Publishing Record (BPR) and *Publishers' Trade List Annual* (PTLA) are two other Bowker tools. BPR is a monthly cumulation of *Weekly Record* (mentioned in the previous chapter). Unlike BIP and FB, it usually lists authors under established forms of name. It is cumulated into annual volumes and five-year sets.

PTLA is a collection of trade lists of over 2,000 American publishers. It is the tool to use when seeking information about the books of a particular publisher.

Cumulative Book Index (CBI) has a broader scope than the above tools, since it includes books published in the English language in all parts of the world. Each year CBI indexes 50,000–60,000 books with full bibliographic information. It is published monthly, except August, with quarterly and permanent annual cumulations.

The *Library of Congress Catalog* (LC) and *National Union Catalog* (NUC) sets, supplements, and cumulations list many more books than the bibliographies described above. The exact titles, subtitles, and dates covered by the various sets and cumulations cannot be briefly noted, but it does not take searchers long to become familiar with the scope of the ones owned by their libraries. The first set published, containing 167 volumes, was *A Catalog of Books Represented by Library of Congress Cards Issued to July 31, 1942*. The title is self-explanatory. Later the scope was expanded to include books reported by other major American libraries and the title became *National Union Catalog*. Published with monthly issues and quarterly, annual, and five-year cumulations, NUC lists books from all parts of the world in every language. The information given is as reliable and accurate as the skills of catalogers can make it. (However, a surprising number of books fall through this cataloging net without being caught.) Two pieces of information frequently needed by searchers—price and publisher's address—are not usually given in LC or NUC.

Figure 6 illustrates which bibliographies are useful for supplying particular types of information. An x means that a tool supplies a particular piece of information enough of the time to make it a useful tool to check. In using BIP and PTLA, searchers usually check only the latest edition, because each new edition supersedes the previous one. Since FB supplements BIP with information on new books, only issues listing books published too recently to be listed in BIP are usually used. In checking BPR, CBI, LC, and NUC, the volume for the year of publication may be checked first, but the searcher will also check the volumes for following years, since books are not always listed as soon as they are published.

Searchers in university and research libraries have available many other tools in addition to these basic six. Most major countries have bibliographies similar to those of the United States. For each country whose books one works with, it is useful to know if there is a bibliography listing books in print, a list of currently published books, a printed library catalog for the largest library of the country, and a bibliography listing books published in the past.

In small libraries, searchers may be hampered by insufficiency of the bibliographic reference collection. The *Li-*

COMPARISON OF MAJOR AMERICAN BIBLIOGRAPHIC TOOLS

	Correct Main Entry and Proper Form of Author's Name (see Ch. 7 & 8 for explanation)	Series, Publisher, Date of Publication	Availability (important for books more than a year or two old)	Price	Publisher's Address (usually listed in special section of tool)
Books in Print (BIP)		X	X	X	X
Forthcoming Books (FB)		X		X	X
American Book Publishing Record (BPR)	X	X		X	X
Publishers' Trade List Annual (PTLA)		X	X	X	X
Cumulative Book Index (CBI)	X	X		X	X
Library of Congress Catalog (LC) and National Union Catalog (NUC)	X	X			

Figure 6.

brary of *Congress Catalog* and *National Union Catalog* will probably not be available, nor may the other five tools all be present.

If during searching it is discovered that the author or title information given on a request is incorrect, it will be necessary to recheck the library's catalog and files to be certain that the book is not present under the correct author and title. If it is discovered that the book is part of a series, it is important to determine whether the library subscribes to the series. The process of preorder searching, as it has been described here, includes four major steps:

1. Checking requests against library catalog and acquisition files.
2. Sorting requests according to whether verification is needed and according to which tools are to be checked.
3. Verifying information on requests and finding additional necessary information.
4. Rechecking requests on which information has been corrected and checking all series in the appropriate files.

These steps are not uniformly perfomed in this sequence. If the information given on a batch of requests is seriously deficient (for example, only the authors' last names are given), it may be necessary to perform step 3 before step 1.

In some libraries, requests are sorted according to difficulty of verification, with the most difficult requests, such as those for foreign books, being given to the most experienced searchers. In other libraries, clerical assistants do the preliminary checking of all requests against the catalog and files, paraprofessionals perform most of the bibliographic searching, and librarians handle only the requests that present special problems.

Illustrated in Figure 7 is a book request that has passed through a library's search procedure. The typed information was included on the request when it was submitted. The current date was stamped on the request when it arrived in the technical services division. The two zeros after PC indicate that the book was not located in the public catalog of the library under either author or title. The underlining in La and France indicates that the searcher was uncertain under

| Library Use Only | CLAYTON JUNIOR COLLEGE |
| | Learning Resources Center |

Library Use Only	CLAYTON JUNIOR COLLEGE Learning Resources Center
Date Received JUN 2 7 '77 PC○ *o* O *o* H○ BIP ✓ BPR CBI PTLA FB NUC ✓ Other LC Card No. 65-15590	Author (Surname first) Beaujour, Michel, ed. Title La France contemporaine Publisher Macmillan Year 1965 List Price Edition or Series Vols. 9.95 8.50 Requested by: Priority J. Jones 1 2 3 Additional purchasing information or comments:

Figure 7.   Book request slip

which word the title would be filed and therefore checked both. The zeros after O and H indicate negative results in checking the "books on order" and "books here" files. A check mark after BIP shows that the book was located in *Books in Print*. The date and corrected price were written in on the basis of the entry in *Books in Print*. However, *Books in Print* did not give the author's first name, which was located in the *National Union Catalog*. The LC card number was also obtained from this source.

After requests have been verified, the next major step is the selection of the vendors from whom the books are to be ordered.

SELECTION OF VENDORS.

Some libraries order all or most of their books directly from publishers, but most libraries find that time in preparing orders, unpacking shipments, and approving invoices can be saved by grouping the books of many publishers together in one order to a library wholesaler or jobber (the two terms are used interchangeably). Although a library may order most of its books from one wholesaler, or different wholesalers for different types of books, it will also probably need to send some orders directly to publishers. In Chapter 2, indications were given of some of the types of publishers who do not usually use book wholesalers. "Rush" requests are also frequently ordered directly from publishers, although local bookstores are another possible source of supply.

Small libraries often do most of their business with one library book jobber; large libraries use different jobbers for different types of books and books from foreign countries. Arrangements with jobbers are not always formalized. If a library decides that the services of a particular jobber sound attractive and sends an order for a group of books of the type handled by the jobber, it is unlikely that the order will be rejected. However, if a library plans to order many books through a particular jobber, it is often useful to make advance arrangements as to how they are to be shipped and billed and how problems are to be handled. The discounts given by the jobber may depend upon the volume of business.

When choosing jobbers, libraries usually consider factors such as these:

1. Type of books handled. Can the jobber supply most of the books needed by the library or most of the books in a particular category, such as medical books or German books?
2. Speed. If the jobber has a large warehouse stock of the type of books needed by the library, his service will be faster than if he has to order the books from the publisher after receiving the library's order.
3. Discount. The discounts offered by different jobbers on particular types of books are important, and they should be later checked to see if practice follows promise.
4. Service. If the library has special billing and ship-

ping requirements, it may be important to select a jobber who will follow them. The number of errors and how they are resolved is also important.

5. Cataloging and processing. Libraries now have a wide choice of processing and cataloging services offered at reasonable prices by major book jobbers.

In addition to using a particular book wholesaler or list of wholesalers and ordering directly from publishers, libraries frequently order from the catalogs and advertisements of bookstores and book dealers who deal in out-of-print books. If it is suspected that some or all of the books in a catalog may be in print, *Books in Print* should be checked to determine whether the prices offered by the dealer are really bargain prices. Even for some very old books, suitable reprint editions may be available.

After a vendor has been selected for each book to be ordered, requisitions or purchase orders are prepared.

TYPING AND PREPARATION OF ORDERS.

Most libraries do not have a free hand in establishing acquisitions routines, since they must abide by regulations and follow procedures set by the institution or governmental unit of which they are a part. Chapter 5 will discuss the influence of these requirements upon ordering procedures and will also cover the accounting aspect of book purchasing.

Use of three-by-five-inch multiple-copy order forms, like use of three-by-five-inch book request cards, is widespread, but by no means universal. (Library catalog cards, which are also three-by-five inches, probably led the way in establishing this size as a standard for many library forms and records.) Also like book request cards, multiple-copy order forms either can be ordered from library supply houses or can be specially designed by a library to meet its own needs. A sample form is illustrated in Figure 8.

The number of parts in the multiple-copy order form

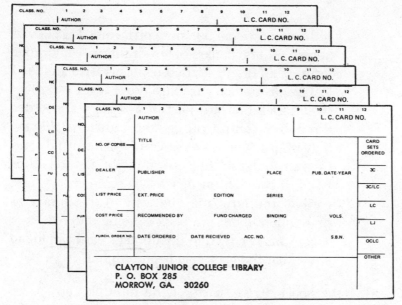

Figure 8. Multiple-copy order forms

varies with the needs of the library. Various parts may be used as follows:

1. One copy is sent to the vendor as an order.
2. A second copy is also sent to the vendor to be used as a report if the book is unavailable.
3. One copy is filed alphabetically by main entry or title in the library's file of orders outstanding.
4. One copy is filed chronologically or numerically by purchase order number. This file can be used to claim long-outstanding orders and to determine when an order is complete.
5. An extra copy of the order form may be filed in the numerical file to be used as the actual claim form sent to the vendor if the book does not arrive when expected.
6. If the book budget is divided into funds, one copy can be filed by fund so that the library can determine the amount currently on order for each fund.
7. One copy may be used to order Library of Congress cards or other printed catalog cards.

8. If the institutional business office needs a copy of library orders, copies of the multiple-copy order forms can be sent to the business office attached to a requisition or purchase order form.
9. In libraries that are part of a system and order through a central office, the individual library may keep one or more copies of the form and send the remainder to the central office. On the other hand, if the central office types the orders, one copy of the form may be sent to the library or branch for whom the book is being ordered.
10. A copy may be filed in the library's card catalog to show that the book has been ordered.

After the books arrive, parts of the multiple-copy order forms used in one of the previously mentioned ways may be redirected for other purposes:

1. The copy previously filed in the orders-outstanding file may be stamped with the date received and filed in a file listing books received but not yet cataloged.
2. Copies filed numerically or by fund may likewise be stamped with the date received and refiled numerically or by fund in files of orders completed. The actual cost of the book will, of course, have to be written on slips used for fund accounting purposes.
3. At least one copy of the form will probably accompany the book through the cataloging process.
4. After the book has been cataloged and the catalog cards filed, a copy of the form may be returned to the acquisitions staff to indicate that the record of the book may be pulled from the process file.
5. A copy of the form, possibly with the original book request stapled to it, may be returned to the person who requested the book indicating that the book has been received and cataloged.

Although librarians have been resourceful in devising a multiplicity of uses for the copies of multiple-copy order forms, individual libraries should keep their ordering systems as simple as possible. If there is only an occasional use for a particular file, the wisdom of maintaining it should be questioned.

EVOLUTION OF ORDERING SYSTEMS.

As one moves from small libraries to large libraries or from the past to the present, one observes the progression of ordering systems through a number of stages.

The first stage is a simple purchase order or requisition that includes a list of all the books ordered. In a small library that orders few books and issues infrequent orders, perhaps only one or two each year, this system may be entirely satisfactory. The book-request cards, in addition to copies of the lists, can be used for information and follow-up on the books ordered.

When a library reaches the stage at which it is ordering books weekly or daily and has many outstanding orders at any given time, lists become cumbersome and do not provide sufficient approaches to books ordered. The library may then find it practical to use multiple-copy book order forms. If at all possible, time should not be wasted typing both a list and multiple-copy order forms. Copies of the multiple-copy order forms attached to a purchase order can substitute for a list.

At a certain stage of development, the disadvantages of ordering many books on one purchase order become apparent. Vendors can seldom supply an order of 50 to 100 or more books in one shipment. Some books will almost certainly be out of stock or not yet published. Unless the library has an automatic cutoff date, it may be many months until the last book is supplied or its order canceled. When a library has hundreds of outstanding orders at any given time, maintaining exact records of the dollar amount outstanding on each order becomes tedious. Also, in order to keep accurate records on each order, it will probably be necessary to instruct vendors to ship and bill books from each order separately. If the vendor has thirty books ready to be mailed to the library, but they were ordered on five different orders, he must put them in five different boxes or packages and prepare five different invoices.

When these conditions become too burdensome to a library, a decision may be made to progress to the next stage of ordering development: a separate purchase order for each book. This may sound like retrogression, but it is actually a simplified procedure. The three-by-five-inch multiple-copy order form, which is serially numbered, is itself the purchase order. The copy sent to the vendor may be printed with shipping and billing instructions, or a form letter may be enclosed. It is, of course, not necessary to mail each order in a separate envelope. Hundreds of orders, or the daily typing output, can be mailed together. The vendor may ship and bill as many orders as he wishes on one invoice, listing the order number by each book. The official file of outstanding orders consists of one copy of each multiple-copy filed numerically. A drawback to this system is that few institutional business offices are prepared to maintain order files consisting of thousands of flimsy three-by-five-inch order slips. Where this system is in effect, the library usually maintains the necessary records and reports regularly to the business office. If this system cannot be put into effect, an alternative plan is to issue blanket orders to vendors from whom the library orders many books, and then follow through with suborders which consist of groups of multiple-copy order forms.

AUTOMATION.

The final level of development in ordering systems is the use of automation, which has been reached only in recent times and only in large libraries (and some special libraries).

In an automated ordering system, the typist typing multiple-copy order forms for each title is replaced by a keypunch operator who punches the same information (author, title, publisher, etc.) onto cards or tapes, which are then fed in batches into a computer once or twice a week. In a system of this type, the computer can be used to print orders, maintain records of encumbrances and payments (by fund if necessary), maintain the file of orders outstanding and books recently received, indicate orders that are overdue and need to be claimed, and provide various types of statistics. Instead of checking files of three-by-five-inch slips for books ordered or recently received, acquisitions staff members check computer printouts to determine whether particular books have been ordered or received. In some libraries, computer-output microfilm (COM) is used instead of printouts. All such automated systems that depend on punching cards or tape are called "off-line systems." In a development known as an "on-line system," the user communicates with the computer by means of terminals permanently connected to the computer by cables or telephone wires instead of via punch cards or tapes. The terminals may have keyboards like a typewriter, cathode-ray tube (CRT) screens like a television set, and a device to print out on paper the information on the screen. Information stored in the computer is available to the user within a few seconds. Additions or changes can be typed in immediately. Since the operator is in direct contact with the computer, this kind of system is sometimes referred to as an "interactive" system. All of the acquisitions functions performed by off-line systems can also be performed by on-line systems. A major advantage of an on-line system is that information can be obtained directly from the computer without checking printouts or waiting for batches to be processed.

Ordering systems are still being developed and reaching higher levels of efficiency. Automated acquisitions systems have already eliminated some of the time-consuming tasks of filing, fund accounting, order follow-up, and checking book requests against a library's holdings. In order for this last task to be automated, a library's entire catalog must be stored in the computer; few libraries have yet achieved this goal. However, some libraries are developing integrated systems in which acquisitions, cataloging, and circulation can use the same data bases and all searching of library files can be done through computer terminals.

Libraries that participate in the OCLC, Inc. network or use other on-line cataloging systems have available a very useful tool for acquisitions searching. They can verify information on most books merely by using their computer terminals. However, the information obtained in such systems may be only cataloging information and may not include price, publisher's address, and whether the book is still in print. The day when full purchasing information on all books and other materials can be obtained by computer searches is still far in the future.

THE BOOK ARRIVES.

Books ordered directly from publishers can be expected to arrive within two or three weeks. Occasionally a local source or a small publisher will manage to supply books in even less time. The first shipment on an order to a book jobber, consisting of books he has in stock in his warehouse, may also arrive in two or three weeks. Books ordered from foreign countries will probably not arrive for several months. If books are temporarily out of stock or not yet published, or if vendors are inefficient or burdened by backlogs of orders, arrival times may be long delayed. These problems will be discussed further in Chapter 5.

In a large library that receives many materials, control of incoming shipments must be carefully maintained. Not all packages and cartons will be properly identified; it is important to keep packing slips and mailing labels until the books are matched with invoices and orders.

The two principal elements of receiving books are matching books with invoices and matching books with orders. The invoice may be incorrect as to number of books shipped, numbers of copies, prices, or titles. On the other hand, the invoice may correctly list the books shipped, but some of them may not be ones that the library has ordered. Either type of problem will require correspondence with the vendor unless a standard procedure for handling such problems has been established. The person receiving books should also ascertain whether the books are in good condition so that damaged books and imperfect copies can be promptly returned for replacements.

Another type of problem encountered in receiving books is finding that the information on the original order form did not correctly or completely describe the book. Author and title information may be inaccurate or the book may be part of a series or set, a fact that was not known at the time the book was ordered. In addition to correcting the appropriate order records, it is important that the person receiving books recheck the catalog and other acquisitions files, if it is possible that the library owns or has previously ordered the book under the correct author, title, or series. If the duplication is discovered at this time, the vendor may give the library permission to return the book for credit.

After it has been determined that the vendor's invoice correctly bills the library for books ordered and received, the invoice is approved for payment. The books are now considered the property of the library and can be stamped with a property stamp or identified with a bookplate. Many libraries stamp the edges of books, because this stamping is difficult to eradicate and can be easily seen when patrons are leaving the library with books. Some libraries use an embossing stamp, perhaps on a secret page, in order to make it even more difficult for the occasional person who tries to obliterate all evidence of library ownership from a book.

"Accessioning" books is an old library tradition. In the past, books were often numbered consecutively as they were added to the library and an accession list was kept, giving author, title, price, and whatever additional information the library found useful. Although the accession list of an old library may be of interest from a historical viewpoint, the strictly chronological arrangement has few practical uses in normal library operations. Most libraries now add whatever purchase or price information they find useful to the shelf list, which is almost always arranged by classification, a more useful arrangement for inventory and other purposes. However, although the chronological accession list may no longer be maintained, many libraries still find it useful to assign a unique, consecutive number to each book as it is added. With the coming of automation the advantages of this identifying number are even more apparent. Although classification, author, and copy numbers can be assigned in such a way that a unique combination of numbers and letters identifies each book, these call numbers are more complex and not as easily handled by computers (or library assistants) as accession numbers.

After ownership identification and accession numbers (if used) have been added to the books, they are ready for cataloging. In many libraries, the original book request and a copy of the multiple-copy order form accompany each book as it goes forward for cataloging.

The next chapter will cover some of the special problems and areas of activity of acquisitions work. Although it is true that many books selected for purchase can be routinely ordered and will be promptly received without any problems being encountered, the route from book request to book in hand is not always a straight and speedy one, or one that can be described in a few words. The steps in book ordering that have been discussed here are illustrated in Figure 9.

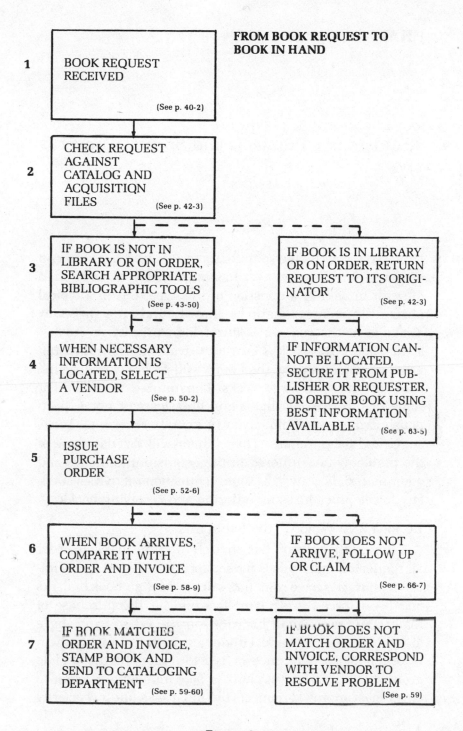

FROM BOOK REQUEST TO
BOOK IN HAND

1 BOOK REQUEST RECEIVED

(See p. 40-2)

2 CHECK REQUEST AGAINST CATALOG AND ACQUISITIQN FILES

(See p. 42-3)

3 IF BOOK IS NOT IN LIBRARY OR ON ORDER, SEARCH APPROPRIATE BIBLIOGRAPHIC TOOLS

(See p. 43-50)

IF BOOK IS IN LIBRARY OR ON ORDER, RETURN REQUEST TO ITS ORIGINATOR

(See p. 42-3)

4 WHEN NECESSARY INFORMATION IS LOCATED, SELECT A VENDOR

(See p. 50-2)

IF INFORMATION CANNOT BE LOCATED, SECURE IT FROM PUBLISHER OR REQUESTER, OR ORDER BOOK USING BEST INFORMATION AVAILABLE

(See p. 63-5)

5 ISSUE PURCHASE ORDER

(See p. 52-6)

6 WHEN BOOK ARRIVES, COMPARE IT WITH ORDER AND INVOICE

(See p. 58-9)

IF BOOK DOES NOT ARRIVE, FOLLOW UP OR CLAIM

(See p. 66-7)

7 IF BOOK MATCHES ORDER AND INVOICE, STAMP BOOK AND SEND TO CATALOGING DEPARTMENT

(See p. 59-60)

IF BOOK DOES NOT MATCH ORDER AND INVOICE, CORRESPOND WITH VENDOR TO RESOLVE PROBLEM

(See p. 59)

Figure 9.

CHAPTER 5

Acquisitions: Problems and Special Concerns

How LONG does it take your library to acquire a book after an approved purchase request has been received? It is often difficult to answer a question of this type, but in a typical library the answer might be that if funds are presently available, if the request is given high priority or "rush" status, and if the book is currently available from the publisher or a local source, the library will probably receive the book within two to three weeks. The number of "ifs" hint at some of the reasons that many libraries can not expeditiously order and do not always promptly receive all books suggested for purchase. This chapter will discuss some of the problems encountered in the acquisition of books and other materials, as well as some acquisitions activities ancillary to the procedures for ordering and receiving books.

BUDGET AND WORK-FLOW PROBLEMS.

A library that always has enough funds available to order all requested materials is indeed fortunate. Even large university libraries have sometimes depleted their book budgets and been forced to declare "freezes" on the purchase of materials. Some small libraries, on the other hand, have always been forced to exist under a system that allows them to order books only once or twice a year. In the middle ground are libraries that have a book budget sufficient to cover most approved requests but must set some low priority or expensive requests aside to be ordered only if special funds become available. Even if libraries are permitted to order continuously, they may be required to space out orders so that an excessive amount is not spent at one time of the year. Libraries may also be expected to encumber all funds well before the end of the fiscal year, leaving the last months of the fiscal year as a time when few, if any, books can be ordered.

Even though the ordering of books may need to be scheduled according to availability of funds, the selection of materials usually proceeds continuously. Therefore, in many libraries there is often a backlog of purchase requests waiting for money. Unless a request is given special priority, it must work its way through this backlog before it can be ordered.

A second reason for delays in ordering is that although requests for purchase may be received continuously, they do not usually arrive at a uniform rate. Some weeks the acquisitions staff may be inundated with new requests; at other times there may be a mere trickle. If ordering proceeds at a standard rate, as allowed by the amount of staff time available, requests will sometimes have a longer waiting time than at other times. Moreover, handling each request individually is not an efficient method of preparing requests to be ordered in libraries that receive hundreds of requests each week or even each day. (The routines of preorder checking and searching described in Chapter 4 are more efficiently performed on batches of requests.) A third reason for delay may be difficulty in obtaining ordering information.

Verification Problems.

In Chapter 4 it was pointed out that it is necessary or advisable to have certain types of information before books are ordered. However, the steps to be taken if this information is not given on a request and cannot be located in bibliographic tools were not described.

Many requests can be ordered without much risk even if the information given has not been verified. A judgment to trust the information given may be made on the basis of the source in which the book was cited or upon past experience with the requester. If the book is not expensive, the risk will not be great. If many unverified requests with unreliable information are ordered, the library will have more orders canceled by vendors, and the person who handles the receipt of books will need more skill in solving problems; but these drawbacks must be weighed against the cost in time of obtaining better verification of requests. It is possible even to order a request on which the price is missing by estimating a price based on the prices of similar books of the same publisher.

Another method of handling unverified requests is to send inquiries to publishers asking for the necessary information. A sample form used for this purpose is illustrated in Figure 10. This is a multiple purpose form that can be used for requesting various types of information and also for

CLAYTON JUNIOR COLLEGE LIBRARY
P. O. BOX 285
MORROW, GEORGIA 30260

TO: Date _____

THIS IS NOT A PURCHASE ORDER. Please expedite as indicated below.

_____ Give price. If not presently available, please indicate.
_____ Correct our author and title information if incorrect.
_____ Send a complete description.
_____ Quote a price if the following out of print book(s) are available
        from you.
_____ If free, please send. If there is a charge, quote price.
_____ Cancel our order. Do not supply.
_____ Billed, but not received.
_____ Received, but not billed. Please send invoice.
_____ Inform as to status of our order. We have not received.
_____ Permission to return material requested. Send disposition instructions.

                        Technical Services Librarian _____

                                LIST OF ITEMS

Figure 10.   Request to publisher or jobber for information

resolving other acquisitions problems. A difficulty encountered in using this method is that it is not always easy to locate addresses for publishers, organizations, and individuals who produce or sell books and other library materials. In the previous chapter, bibliographic tools listing publisher's addresses were indicated. Another frequently used source is *American Book Trade Directory* (R. R. Bowker, various editions). Many different sources are used for addresses of organizations and individuals. If a library has a collection of telephone directories, the directory for a particular city may be used when it is known that a publisher is located there. *The Encyclopedia of Associations* (Gale Research Company, annual) is a useful source for addresses of national organizations.

Sometimes the additional information needed for ordering a book can be obtained by contacting the person who initiated the request. However, it should not be assumed that requesters are always able to supply complete ordering information. In academic libraries, faculty members frequently suggest books on the basis of bibliographic citations in books and journals. Prices and publishers' addresses are not customarily given in bibliographies. Since there are many bibliographic and reference tools available to searchers and a number of approaches to be taken in solving problems, it is not often that a technical services division must report to a requester that a book cannot be ordered because of insufficient information.

NOT-YET-PUBLISHED BOOKS.

Occasionally a requester will indicate on a book request that a book has not yet been published and will list the expected date of publication. More often searchers become aware of the "not-yet-published" status when they do not find the book listed in sources such as *Books in Print* and discover the future date of publication by checking *Forthcoming Books* or the publishers' catalog or by writing the publisher. However, in many cases a book is ordered from the publisher or a book jobber and the library does not learn that is has not yet been published until it receives a report from the vendor. The fact that a book has been advertised or that it is listed in a publisher's catalog does not mean that it has been published. Publishers who frequently advertise books that are not yet published, give publication dates that are not observed, and sometimes cancel publication plans unintentionally create many problems for acquisitions departments. In the past, publishers of reprint editions have been among the worst offenders, but hopefully the many complaints by librarians will have some effect upon them.

Ordering books far in advance of publication dates, especially if the dates are uncertain, may unnecessarily tie up library funds and increase problems in completion of orders. Many libraries file book requests with future publication dates and order them only as the date of publication approaches.

Out-of-Stock Books and Claiming.

If a library orders at one time 100 different titles from a book jobber, it unlikely that three months, or even six months later, all of the books will have arrived. A few books may not yet be published, and a few others may be out of print, but in many cases the leading cause for nonfulfillment will be that the books are out of stock. Frequently, books remain in an out-of-stock status for many months and sometimes a year or longer. The publisher may then have more copies printed or he may let the book go out of print. Even if a library orders books directly from publishers, the "out-of-stock" problem will often prevent orders from being promptly completed.

After issuing orders, a library will frequently receive reports from vendors, such as:

NYP   not yet published
TOS   temporarily out of stock

OSB   out of stock, backordered
OSC   out of stock, canceled. Reorder later.
OP   out of print

The symbols used will vary. These reports should be systematically recorded. Periodically, it will be necessary to analyze all old orders to determine which ones require a follow-up or claim. Much claiming is undesirable, because it requires excess labor by both the library and the vendor. Recent vendor reports, expected dates of publication, and past experience with particular vendors and types of books should all be considered before claiming.

OUT-OF-PRINT BOOKS.

If a book is out of print, it is no longer available from the publisher. The date of publication is not always a good indication of whether a book is in print or out of print. Some books stay in print for decades. Others go out of print within a year or two. The fact that a book is out of print may be indicated on a book request, may be discovered during preorder searching, or may be reported by the publisher or book jobber in response to an order or query. It must be remembered, however, that a requester's indication that a book is out of print may be in error and that book jobbers also sometimes erroneously report books as out of print. *Books in Print* does not include all in-print books of all publishers. If there is doubt as to whether a book is out of print, the question can be resolved by writing the publisher.

Requests for out-of-print books are sometimes accompanied by dealers' catalogs offering the books for sale. Some out-of-print dealers present complete bibliographic information in their catalogs, but others do not. Enough information must be obtained through preorder searching to determine whether or not the library already has the books or has them on order. In some cases, the prices should also be compared with those listed in auction records (such as *American Book-Prices Current*, whose publisher varies), catalogs from other dealers, or for reprint editions in *Books in Print*. Even if orders from dealers' catalogs are placed promptly, some of the books will probably have already been sold. On the other hand, even after a long delay, some books may be still available; speed in processing requests from out-of-print catalogs is desirable, but not always necessary since not all books listed in catalogs are quickly sold.

For books that are determined to be out of print by preorder searching or through order cancellations, acquisitions personnel must find their own sources of supply. First, however, it may be desirable to check with the requesters to be certain that there is a definite need for the particular books requested. Obtaining out-of-print books is often a lengthy and costly process. Sometimes it may be possible to substitute similar books that are readily available.

One frequently used method of searching for out-of-print books is to list them with an out-of-print dealer from whom the library has received offers of service or who has advertised in library journals. Another method is to search incoming out-of-print catalogs or the library's collection of recent dealers' catalogs. However, this method may be like searching for a needle in a haystack, unless the item sought is of the type frequently bought and sold, for example, sets of authors' complete works and basic reference sets.

Finally, copies of many out-of-print books can be purchased in microform or hard copy reproductions. If a library has access to a copy of a book through Interlibrary Loan, it can produce its own copy provided there is no copyright problem and production facilities are available.

Large research libraries and other libraries that purchase many out-of-print books use other methods also, such as bidding at book auctions, purchasing private collections offered for sale, and advertising their needs.

MULTIPLE-VOLUME SETS AND STANDING ORDERS.

Multiple-volume sets are also referred to as terminal sets or in-progress sets. Unlike serials, which will be discussed in a later chapter, they are not intended to be continued indefinitely, but reach completion with a specified number of volumes. Some sets consist of only two volumes; others contain a hundred volumes or more. If all volumes of a set are published at the same time, fewer problems are created for acquisitions personnel than if the volumes are published one at a time over a long period of time. Book requests do not always indicate whether all volumes of a set, such as an author's complete works, should be purchased or only a volume recently reviewed. Small libraries may in some cases decide to order only volumes specifically requested. Large libraries are more likely to order all volumes of multiple-volume sets for which some volumes have been requested. To make the library's wishes clear to the vendor, it is important to place a note on the order, such as: "Volume 1 only" or "Volume 1 and future volumes as published." The latter note creates a standing order. A record must be kept of this order until all volumes have been received.

Other books for which libraries often place standing orders are books published in annual or frequent new editions, such as *The World Almanac* and *Who's Who in America*, and books appearing in monographic series, such as *Twayne's United States Author Series*. Most book jobbers handle these types of standing orders, sometimes referred to as continuations, and some serials subscription agents also supply them.

With the tight budgets of recent years, libraries have become more cautious in placing standing orders, which can quickly use up a major part of the book budget, substantially decreasing the amount of money left for discretionary purchases.

On-Approval Plans and Blanket Orders.

Many publishers encourage libraries to place standing orders for all of their publications or all publications in particular categories. The inducements are large discounts and usually the privilege of returning all volumes that the library does not want to keep. Book jobbers also frequently offer to supply books based on an analysis of the library's needs with return privileges and good discounts.

The library has the advantage of being able to examine books before purchase decisions are made. However, this advantage may be more illusory than real. Vendors usually offer on-approval plans expecting return rates of less than five to ten percent: once a library has the books in hand, it is easier to keep them than to return them.

For large libraries that normally acquire almost all books in certain categories, mass purchasing instead of title-by-title selection can be an efficient procedure. If a university library finds that it sooner or later orders almost all books published by university presses, it may decide to place a standing order with a jobber to receive all of them as soon as they are published. Another situation in which blanket orders may be desirable is when books are ordered centrally for a large system of libraries. Single copies of books can be received on the blanket orders. After they are examined and evaluated, a decision can be made on how many additional copies to order.

On-approval plans are more popular in times of growing, liberal book budgets than when libraries do not have funds adequate to order even all those books specifically requested. If a college library reaches the point where for each book accepted under an on-approval plan, it must reject a request submitted by a faculty member, the desirability of maintaining the plan will probably be reconsidered.

MONEY MANAGEMENT AND ACCOUNTING.

Large acquisitions departments that handle materials budgets of a million dollars or more obviously need people with business and accounting skills. However, even in small libraries, money may be wasted if purchases are not made efficiently and funds are not managed wisely.

In many situations, libraries and institutional business offices work together in making expenditures and accounting for them. Few librarians are in a position to write a check. If librarians were able to write checks for library purchases, perhaps they would not be so irritated by requests for prepayment, which under present conditions often require justification and extra paperwork before the business office will issue a check.

Ordering books is different from ordering supplies and equipment. Since each book title ordered is a unique item, ordering 100 different books is a different type of procedure from ordering 100 tables or chairs. Librarians are usually more skilled in the intricacies of book buying than procurement officers. Book purchasing can generally be performed more efficiently when the library is given the authority to send orders directly to one or more vendors, rather than having to send requisitions to an institutional purchasing office. If the purchase of library materials is not exempt from bidding requirements, bids can be sought specifying discount and service on categories of books, such as domestic trade books, instead of requesting jobbers to bid on individual titles.

Frequently some financial records are kept in the business office and others in the library. Cooperation is vital. One type of record usually kept by the library itself is the record of expenditures within the particular funds into which the materials budget has been subdivided. These funds may be for types of materials, such as books, periodicals, and audiovisual materials; departments of a public library, such as reference, adult, and children's departments; academic departments of a college or university; or by subject, regardless of requester. How funds should be allocated and even whether they should be allocated at all is a frequently debated question.

In maintaining records of funds, encumbrances as well as expenditures must be subtracted from the original allotments. As books are ordered from a fund, the prices are subtracted from the balance in the fund; since this money is now encumbered, it is no longer free to be spent on other books. When a book arrives, the encumbrance is canceled and the cost price becomes an expenditure. Copies of the multiple-copy order form are often filed by fund as records of encumbrances and expenditures, or a ledger record of funds may be maintained.

If many books are ordered on one purchase order, completion of orders may be a problem. As long as even one book is outstanding on an order, the order is open and an encumbrance must be maintained. To avoid this problem, school libraries, and some other small and medium-sized libraries, specify cutoff dates on orders, perhaps allowing the vendor sixty to ninety days to send as many books as possible, after which any books not supplied are canceled. The canceled books can then be reordered at a later date, if the need for them still exists. If an exact amount, such as $500, must be spent within a specified time, the library may send an order to a jobber for books with list prices totaling two or three times that amount with the request that a shipment with actual cost of $500 be sent within the allotted time. Large libraries seldom need to use such methods, as they usually have more control over their ordering procedures and can keep orders open as long as necessary.

GIFTS.

Gifts are often a mixed blessing. Libraries of all sizes and types receive gifts and offers of gifts. If a library is small and struggling, donors assume that any book, regardless of age or condition, will be received with gratitude. If a library is huge and broad in scope, donors may think that it will welcome all materials, no matter how esoteric. In small libraries, many gift books are not suitable for the collection. In large libraries, most gift books will probably duplicate items already owned. In spite of the fact that many books not needed will be received, and time will have to be spent on disposing of them in a suitable manner, most libraries hesitate to refuse gifts. Libraries do not like to give the impression that they are so rich that they do not need to consider gifts. Moreover, there is always the thought that some truly valuable item may be contained in a gift collection or that some day the donor will make a more worthwhile gift to the library. If it can be determined that the library already has the material offered or has no need for it, the offer should be courteously declined, perhaps with a suggestion as to other libraries that might appreciate the gift. When gift collections are accepted, it should be with the understanding that the library will dispose of unneeded items according to its own discretion. Procedures for acknowledging gifts should be established. Libraries should not make appraisals for tax purposes, because they are interested parties in the transaction, but sometimes a general indication of approximate value can be given.

In another category are gifts of valuable rare books, endowment funds, and grants from foundations. Gifts of these types are usually encouraged and sometimes actively solicited.

Another type of gift is the book, pamphlet, or periodical that arrives unsolicited in the mail, often without indication of why or from where it is being sent. Time must be spent in verfying that there is no outstanding order or request for the item and in evaluating its usefulness to the collection.

EXCHANGES.

Closely related to the subject of gifts is the area of exchanges, usually meaning exchanges with other libraries. University and research libraries frequently have exchange arrangements with libraries all over the world, according to which they send publications of their institutions and in exchange receive publications from other institutions. Sometimes the only way in which libraries can obtain certain publications of institutions and learned societies in foreign countries is by agreeing to send publications in exchange.

Another type of exchange is the exchange of unwanted gifts and duplicate materials. Lists of books, periodicals, and other unneeded items are typed and sent to other libraries. The first library requesting an item gets it. There is no attempt to balance items sent to a library with items received from that library, since the chief motive is to dispose of unwanted material in a useful manner.

LEASE PLANS.

A lease, or rental, plan is a plan by which a library pays a monthly charge for which it receives a specified number of new books. The books may usually be kept as long as the library needs them, but a limit is set on the total number of books the library may have on hand at any time. The library returns books no longer in heavy use, and it may also purchase books at a reduced price. An example of a small rental plan is one in which a payment of $50.00 monthly is made to receive 10 new books a month, with the total inventory not to exceed 100 books, and the privilege of purchasing any of the books at one-fourth price after they have been held six months. Two well-known lease plans are Josten's Lease Plan and Bro-Dart's McNaughton Plan.

A lease plan is useful if there are books of passing interest—current best-sellers, for instance—that a library wishes to make currently available to its patrons but does not wish to add permanently to its collection. It is also a means of providing extra copies of best-sellers during their period of highest popularity.

How to Be Successful in Acquisitions.

Acquisitions personnel are sometimes swamped with incoming purchase requests, invoices, book advertising, publishers' and dealers' catalogs, gift materials, book shipments, and miscellaneous materials being acquired by the library. One measure of success is steadiness in keeping everything moving so that one is not buried in paperwork or blockaded by unprocessed materials.

Another measure of success is the expenditure of all funds available in the most useful manner possible. The need for books, periodicals, and other materials is usually greater than the amount allowed by the materials budget, but there are often deadlines by which funds must be spent, unexpected cancellations and discounts, and unpredictable increases and decreases in funds—all of which make acquisitions staff fearful that they will lose money by not getting it encumbered or spent fast enough.

Prompt ordering of materials requested, location of sources for difficult-to-acquire materials, wise spending of funds, and quick and efficient moving forward of materials received are all major acquisitions goals.

THE UNNECESSARY DUPLICATE: TEN REASONS WHY IT GETS INTO THE LIBRARY.

One particularly annoying acquisitions failure is the unintentional duplicate. Since considerable time is spent in searching and verifying with the purpose of avoiding duplication, a book that is not revealed to be a duplicate until the cataloging process or even later reflects on the efficiency of acquisitions routines. Unfortunately, completely avoiding unnecessary duplicates would be likely to require greater expenditures in staff time than the money lost by purchasing a few such books. A list of some of the reasons why these duplicates are acquired is revealing of the complexity of the acquisitions process:

1. Card misfiled in card catalog. It is perhaps an exaggeration to say that for every card misfiled in the card catalog, a duplicate book will be acquired, but it illustrates the importance of correct filing.
2. Card temporarily removed from the card catalog without a temporary slip inserted.
3. Errors in spelling of author's name and/or title that are not corrected during the verification process.

4. Book ordered under wrong entry. If acquisitions files are arranged by author or other main entry, this can easily happen when the correct main entry is not verified in authoritative sources. Even if files are arranged by title, duplication can occur if there are slight variations in the wording of the title. Moreover, the error in main entry or title may have occurred in the order for the first copy, so that the searcher responsible for checking the second request for the book would have to be psychic to know that a copy had been ordered. (In small libraries, where one person handles all requests, an excellent memory might suffice.)
5. Slip misfiled in acquisitions file.
6. Slip temporarily removed from acquisitions files for any reason.
7. Confusion of editions. A book thought to be a new edition may turn out to be only a new, unrevised printing.
8. Same book published under several titles.
9. Book not identified as being part of a series for which the library has a standing order.
10. Correct entry for series not determined, although book was known to be part of a series; so the library record of the series was not located.

CHAPTER 6

How to Catalog

What Is Cataloging?

A LIBRARY is more than a collection of books and other materials. A warehouse filled with books is not a library. In order to qualify as a library, a collection of books must be organized for use. Cataloging is the process by which books are made accessible to the intended users. The physical arrangement of the books on the shelves is one means by which access can be made convenient. A systematized list of the books, or catalog, is another.

To better understand the nature of cataloging, consider these four basic elements:

1. Entering books into a catalog by author and title.
2. Describing the books in such a way as to identify each book as a unique item.
3. Selecting words or phrases to identify the subjects of the books.
4. Organizing the books according to a logical classification of knowledge.

Many of us have become accustomed to libraries in which books are arranged on the shelves according to a particular classification of knowledge and listed in a card catalog by author, title, and subject entries, but specific techniques should not be confused with the basic elements noted above. In the past, for example, books were often assigned shelf positions according to their order of accession, and catalogs were in book form. Now, however, the book catalog is making a comeback, and in some libraries patrons use computer terminals to locate books by author, title, or subject. Moreover, classifications systems should not be thought of only as means of arranging books on the shelves, because the systems can also be used as methods of arrangement in printed or card catalogs.

Not all materials in libraries receive all four elements of the cataloging process. For example, in some libraries, pamphlets are put in files under subject headings but are not classified, entered by author or title, or described individually in the library's catalog. Periodicals are often arranged alphabetically, rather than according to a subject classification, but they may appear in the catalog under title and subject.

Sometimes the word *cataloging* is given a very specific meaning. Unless an item has been fully and accurately cataloged, it is not considered to have been cataloged at all. (This is similar to saying that poetry that is not good poetry is not really poetry, but merely verse, or that music that is not good music is not music, but sound.) Also, the function of classification is sometimes separated from the rest of the cataloging process, so the phrase "cataloging and classification" must be used to describe the complete operation. In this book, "cataloging" is used in its broad sense, to cover all processes connected with maintaining a library catalog, as well as the systematic arrangement of the materials on the shelves.

THE CATALOGING MYSTIQUE.

Cataloging should not be considered a mysterious procedure properly done only by professional librarians who have studied it extensively and been introduced to its intricacies through many years of experience. Cataloging is performed in many types of situations, from small church, school, and business libraries to large university libraries, and not all situations require equal skill. Moreover, a person participating in the cataloging endeavor may be responsible for only one simple part of the process. In large libraries and libraries with highly specialized collections, some of the decisions made during the cataloging process may be very difficult ones, especially since they may affect the success of the entire library operation. These decisions often can best be made by professional librarians. However, in large libraries, as well as small libraries, there are many opportunities for nonprofessionals to contribute to the cataloging operation. In the discussion of cataloging in the remainder of this chapter, as well as in the following chapters, little attention will be given to the job levels of the workers who perform the various activities.

ORIGINALITY VERSUS CONFORMITY: WHY SHOULD WE FOLLOW RULES?

Theoretically it would be possible for the person faced with the responsibility of organizing a library collection to study the objectives of the library, the needs of the users, and the nature of the collection, and then devise his own system for arranging the books and listing them in a catalog. However, there are reasons that it is usually desirable to follow standard library practices, even if one is a genius who could perhaps devise a superior classification or set of cataloging rules. Library users who go from one library to another expect to find the books arranged according to one of the two principal classifications and the catalog based on a standard set of cataloging rules. Also, a cataloger cannot look forward to a collection remaining forever under his jurisdiction. Someday other catalogers will need to continue the work and it will be difficult for them, if the collection has been cataloged by unique rules known to one person alone. Finally, if every library were to use its own special cataloging rules, every book published would have to be cataloged separately by each library. The ease and cost saving of centralized and cooperative cataloging would be impossible to achieve.

Cataloging practices in libraries are far from uniform, but most libraries base their policies on standard rules and make departures only when necessary or expedient. The Anglo-American Cataloging Rules are a detailed, complex set of rules covering author and title entries and the form in which descriptive information is given. Small libraries that do not use the rules themselves are likely to use cataloging manuals or textbooks containing simplified versions of them. Most American libraries select their subject headings either from *Sears List of Subject Headings* (used mainly by small to medium-sized libraries) or from the more extensive list of subject headings published by the Library of Congress. Almost all school libraries and small public libraries use the Dewey Decimal Classification. Other libraries usually use either the Dewey Decimal Classification or the Library of Congress Classification.

Special libraries and information services are more likely to depart from standard cataloging rules and to use special classifications and subject headings than are general libraries, which cover all subjects. Since these libraries serve special purposes, special classifications and subject heading lists (or thesauri) must sometimes be developed.

The Library of Congress, located in Washington, D.C., is the largest library in the United States. As its name indicates, it was organized for the use of the United States Congress, but it has undertaken numerous other missions, including services to other libraries. Since 1901 the Library of Congress has been selling printed catalog cards to libraries. Through this and other services, the Library of Congress has been an influence toward standardization of cataloging throughout the country.

The Lone Cataloger.

In many small libraries one person is responsible for all of the cataloging that is done. Moreover, this person is likely to have other responsibilities as well. Even in medium-sized libraries, such as some college and public libraries, there may be only one cataloger. However, when a person assumes the responsibility for the cataloging of a library, there are usually precedents that can be followed, manuals and textbooks that can be consulted, and nearby librarians who are willing to give advice; so the new cataloger need not feel completely alone.

To catalog a library collection from the very beginning is preferable to taking over the cataloging of a collection that has been organized over the years by persons who have not used standard cataloging procedures. It is easier to do the job right from the beginning than to redo the incompetent work of others. However, most library collections, although they may not be cataloged in the best possible manner, have received the best efforts of the catalogers who have worked with them. The new cataloger should therefore not be too hasty in making major changes in policies that have been followed for years. In most libraries, new catalogers can build upon the work of those who preceded them. Unless a structure is completely unsound, there are usually ways to add on or remodel without destroying all that has been previously constructed. New catalogers should also consider how the decisions they make today will affect the work that must be done by their successors.

Subsequent chapters in this book will give some guidance in making decisions on the classification and cataloging rules to be used by a library, but other books and articles on cataloging should also be consulted. Even more important, the opinions of other librarians should be sought. These decisions should not be made lightly, because reclassification and recataloging are expensive, tedious procedures.

Even if little cataloging needs to be done, either because the collection is very small or because most books arrive already processed, cataloging tools and guides should be available. Following are some basic publications:

1. Dewey, Melvil. *Decimal Classification and Relative Index.* 18th ed., 1971. 3 volumes. Forest Press, 85 Watervliet Ave., Albany, NY 12206.
   or
   Dewey, Melvil. *Abridged Dewey Decimal Classification.* 10th ed., 1971. Forest Press. (designed for small general libraries, especially elementary and secondary school and small public libraries)
2. Sears, Minnie Earl. *Sears List of Subject Headings.* Edited by Barbara M. Westby. 11th ed., 1977. H. W. Wilson Co., 950 University Ave., Bronx, NY 10452.
3. Piercy, Esther J. *Commonsense Cataloging.* Revised by Marian Sanner. 2nd ed., 1974. H. W. Wilson Co.
4. Bernhard, Genore H. *How to Organize and Operate a Small Library.* Rev. ed., 1976. The Highsmith Co., Inc., P. O. Box 25, Fort Atkinson, WI 53538.

For small libraries, which often use the Dewey Decimal classification and Sears subject headings, the first two books are useful in answering reference questions as well as in cataloging. Piercy and Bernhard are practical, nuts and bolts type manuals for organizing small libraries. Most libraries, no matter how small, can afford Dewey and Sears and at least one or two books giving guidance in library organization.

5. *Anglo-American Cataloguing Rules.* 2nd ed., 1978. American Library Association, 50 East Huron, Chicago, IL 60611. (The first edition, published in 1967, is, unless otherwise stated, the one referred to in this book. The new rules will not be im-

plemented by the Library of Congress or most other libraries until 1981.) Most libraries should have these rules available in their entirety rather than depending on the excerpts and interpretations given in various cataloging texts. The American Library Association also publishes other books useful to catalogers, and these are listed in its catalog of publications.

6. Copies of the *Library of Congress Classification* schedules and the *Library of Congress Subject Headings* list can be purchased from: Cataloging Distribution Service, Library of Congress, Building 159, Navy Yard Annex, Washington, DC 20541. The list of subject headings is available on microfiche as well as in a two-volume edition. A price list of publications, as well as information on ordering Library of Congress catalog cards, can be obtained from the above address.

7. *Cutter-Sanborn Three-Figure Author Table.* Distributed by Libraries Unlimited, Inc., Box 263, Littleton, CO 80120. About $10.00. A table such as this is needed if Cutter numbers are used with the classification. Chapter 11 of this book discusses the use of Cutter and other author numbers.

After the cataloger has made the initial decisions on cataloging rules and classification, or become familiar with existing library policies, and has assembled the necessary tools, the various steps in the cataloging procedure can be undertaken.

STEPS IN CATALOGING A BOOK.

To understand the steps involved in cataloging a book, imagine that you are working in a small library that receives most of its books already processed. One day your boss hands you a book that has been received as a gift and tells you to catalog it and add it to the collection. Since very few books are cataloged by your library, each book that needs to be cataloged is treated as an individual item. In this particular case, you know that you are responsible for all of the steps in the cataloging process and must, by yourself, prepare the book for circulation. The manner in which you would proceed would, of course, be affected by factors such as the type of catalog maintained by your library, cataloging tools available, and the cataloging policies of your library; but an effective procedure would still probably contain most of these steps:

1. Check the library's catalog and order files to determine whether the gift book is a new title or an added copy. Accession the book and stamp it with a property stamp. Chapter 4 of this book discusses the step of checking the catalog and files, since this is basically an acquisitions procedure. In a large library, gifts are normally checked against the catalog and order files before being forwarded to the catalog department.

2. Select the main entry for the book. If the authorship of the book is obvious, there will be no problem. Chapter 7 explains the concept of main entry and the complications that can occur in selecting the main entry.

3. Decide what added entries will need to be made for other persons associated with the book, such as joint authors and editors. Select the correct form of name for each. Also decide whether an entry should be made under title. Chapter 8 discusses proper form of names and added entries.

4. Record the name of the author, title, place of publication, publisher, date, paging, illustrations, and other elements of bibliographic description according to the rules followed by your library. See Chapter 9 for a detailed description of this step.

5. Select appropriate subject entries, using the list of subject headings followed by your library. See Chapter 10.
6. Classify the book according to the classification system used by your library. See Chapter 11.
7. Type a set of catalog cards. See the concluding section of Chapter 9 for advice on typing cards and Chapter 12 for ways in which this step can be avoided.
8. File the catalog cards for the book in the card catalog and the shelf list card in the shelf list. Chapter 13 covers filing rules and problems in the maintenance of catalogs.
9. Type a book card and pocket, paste in the pocket, attach a plastic jacket, and type and attach a spine label. Chapter 14 discusses these procedures.

The above steps are not always performed in this order, nor do experienced catalogers always think of their work as being divided into many separate steps. However, if the beginner attempts to look at cataloging as one process rather than considering the component parts separately, it may seem more difficult and confusing than it actually is.

Even in small libraries, there is likely to be some division of labor within the cataloging process, with the result that the person who selects the catalog entries and determines the classification is usually not the same person who types the catalog cards and pastes in the pockets.

DIVISION OF LABOR IN A LARGE CATALOG DEPARTMENT.

In the catalog departments of large libraries, the work is often divided among many professional librarians, paraprofessional assistants, and clerical workers. The division of responsibility is usually based upon such factors as type of material, subject matter, language, whether cataloging copy is available, whether the book is new or is added copy, and the difficulty of various steps in the cataloging process.

Books, serials, and audiovisual materials are three major types of materials acquired by libraries and may be handled by separate sections of a catalog department. Other categories, such as microforms, maps, and music scores are also sometimes handled separately.

In order to take advantage of the special subject backgrounds and language abilities of the cataloging staff, materials may be divided by subject or language. For example, a catalog department may have separate sections for the humanities, the social sciences, and the natural sciences. Books in languages other than English may be assigned to particular catalogers.

Most large libraries accept as much help as they can get from the cataloging done by other libraries. In the past this frequently meant the purchase of Library of Congress card sets, but today faster and more economical means of obtaining cataloging copy are widespread. (See Chapter 12.) However, cataloging copy is never available for all of the books to be added; so another basic division may be made between cataloging with copy and original cataloging, which is the more difficult.

Added copies, replacements, and even added editions require fewer decisions than new titles and thus are sometimes handled by paraprofessionals or clerical assistants in a separate section of the catalog department.

One of the most basic and necessary of the divisions of cataloging duties is according to the education, training, and skills of the various members of the cataloging staff. As one moves from typing catalog cards to selecting catalog entries, and classification to revision of cataloging, overall supervision, and establishing policies and procedures, higher levels of responsibility are involved. Also, a division is sometimes made between different parts of the cataloging process, such as descriptive cataloging and subject cataloging, with some staff members specializing in one or the other.

Since there are a number of ways in which the cataloging work load can be divided, and which type of division takes precedence is variable, the possible ways in which a large catalog department can be organized are multitudinous.

OTHER CATALOGING SITUATIONS.

In addition to medium-sized libraries with several persons employed in cataloging, there are processing centers for school or public library systems, which catalog books for a group of small libraries. The number of volumes handled by such a center may be as great or greater than the number handled by a large library's catalog department. However, the nature of the work to be done is likely to be different. Many of the books will probably be added copies. Fewer of the books will be foreign books, and a higher proportion will probably be fiction and other easy-to-catalog books. However, there are likely to be some materials, such as audiovisual materials, that present cataloging problems. In a large processing center, the sheer volume of materials handled demands that there be good organization and efficient processing procedures.

Although special cataloging situations may require special knowledge and skills, all participants in the cataloging process, as well as other library staff members, can benefit by understanding the basics of cataloging, which are discussed in the following chapters.

CHAPTER 7

Choice of Main Entry

THE CONCEPT OF MAIN ENTRY.

THE CARD catalog of a library usually has more than one card for each book in the library. There may be one card filed under author, one under title, and one under subject. If a book has more than one author, title, or subject, there will be additional cards. If the library has a book catalog instead of a card catalog, there will still probably be more than one entry in the catalog for each book. Since library catalogs vary in format, it is more precise to speak of author entries, title entries, and subject entries rather than author, title, and subject cards when discussing approaches to books afforded by library catalogs.

Although most books are entered more than once in a library's catalog, traditionally one entry has been considered the main entry. An understanding of the concept of main entry and how the main entry is selected is essential to a knowledge of cataloging practices.

WHO IS AN AUTHOR?

The concept of main entry is closely related to that of authorship. Often we think of an author as "the person who wrote the book." However, this definition of authorship does not cover all cases.

The author of a book may not have literally written the book. In the case of the "as told to" book, a famous person tells his story to someone, often a professional writer, who then writes the story, perhaps with many deletions, grammatical corrections, and changes in sequence. Authorship of a book of this type is attributed to the person who tells the story as long as most of the book is written as though in his words. (However, a brief interview with a famous person submerged in a biography of him would not cause us to attribute authorship to him.) From this example, we can see that a person need not even be literate to be an author; if he is famous or unusual enough for readers to be interested in his story, he can tell it to someone or record it on tape.

It is also possible to unintentionally and unknowingly become the author of a book. If you have written letters or a diary of literary or historical significance, after your death someone may edit and publish your writings, and you, not the editor, will be considered by catalogers as the author of the book as long as your writing comprises the major part of the book.

Another example of a type of book that is not literally "written" by its author is one consisting principally of reproductions of paintings or photographs. The painter or photographer is considered the author of such a book.

One final exception to the definition of "author" as the person who wrote the book is the concept of corporate authorship. If a corporate body, such as a society, institution, government agency, or conference, prepares and issues official reports, statements, or studies, catalogers may consider the corporate body to be the author.

The concept of authorship is not so simple as it appears at first glance. To give an adequate definition of "author," we must make a rather complicated statement: the author is the person or corporate body chiefly responsible for the intellectual or artistic content of a work.

Are Main Entry and Author Entry Always the Same?

If a book is written by one individual person, the author is always the main entry. If a book is written by two or three authors, the first named author becomes the main entry, unless principal responsibility is attributed to someone else. If, however, a book is written by four or more authors, the title becomes the main entry. The title is also used as the main entry for many collected works, such as collections of articles, essays, and poems. A special type of title entry, the uniform title, is used as the main entry for works which have been published in many editions and translations under various titles. The uniform title "Bible," with various subheadings, is used for the Bible and any of its parts, regardless of the wording on the title page.

Some author entries, such as entries for joint authors, are not main entries and some main entries, such as the title entries referred to above, are not author entries. Therefore, although author entries and main entries are often the same, this is not true for all books.

Is Main Entry an Outmoded Concept?

Since choice of main entry as presently practiced is not always easy, it is sometimes recommended that title be used as main entry for all books to eliminate difficult decisions. Although it is usually easier to determine the title of a book than to attribute authorship, some books also present title problems. The title on the spine or front cover may be different from the title on the title page, there may be a series title as well as a title for the individual work, and some titles such as *Report*, *Poems*, or *Stories* are not distinctive or easily remembered. If a title page reads *John Jones' Early Poems* or *Tenth Annual Report*, what should the title entry be? These examples show that main entry under title would also require a set of rules, although perhaps not a very lengthy one. Moreover, even if the main entry were always under title, decisions would still have to be made on added entries for the persons responsible for a book; so the problem of attributing authorship would not be completely eliminated.

The question may also be raised as to whether computer technology will eliminate the need for choice of main entry by providing a great number of access points to a work, all of equal status. However, for the student of technical services to assume that he does not need to learn the rules of main entry because the need for them will soon vanish is similar to a student's objecting to being required to learn multiplication tables because he expects to use calculators in the future. Whatever the future may bring, the Library of Congress, commercial cataloging services, networks such as OCLC, and almost all libraries still use certain rules for main entry. Knowledge of these rules is basic to an understanding of cataloging as presently practiced.

What Difference Does It Make Which Entry Is the Main Entry?

In the past, when catalog cards were handwritten or individually typed, an effort was made to reduce the time required by considering one card, usually the author card, as the main card and including full information on this card only. The title card in some libraries contained only the call number, title, and name of author. Subject cards also contained abbreviated information. Most libraries today either purchase catalog cards or duplicate cards from a master copy. All of the cards in a set are essentially alike except for headings typed above the main entry on all except the main entry and shelf list cards. This is called the unit card system. However, there may still be instances in which a main entry card contains more information than the other cards. The holdings of serials may be recorded on main cards only, since these holdings must be frequently updated, and when cards do have to be typed, tracings and the full contents of sets may be indicated only on the main card.

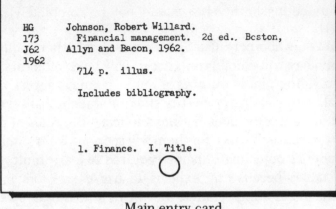

Main entry card

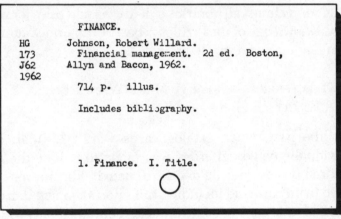

Subject card

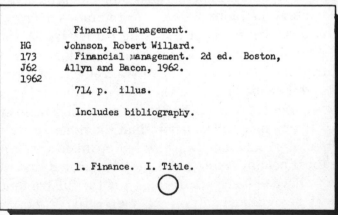

Title card

Figure 11.   Set of catalog cards prepared by library

Although choice of main entry no longer determines the amount of information to be given on a catalog card to the extent that it once did, it is still necessary to identify the main entry in order to type a set of cards correctly. The main entry is the item on the card above which all other headings are typed. (See Figure 11.)

When typing book cards, Library of Congress card orders, and similar forms, it is necessary to know what, if anything, to put in the author position on the card or form. If a cataloger has entered a book under title, the library assistant should not try to attribute the book to a person who happens to be named on the title page. Shown in Figure 12 are two book cards typed for *The World Almanac and Book of Facts*, which is entered under title.

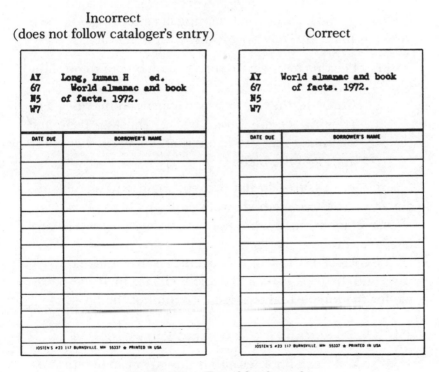

Incorrect
(does not follow cataloger's entry)

Correct

AY	Long, Luman H ed.
67	World almanac and book
N5	of facts. 1972.
W7	

AY	World almanac and book
67	of facts. 1972.
N5	
W7	

Figure 12. Typed book cards

A knowledge of main entry is also needed for searching some bibliographies, such as the *National Union Catalog*, which is arranged by main entry. Many libraries also arrange their order files and other similar files by main entry.

The choice of main entry even influences the location of books on the library's shelves. Most libraries use call numbers for books that include both a classification number and a Cutter number or other designation derived from the author's last name. If a book is not attributed to an author, the Cutter number or other author number is still derived from the main entry. If titles were used as main entries for all books, books on a particular subject would not be arranged by author or other main entry as they are now.

WRONG WAYS TO SELECT MAIN ENTRY: THE MISTAKES OF THE UNINITIATED.

Persons who have not had training in cataloging will often guess at main entry by one of these three methods:

1. Looking for the name of a person on the spine of the book.
2. Choosing the first name to appear on the title page.
3. Looking for the word "by" on the title page and assuming that the name that follows is that of the author of the book.

Since most books do not present main entry problems, any of these three methods will result in a high percentage of correct main entries, but not high enough to meet library needs and requirements.

The correct way to select main entry is to examine the title page and the book itself and decide who is chiefly responsible for the intellectual or artistic content of the book.

THE ANGLO-AMERICAN CATALOGING RULES.

Most American libraries either directly or indirectly base their choice of main entry on *Anglo-American Cataloging*

Rules (AACR). If a library purchases catalog cards from the Library of Congress or a commercial cataloging service, these cards will almost always have entries derived according to this code. The rules are complex, because they cover materials published in all languages and cover types of books such as incunabula (books published before 1500), seldom acquired by small or medium-sized libraries. However, it is not necessary to memorize all of the rules in order to be a good cataloger. It is only necessary to understand the rules well enough to be able to identify books that present a main entry problem and then to be able to consult the code to determine the best choice of entry.

BASIC RULES FOR CHOICE OF MAIN ENTRY.

Ten basic rules for choice of main entry, and catalog cards illustrating the rules, follow. These rules are based on the *Anglo-American Cataloging Rules* but have been simplified. In all cases they retain the spirit, if not the letter, of the law.

1. If a book is written by one person, enter it under that person.

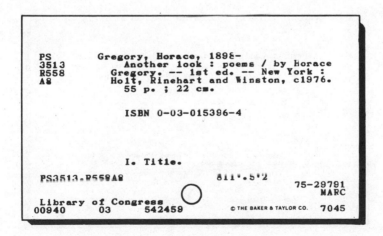

```
PS          Gregory, Horace, 1898-
3513            Another look : poems / by Horace
R558        Gregory. -- 1st ed. -- New York :
A8          Holt, Rinehart and Winston, c1976.
                55 p. ; 22 cm.

            ISBN 0-03-015396-4




                I. Title.

PS3513.R558A8                   811'.5'2
                                            75-29791
                                             MARC
Library of Congress
00940      03        542459    © THE BAKER & TAYLOR CO.   7045
```

Figure 13.   Book by one author

2.   If a book is written by two or three people, enter it
     under the first person named (unless principal
     responsibility is attributed to one of the other
     people by wording or typography).

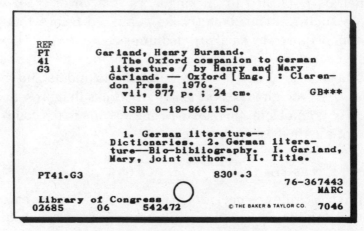

Figure 14.   Book by two authors

3.   If no one is represented as the principal author,
     and there are more than three authors, enter
     under title. The title page of the book below names
     four authors in addition to the collaborator.

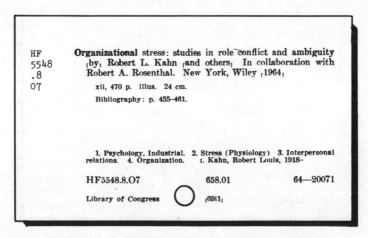

Figure 15.   Book by more than three authors

4.   Enter a translation under the author of the original work.

```
DC          Folz, Robert.
73              The coronation of Charlemagne, 25
F613        December 800 / Robert Folz ; trans-
            lated by J. E. Anderson. —
            London : Routledge & K. Paul, 1974.
                xii, 266 p., [12] leaves of
            plates : ill. ; 22 cm.
                Translation of Le couronnement
            imperial de Charlemagne, 25 decembre
            800.
                Bibliography: p. 250-257.
                Includes index.
                ISBN 0-7100-7847-1
                1. Charlemagne, 742-814.   I.
            Title.
DC73.F613                       944'.01'0924 [B]
                                         75-300794
                                               MARC
     Library of Congress     ◯
     02432     15      542311      © THE BAKER & TAYLOR CO.   7040
```

Figure 16.   Translation

5.   Enter an edition that has been revised, enlarged, or condensed by another person under the original author (unless the new edition clearly indicates that the work is no longer that of the original author).

```
REF
QM          Gray, Henry, 1825-1861.
23.2            Anatomy of the human body, by
G73         Henry Gray.  29th American ed.,
1973        edited by Charles Mayo Goss. With
            new drawings by Don M. Alvarado.
            Philadelphia, Lea & Febiger, 1973.
                xvii, 1466 p.  illus.   27 cm.
                First ed. published in London in
            1858 under title: Anatomy, descrip-
            tive and surgical.
                Includes bibliographies.

                1. Anatomy, Human.  I. Goss,
            Charles Mayo, 1899-      ed.  II.
            Title.
QM23.2.G73 1973                 611
IODN 0-8121-0377-7                        73-170735
                                               MARC
     Library of Congress     ◯
     21597     04      817259      © THE BAKER & TAYLOR CO.   6297
```

Figure 17.   New edition

6. If a work or group of works by one person is edited by another person, enter under the original author.

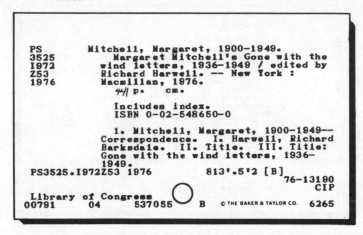

```
PS        Mitchell, Margaret, 1900-1949.
3525          Margaret Mitchell's Gone with the
I972      wind letters, 1936-1949 / edited by
Z53       Richard Harwell. -- New York :
1976      Macmillan, 1976.
              441 p.    cm.

              Includes index.
              ISBN 0-02-548650-0

              1. Mitchell, Margaret, 1900-1949--
          Correspondence.  I. Harwell, Richard
          Barksdale.  II. Title.  III. Title:
          Gone with the wind letters, 1936-
          1949.
PS3525.I972Z53  1976           813'.5'2 [B]
                                            76-13190
                                              CIP
Library of Congress
00791     04      537055      B   © THE BAKER & TAYLOR CO.   6265
```

Figure 18. Work by one author edited by another

7. Enter a collection of articles, essays, stories, or poems by different authors under title. The 1967 *Anglo-American Cataloging Rules* prescribed entry under the editor or compiler for most such works, but the rule was revised in a between-edition change. Three examples, one of the 1967 rule and two of the current practice, follow.

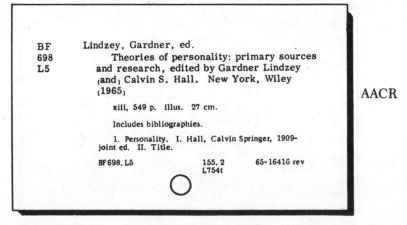

```
BF        Lindzey, Gardner, ed.
698           Theories of personality: primary sources
L5        and research, edited by Gardner Lindzey
          [and] Calvin S. Hall.  New York, Wiley
          [1965]
                                                        AACR
              xiii, 549 p.  illus.  27 cm.

              Includes bibliographies.

              1. Personality.  I. Hall, Calvin Springer, 1909-
          joint ed.  II. Title.

          BF 698. L5           155. 2        65-16416 rev
                               L754t
```

Figure 19. Collection of works by different authors

PR
6052
R8
Z7

The Happening worlds of John Brunner : critical explorations in science fiction / edited by Joe De Bolt ; pref. by James Blish ; response by John Brunner. — Port Washington, N.Y. : Kennikat Press, 1975.

216 p. ; 23 cm. — (National university publications) (Literary criticism series)

"A Brunner bibliography": p. 195-209.
Includes indexes.
ISBN 0-8046-9124-X : $12.95

LC

1. Brunner, John, 1934- —Addresses, essays, lectures.   I. De Bolt, Joe.

PR6052.R8Z7   823'.9'14   75-31968
                                                      MARC

Library of Congress   75

PS
589
I2

I hear my sisters saying : poems by twentieth-century women / edited by Carol Konek and Dorothy Walters. — New York : Crowell, c1976.
xiv, 295 p. ; 21 cm.

Includes indexes.
ISBN 0-690-01092-3
ISBN 0-690-01107-5 pbk.

LC

1. American poetry—Women authors.
2. American poetry—20th century.
3. Women—Poetry. I. Konek, Carol.
II. Walters, Dorothy, 1928-
811'.5'408

PS589.I2

76-4973
MARC

Library of Congress
02106   13   543481   © THE BAKER & TAYLOR CO.   7060

Figure 19. (continued)

8. Enter under corporate body a work that is the result of corporate activity or effort. Two examples follow.

9. If a book is composed principally of reproductions of drawings, paintings, photographs, or other works of an artist, and the text is clearly a minor part of the publication, enter under artist.

MAIN ENTRY   **99**

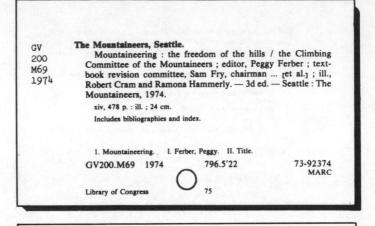

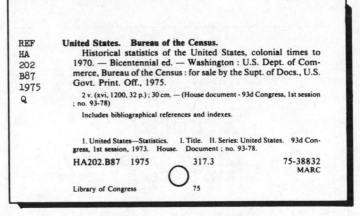

Figure 20. Works resulting from corporate effort

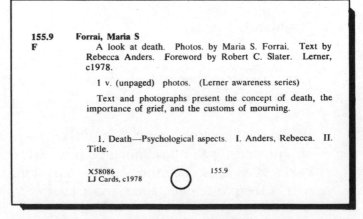

Figure 21. Reproductions of works by an artist

10. Use the uniform title *Bible* for the Bible and any of its parts. Also use uniform titles for other sacred works and anonymous works whose editions and translations have appeared under many titles, such as the *Koran*, *Arabian Nights*, and *Beowulf*.

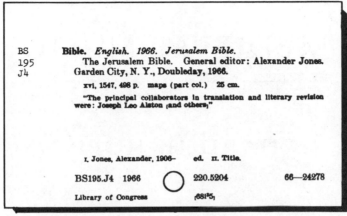

Figure 22.　Sacred works

The above rules do not cover all main entry problems. Choice and form of name for personal and corporate authors will be discussed in Chapter 8. Main entries for serial publications and audiovisual materials will be discussed in the chapters on these types of materials.

When you are having a problem determining main entry and none of the above ten rules seems to apply, consult your volume of *Anglo-American Cataloging Rules*. It contains rules to cover many other problems in choice of main entry. If your library has the *National Union Catalog*, you may find the book you are cataloging, or you may be able to find similar works listed, which will give you a clue as to how your problem book should be entered. Checking to see how similar works have been entered in your library's catalog is another useful procedure.

SAMPLE TITLE PAGES.

Five title pages are shown in Figures 23 through 27. Examine them and make a guess as to the main entry selected by the Library of Congress. Reproductions of the Library of Congress cataloging for the books and brief explanations will follow.

MEDIEVAL MUSIC

RICHARD H. HOPPIN

The Ohio State University

W · W · Norton & Company · Inc · New York

Figure 23.   Title page A

COMMONSENSE CATALOGING

A Manual for the Organization of Books and Other Materials
in School and Small Public Libraries

ESTHER J. PIERCY

SECOND EDITION

Revised by MARIAN SANNER

THE H. W. WILSON COMPANY   NEW YORK   1974

Figure 24.   Title page B

Sears List
of
Subject
Headings

11th Edition   *Edited by*
BARBARA M. WESTBY

New York
The H. W. Wilson Company
1977

Figure 25.   Title page C

CHINESE FAMILY LAW AND SOCIAL CHANGE

in Historical and Comparative Perspective

Edited by
DAVID C. BUXBAUM

UNIVERSITY OF WASHINGTON PRESS
Seattle and London

Figure 26.   Title page D

THE
UNITED STATES
Congressional
Directories
1789–1840

EDITED BY
Perry M. Goldman
&
James S. Young

1973
Columbia University Press
New York and London

Figure 27.   Title page E

Hoppin, Richard H
    Medieval music.
    (Norton introduction to music history series)
    Bibliography: p.
    Includes index.
        1. Music—History and criticism—Medieval,
    400–1500.   I. Title.
    ML172.H8   780'.902   78–7010

                    ISBN 0 393 09090 6

Figure 28.
CIP data for
Title page A

This book is written by an individual. It is one of many books that present no problem in choice of main entry.

Figure 29.
CIP data for
Title page B

Piercy, Esther J
    Commonsense cataloging.

    Bibliography: p.
    1. Cataloging.   I. Sanner, Marian, ed.   II. Title.
Z693.P54   1974   025.3   73-7573
ISBN 0-8242-0009-8

This book is an example of Rule 5 above that works of an author revised by another author are usually entered under the original author. It also illustrates the basic concept of entering a work under the person chiefly responsible for the intellectual content of the work.

Sears, Minnie Earl, 1873-1933.
    Sears list of subject headings.

    First-5th ed. published under title: List of subject
headings for small libraries.
    Bibliography: p. xxxiii-xxxiv.
    1. Subject headings. I. Westby, Barbara Marietta.
II. Title. III. Title: List of subject headings.
Z695.S43   1977   025.3'3   77-807
ISBN 0-8242-0610-X

Figure 30.
CIP data for
Title page C

Although the problem presented by this book is similar to that presented by the previous book, it also illustrates another important cataloging rule. Books often cannot be cataloged on the basis of the title page alone. In this case it is necessary to consult the preface of the book to locate the author's full name.

Main entry under title:

Chinese family law and social change in historical and comparative perspective.

(Asian law series; 3)
"A collection of papers delivered (and discussed) at a conference sponsored by the University of Washington Law School in August 1968."
Includes index.
1. Domestic relations—China—History—Congresses. 2. Domestic relations—Taiwan—History—Congresses. 3. Domestic relations—Asia—History—Congresses. 4. Sociological jurisprudence—Congresses. I. Buxbaum, David C. II. Washington (State). University. School of Law. III. Series.
Law   301.42'0951   76-7781   ISBN 0-295-95448-5

Figure 31.   CIP data for Title page D

If the Library of Congress had cataloged this book a few years earlier, it would have been entered under editor. This book is an illustration of Rule 7 above and of the fact that cataloging rules are not static.

United States. Congress.
  The United States Congressional Directories, 1789–1840.

  Includes bibliographical references.
  1. United States. Congress—Registers.
I. Goldman, Perry M., ed. II. Young, James Sterling, ed. III. Title.
JK1011.U53   328.73'0025   73-15907
ISBN 0-231-03365-6

Figure 32.
CIP data for
Title page E

This is an example of a main entry under corporate body. Directories of an organization are frequently entered under the name of the organization. Title main entry or entry under editor might seem reasonable for this book, but examination of the contents of the book and the current AACR rules probably led to this choice of entry. Notice that with corporate main entries it is particularly important to use the correct form of name, in this case "United States. Congress" not just "Congress."

CHAPTER 8

Proper Form of Names and Added Entries

AFTER it has been decided to enter a book under the name of a particular person or corporate body, the correct form of name for that person or corporate body must be selected. Moreover, one entry, no matter how correct, is seldom sufficient. Library users may look for the book under the names of other persons associated with the book, under the title, under the name of a series of which the book is a part, or possibly under the title or author of one portion of the book. The complete process of establishing author and title entries may be subdivided into these steps:

1. Selecting the main entry.
2. Establishing the correct form of name for the main entry.
3. Deciding what added entries should be made for other persons or corporate bodies associated with the book.
4. Establishing the correct form of name for each of these additional entries.
5. Deciding what cross-references need to be made for alternative forms of the names selected in steps two and four.
6. Deciding whether an entry should be made for the title.
7. If the book is part of a series, deciding whether an entry for the title of the series should be made.

8. If the book consists of a number of parts, deciding whether any part is important enough to warrant a separate author and/or title entry.

THE PROBLEM OF NAMES.

Many cataloging difficulties are merely reflections of problems and inconsistencies in the organization of human society and intellectual activity. One source of many cataloging problems is the way in which names are used to refer to persons and organizations. Many people are not happy with the name they were given at birth and use their middle name, a nickname, or initials. The name of a woman may change a number of times during her life as she marries or remarries. When writing a book, an author may decide to use a pseudonym. Complicating the problem is the fact that libraries contain many books written by authors from other times and places with differing practices on surnames and given names.

Societies, institutions, and government agencies change their names even more frequently than persons. Like people, they may have an official name that is seldom used and a popular name by which they are commonly identified. In addition, they can merge, be absorbed, and subdivide.

As with choice of main entry, *Anglo-American Cataloging Rules* (AACR) is the basic authority for determining the correct form of name.

PERSONAL NAMES.

The basic AACR rule for personal names is to enter a person under the name by which he is commonly identified whether it is his real name, assumed name, nickname, or other name. The form of name of an author is ordinarily determined from the way it appears in his works issued in his language. This rule seems simple and sensible, but there are many complications.

Fullness of Name.

If the forms of name appearing in different books by an author vary in fullness, the fullest form is usually used. Initials used for forenames should be spelled out when necessary to distinguish between two persons. A first forename represented by an initial should always be spelled out if the surname is a common one. The reason for this rule is that there may be numerous books by persons with the same surname and first initial. In one five-year cumulation of the *National Union Catalog*, 1968-1972, there are over 300 authors listed with the surname "Smith" and the first initial "J."

Nicknames.

If a person consistently uses a particular nickname and is commonly identified by that name, it is the form of name used. The heading "Carter, Jimmy" is used even though we know that his given name is James Earl Carter, Jr.

Pseudonyms.

If all of the works of an author appear under one pseudonym or if he is primarily identified by a pseudonym, the entry is made under pseudonym. The children's books by Dr. Seuss are entered under "Seuss, Dr."

If an author uses a number of different pseudonyms, or his real name and one or more pseudonyms, the real name is preferred. All of the works of the author, regardless of the names used, are thus kept together. There is an alternative rule given in AACR providing for entry of each work under the pseudonym used for it. This rule is followed by many public libraries. As an example, Eleanor Hibbert has used the pseudonyms Jean Plaidy and Victoria Holt, as well as a variety of less well known pseudonyms. The Library of Congress enters all of these books under the heading "Hibbert, Eleanor," but many public libraries use the various pseudonyms because their patrons will almost certainly look for the books under these names. As with choice of main entry, selection of the form of name may affect the shelf location of a book. This is particularly true of fiction since many libraries shelve fiction alphabetically by author. Readers of Jean Plaidy novels will expect to find them in the fiction section under *P* rather than *H*, which is one reason for entering under pseudonym in cases such as this.

Names with Prefixes.

The rules for names with prefixes are complicated because they give preference to the way in which the name would be entered in alphabetical lists in the author's own language. It is thus necessary to take into account the author's nationality when determining the entry element. A few rules are shown below:

Nationality	*Examples*	*Rule*
English, American, Italian	De La Mare, Walter Van Buren, Martin Da Ponte, Lorenzo	Enter under the prefix in most cases

French, German, Spanish, Dutch	Gaulle, Charles de
	Goethe, Johann
	  Wolfgang von
	Figueroa, Francisco
	  de
	Gogh, Vincent van
		Do not enter under the prefix if it is a preposition

French, German	Le Rouge, Gustave Zur Linde, Otto	Enter under the prefix if it consists of an article or the contraction of an article and a preposition
Spanish	Las Heras, Manuel Antonio	Enter under the prefix if it consists of an article alone

Since there are many other rules on prefixes and the rules generally require correct identification of the author's nationality and enough knowledge of the language to distinquish a preposition from an article, the best procedure when in doubt is to search under both the prefix and the following element until the name is located in an authoritative source.

Compound Names.

Hyphenated surnames are always entered under the first element. Most other compound surnames are also entered under the first element, with the exception of Portuguese names, for which the entry is usually the last element. However, except for Czech, Hungarian, Italian, and Spanish names, entry is not made under a married woman's original surname. Also, entry is not made under a name that can be presumed to be a middle name rather than part of the surname. Examples:

> Day-Lewis, Cecil (hyphenated surname)
> Johnson Smith, Geoffrey (compound surname)
> Silva, Ovidio Saraiva de Carvalho e (Portuguese name—entry under the last element)
> Molina y Vedia de Bastianini, Delfina (Spanish name—entry not under last element)
> Stowe, Harriet Beecher (name not entered under original name)
> Adams, John Jerome (name not entered under middle name)

Special Problems with Foreign Names.

Names, such as Russian names, that are not originally written in the Roman alphabet frequently appear in library headings in unfamiliar forms because they have been transliterated (changed from one alphabet to the other) according to a particular system. Examples:

> Evtushenko, Evgeniĭ Aleksandrovich (instead of Yevtushenko, Yevgeny)
> Chaĭkovskiĭ, Petr Ilich (instead of Tchaikovsky, Peter)

With some Asian names, such as Chiang Kai-shek and Mao Tse-tung, the first name is actually the surname and serves as the entry element. Examples:

Chiang, Kai-shek
Mao, Tse-tung

Entry under Given Name or Byname.

A person whose name does not include a surname is entered under the form of name by which he is primarily identified in reference sources. Royalty, saints, and popes are also commonly entered under forenames. Examples:

Plato
John the Baptist
Joseph, Nez Percé chief
Elizabeth II, Queen of Great Britain
Francis of Assisi, Saint
Augustine, Saint, Bp. of Hippo
Gregory I, Pope

Additions to Names.

The years of a person's birth (and death for persons no longer living) are added when necessary to distinguish between persons with the same name.
Examples:

Keats, John, 1795–1821. (the English poet)
Keats, John, 1920– (author of *The Sheepskin Psychosis, A Crack in the Picture Window,* and other popular works)

Distinguishing terms are sometimes used to identify names when dates are not available.
Examples:

Brown, George, Captain.
Brown, George, Rev.

The basic AACR rule advises directly entry under the name of the corporate body except when subsidiary rules provide for entry under a higher body of which it is part, under the name of the government of which it is an agency, or under the name of the place in which it is located. Examples:

> American Library Association. (basic rule)
> Princeton University. Bureau of Urban Research. (The bureau is entered under the university of which it is a part.)
> U.S. Supreme Court. (Library patrons may look directly under "Supreme Court," but this entry is logical since the Supreme Court is part of the United States Government and there are other supreme courts, such as state supreme courts.)
> Cohoes. City Library. (If the name of an institution consists only of a common word or phrase, it is entered under the municipality in which it is located.)

A rule suggesting main entry under uniform title for certain types of books was given in the last chapter. Examples of uniform title headings are:

> Bible. English. Revised standard. 1959.
> Koran. English. Selections.
> Chanson de Roland.
> Book of the dead.

Some examples of other types of headings follow:

> Illinois. Laws, statutes, etc. (laws)
> U. S. Constitution (constitution)
> Catholic Church. Liturgy and ritual. (liturgical works)
> Symposium on Protein Metabolism, University of Toronto, 1953. (conference)
> International Geological Conference. 15th. Pretoria, etc., 1929. (conference)

The rules described above are only a few from the many given in AACR. They have been selected to illustrate the multiplicity of potential problems in choosing form of name and to indicate some of the types of names most likely to cause problems. They should thus be given special attention. Not all libraries enter the names cited in the examples in the ways prescribed. The policies of libraries and cataloging services vary. Moreover, many library catalogs were begun long before *Anglo-American Cataloging Rules* was published in 1967 and contain entry forms established in accordance with other codes. Most libraries, including the Library of Congress, do not always change established forms of names when a new code is adopted, although they do usually change the form of name if an author changes his name or becomes commonly identified by a different name.

LIBRARY POLICIES ON NAMES.

Traditionally, one of the objectives of library cataloging has been to bring together all of the works of a particular author. Two problems are involved in meeting this objective. If two or more people have the same name, the names must be distinguished either by adding dates or by some other means. If this is not done, the works of a number of different people with the same name may be interfiled.

The other problem in bringing together the works of each author is establishing a uniform form of name for any author who has used more than one form of name. The simplest method of selecting forms of names would be to always use names as given on title pages. However, this would mean that some authors might be listed in the catalog under a variety of names since the title pages of their books use different forms of names. For example:

G. B. Shaw   Bernard Shaw
G. Bernard Shaw   George Bernard Shaw

Establishing correct forms of names is not always a complicated process. Many libraries purchase printed cards for most of their books or base their cataloging on information located in such sources as the *National Union Catalog*. The headings used by these sources are often accepted without further checking. Occasionally when a catalog card is filed, it may be noticed that the library has previously used a different form of name for the author. The cataloger must then make a decision on the correct form of name and change either the old or new cards. However, in some libraries, especially older libraries and large libraries, where more discrepancies and problems can be expected, all entry points on printed cards and cataloging copy are checked in the card catalog during the cataloging process. *Cataloging with Copy* by Arlene Taylor Dowell (Libraries Unlimited, 1976) contains a detailed discussion of the problems of integrating name entries from outside cataloging copy into the local catalog.

A "no conflict" rule is frequently used for original cataloging. The name of the author as it appears on the title page is checked against the library's catalog. If the author is already listed in the catalog, the established form of name is used for the new book. If the name on the title page does not appear in the catalog but does not conflict with any other name, it is used in the title page form. If there were another author with the same name already listed in the catalog, this would be considered a conflict, and an effort would be made to distinguish between the two authors by completing parts of the names designated by initials or by adding birthdates. The Library of Congress catalogs, the *National Union Catalog*, and other reference works as well as the *Anglo-American Cataloging Rules*, are frequently consulted by catalogers when there are name entry problems.

Different types of libraries have different policies on names. Public and school libraries are particularly anxious to use the form of name most likely to be sought by their patrons. For example, they may use the name Michelangelo instead of the full name, Buonarroti, Michelangelo. Large academic libraries often follow Library of Congress practices. The larger the library, the more important it is to establish a uniform form of name for each author.

Many libraries maintain a name authority file on three-by-five-inch cards that list the name headings used in the catalog and the cross-references made to them from other forms. The bibliographic sources in which the name was verified may also be listed. Often, this file includes only names for which cross-references have been made, problem names, and/or names for which the library has decided to use a form of name different from that used by the Library of Congress. The library's own catalog and the *National Union Catalog* serve as a name authority file for other names. A name authority card that uses an *x* to indicate the cross-references made is shown in Figure 33.

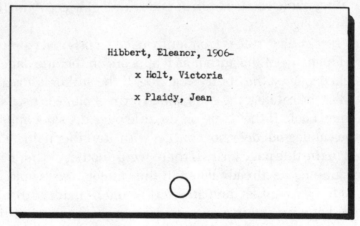

Figure 33. Name authority file card

CROSS-REFERENCES.

Whenever a form of name significantly different from that on the title page is used for an entry, a cross-reference should be made. (By significantly different it is meant that the two names would not file immediately adjacent to each other.) An example of one type of format used for cross-references is shown in Figure 34.

Neither printed catalog cards nor CIP data suggest re-

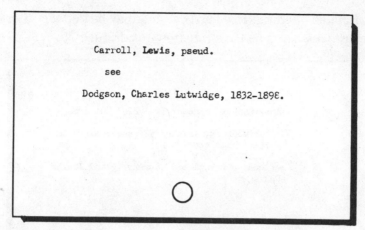

Figure 34. Cross-reference

quired cross-references; therefore, even if a library receives its books already cataloged, cross-references may still need to be made. After it has been decided that a name requires a cross-reference, the catalog or name authority file must be checked for that cross-reference, which may have already been made. It can be seen that appropriate cross-references cannot be made by commercial or centralized cataloging services that do not know what entries and references are already present in a particular local catalog.

Compound names, names with prefixes, and names not entered under the last element also require cross-references:

Lewis, Cecil Day *see* Day-Lewis, Cecil.
Maurier, Daphne du *see* Du Maurier, Daphne.
Kai-shek, Chiang *see* Chiang, Kai-shek.
Aquinas, Thomas *see* Thomas Aquinas.

Names of corporate bodies frequently require cross-references:

U.S. State Dept. *see* U.S. Dept. of State.
Supreme Court, U.S. *see* U.S. Supreme Court.
American Red Cross *see* American National Red Cross.
William Hayes Fogg Art Museum *see* Fogg Art Museum.

Related headings in a card catalog may be tied together by references, such as the one shown in Figure 35.

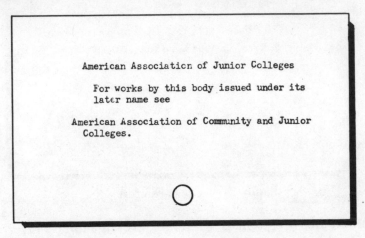

American Association of Junior Colleges

For works by this body issued under its later name see

American Association of Community and Junior Colleges.

Figure 35.   Cross-reference

The use of cross-references alleviates problems of entry because an alternative route to a book can be provided when a difficult decision must be made between forms of names. However, cross-references should be recorded so that they can be removed from the catalog when books are withdrawn and the entries to which the cross-references refer are removed from the catalog. One method used is to trace each cross-reference on the reverse side of a card for the heading to which it refers. If this card is removed from the catalog, the reference is traced on another card with the same heading. If there are no other cards with the same heading, the cross-reference is removed.

NAME ADDED ENTRIES.

Although the term *added entries* covers title entries, series entries, analytical entries, and in some usages, even subject entries, its most distinctive use is for catalog entries made under the names of persons or organizations other than the one chosen for the main entry. An added entry should be made for any person or corporate body associated with a publication under whose name a catalog user might reasonably expect to find it listed. The primary purpose of name added entries is to help library users locate books either when they are unfamiliar with library rules of entry or when they are uncertain as to the authorship of a particular book. These entries also enable the catalog to display more fully the publishing activities of a person or corporate body. The catalog user can find listed in one place not only the books for which a person was chiefly or solely responsible, but also books for which he was a joint author or editor, or contributed in some other major way. Another reason for making added entries, although of less practical importance, is the desire to give credit where credit is due. The person whose name appears second on a title page may have worked just as hard and contributed just as much as the person whose name appears first.

According to the *Anglo-American Cataloging Rules*, when two or three authors have worked together to produce a book, an entry, either main entry or added entry, should be made for each. If four or more persons have collaborated, an entry is usually made only for the first person named.

Added entries are made for editors, translators, and illustrators only under certain circumstances. If a collection of stories, poems, or articles by different authors is entered under title, an added entry is made for the editor or compiler, if one is named on the title page or elsewhere in the work. An added entry is made for the editor of an individual author's work if he has added significantly to the work. An added entry is made for the translator only if the translation is in verse or if the work has been previously translated by many different translators. Added entries are not made for illustrators unless the illustrations are an important feature of the publication.

Whenever possible, it is desirable to make at least one personal name entry for books whose main entries are under corporate names, titles, or special headings. Many people assume that all books have individuals as authors and will thus look for a book under the name of the first person listed on the title page or a name displayed prominently elsewhere on the publication, as in some children's books. On the other hand, when the main entry is not under the name of the corporate body that had responsibility for the content of the work, as opposed to being only the publisher or issuing body, an added entry should be made for the corporate body.

After it has been decided what name added entries should be made, the correct form of name for each entry should be established in the same manner as for main entries. Cross-references should also be made when necessary.

TITLE ENTRIES.

The simplest practice would be to make title added entries for all books (except, of course, those for which the main entry is the title). Even if this practice is followed, however, an awareness of types of title entry traditionally not made is necessary in order to understand the cataloging observed on printed cards and in other libraries.

Title entries are not always made for all books, because some entries are considered to be unnecessary and other entries might confuse catalog users. Titles such as *Collected Works, Letters, Poems,* and *Bulletin* occur frequently, but they are not meaningful without the author's names. Titles that are long and involved are not easily remembered and will not be frequently sought by library patrons. If a title is the same as a subject heading, it will file near it in a diction-ary catalog. It may confuse library users if entries are made for titles that consist solely of the names of people because the names as given in the titles, often with forenames first, are not likely to be the same as the proper forms of name used for other entries.

On the other hand, a reason for making title entries for all books is consistency. The complexities involved in selecting main entries and proper forms of names have already been discussed. If a catalog user has a choice between checking a list of books in a library catalog under author or under title, the title search is the simplest procedure, but it can be recommended only if the catalog contains title entries for all books. In many libraries, the user cannot know which books will have title entries unless he knows all the present exceptions to title entry and the policies from past years.

After a decision has been made on whether or not to make an added entry for the main title, the title page and the book itself should be examined to determine whether there are other titles, such as a different title on the spine or a distinctive part of the main title, that require added entries.

SERIES ENTRIES.

Cataloging rules leave considerable discretion to individual libraries as to whether added entries should be made for series. Some examples of series familiar even to many small libraries are:

The Reference shelf.
The Chronicles of America series.
Norton critical editions.
U.S. Dept. of Agriculture. Yearbook of agriculture.

If a series is of the type that may be cataloged as a collected set under one call number by some libraries, it is desirable for libraries that classify the volumes separately to make an added entry for series. An added entry should also be made for the series if the book is likely to be identified as part of a series by reference works or by library patrons. The fact that a series is numbered counts as a point in favor of making an entry. However, if the series is a "publishers series," including books that have little in common except the format, there is less reason to make the series entry.

A series entry can be made in the same manner as other added entries by typing the name of the series above the main entry on a catalog card. If a library holds many volumes of a series, the series cards for the individual volumes may consume considerable space in the catalog. Therefore, some libraries type special cards for series, listing several volumes on each card.

If series entries are made for some, but not all series, it is desirable to be consistent in making or not making entries for particular series. When observing series cards for some books of a series, library patrons (or staff members) may reasonably conclude that they represent the library's entire holdings in the series. A library can achieve consistency in series entries by maintaining a series authority file, which contains a card for each series of which any part is held by the library. Whether or not a series added entry is made is indicated on each card. Libraries using Library of Congress printed cards may have a policy of always following Library of Congress practice, but this will not always result in consistency because Library of Congress practice changes from time to time and the Library of Congress catalogers are not always consistent in making series entries. Moreover, this policy may result in the library making more series entries than needed while at the same time neglecting entries for the few series that are really important to the patrons of the library.

ANALYTICAL AUTHOR AND TITLE ENTRIES.

An analytical entry may be made under author and/or title for one or more of the articles, essays, stories, plays, or other works contained in a book or work. Unlike most types of added entries, analytical entries may sometimes be made by small libraries even when they are not made by large libraries because small libraries that do not have a separately published edition of a work may wish to draw attention to a larger work in which the item can be found. In addition, large libraries have more reference works that identify items in collections than do small libraries. Analytics may be made for all of the items in a collected work or only those likely to be sought by users of the library. They can be made for the parts of a one-volume work and for the parts of a multivolume set or series. The appropriate heading can be typed at the top of the unit card for the comprehensive work or a special analytic card may be used. (Analytical entries for serials will be briefly discussed in Chapter 17.)

One type of analytical entry is shown in Figure 36.

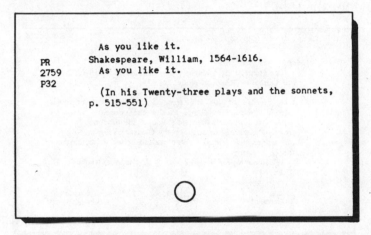

```
                As you like it.
    PR          Shakespeare, William, 1564-1616.
    2759          As you like it.
    P32
                (In his Twenty-three plays and the sonnets,
              p. 515-551)
```

Figure 36.   Analytical entry

SAMPLE CATALOG CARDS.

The problems and decisions related to selecting proper forms of names and added entries are too numerous to be briefly summarized. Even experienced catalogers are occasionally faced with decisions for which they do not know the rule or for which there are no rules. Shown in Figures 37 through 41 are five printed cards illustrating only a few of the many types of decisions that must be made. (Added entries are indicated at the bottom of the cards following the subject headings. Arabic numerals are used for subject headings. Roman numerals are used for added entries. As was previously mentioned, cross-references are not shown on printed cards.)

Figure 37 represents a book for which it was important to decide the correct form of name for the author under whom the main entry was made. A cross-reference should be made from Ali, Muhammad. If the cataloger thinks that some library patrons will look under Clay, Cassius, the champion's name from birth until 1964, he could make a cross-reference from that name. Notice that added entries were made for the author who collaborated with Muhammad Ali and for the title.

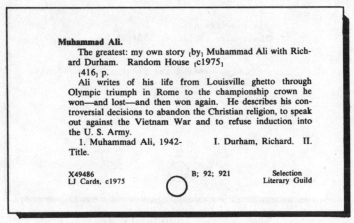

Figure 37. Name-form problem

From the author statement that follows the title of the card in Figure 38, we know that an initial was used for the first author's middle name on the title page of the book. The cataloger completed the name. An added entry was made for the joint author. No entry was made under the title, because it is not distinctive and is the same as the subject. Many libraries, especially those with a divided catalog that separates subjects from titles, will want to add a title entry. No entry was made for the series, which is an unnumbered publisher's series.

A cataloger using the printed card shown in Figure 39 may need to check the library's catalog to see whether books

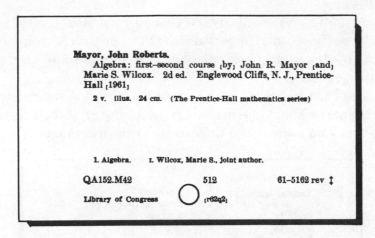

Mayor, John Roberts.
Algebra: first–second course ₍by₎ John R. Mayor ₍and₎ Marie S. Wilcox. 2d ed. Englewood Cliffs, N. J., Prentice-Hall ₍1961₎

2 v. illus. 24 cm. (The Prentice-Hall mathematics series)

1. Algebra. I. Wilcox, Marie S., joint author.

QA152.M42   512   61–5162 rev ‡

Library of Congress   ₍r62q2₎

Figure 38. Name-form change; omission of title entry

by this author are entered under Clemens or Twain and whether an appropriate cross-reference has been made. If the library uses the pseudonym, the heading on the card must be changed. Notice that although the names of the people who wrote the introduction and did the illustrations are indicated on the card, added entries are not made. It is not necessary to make added entries for everyone whose

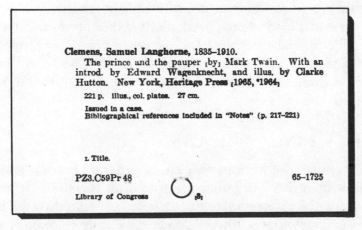

Clemens, Samuel Langhorne, 1835–1910.
The prince and the pauper ₍by₎ Mark Twain. With an introd. by Edward Wagenknecht, and illus. by Clarke Hutton. New York, Heritage Press ₍1965, °1964₎

221 p. illus., col. plates. 27 cm.

Issued in a case.
Bibliographical references included in "Notes" (p. 217–221)

I. Title.

PZ3.C59Pr 48   65–1725

Library of Congress   ₍3₎

Figure 39. Pseudonymous author

contribution is described on a catalog card. The reverse is not true, however. If an added entry is made for a person, his relationship to the book must be shown somewhere on the catalog card.

The card in Figure 40 represents a book for which two title entries should be made. The second part of the title is for a separate novel and thus requires its own entry.

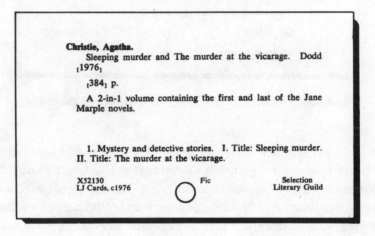

Figure 40.   Two books in one volume

A series entry was made for the book represented in Figure 41. Series entries are often made for the series of societies and institutions, particularly if they are numbered.

For additional examples of added entries made on printed cards, see the cards illustrating problems of main entry that were included in Chapter 7. Note the added entries indicated in the tracings.

RULES FOR A VERY SMALL LIBRARY.

For those who work in very small general libraries, such as church, school, or public libraries with less than 10,000 volumes, the elaboration or rules needed to maintain order in the catalogs of large libraries may have little relevance. If printed cards are used or if most books arrive already

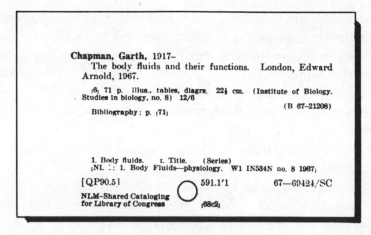

Chapman, Garth, 1917–
    The body fluids and their functions. London, Edward
Arnold, 1967.

    ₍6₎ 71 p. illus., tables, diagrs. 22½ cm. (Institute of Biology.
Studies in biology, no. 8) 12/6

    Bibliography: p. ₍71₎

                                    (B 67–21208)

    1. Body fluids.   ɪ. Title.   (Series)
    ₍NL ⠴₎ 1. Body Fluids—physiology. W1 IN534N no. 8 1967₎

[QP90.5]   591.1′1   67—69424/SC

NLM–Shared Cataloging
for Library of Congress   ₍68c2₎

Figure 41.   Tracing indicating series entry

cataloged, the remaining books will probably be cataloged in
a manner consistent with that of the outside cataloging
received. If original cataloging is done for all or most books,
policies such as the following may be used.

Form of name: Accept the form of name given on the title
page, unless the author is already listed in a different way in
the library's catalog. When there is a choice to be made
between forms of name or when there is a question as to
which element of the name should be the entry point (as
with names with prefixes), consult encyclopedias, biographical dictionaries, and other tools to determine the form
of name most frequently used. Although an attempt should
usually be made to keep together all the works of an author,
an exception can be made for authors writing under several
pseudonyms, which may be entered under the various
pseudonyms.

Cross-references: Be liberal with cross-references from
one form of name to another.

Added entries: Do not routinely make added entries for
joint authors, translators, illustrators, or editors. Make added
entries only for names under which library patrons are likely
to seek a book. For example, if the library acquires the
collection of Margaret Mitchell's letters published in 1976,

the main entry should be under Mitchell, but an added entry should be made for the editor, Richard Harwell, because library users are likely to look for the book under his name. For the same reason, if a main entry is under title or the name of a corporate body, whenever possible make an added entry for the person most prominently associated with the book.

Titles: Make a title entry for every book without exception.

Series: Do not make entries for series unless the library users regularly request certain books by series name.

Analytical entries: Make analytical entries for stories, plays, or articles in collected works if they are likely to be frequently requested by patrons.

CHAPTER 9:

Descriptive Cataloging:
From Simple to Complex

THE OBJECTIVES OF DESCRIPTIVE CATALOGING.

THE PREVIOUS two chapters have discussed the most difficult aspects of descriptive cataloging—choosing the main and added entries, and establishing their correct forms. The remainder of descriptive cataloging involves the recording of other necessary information about books.

One objective of descriptive cataloging is to describe a book in such a way as to distinguish it from all other books. The author and title alone are usually enough to distinguish between different works, but not all books with the same author and title are identical because some works are published in many different editions. Some editions may be revised or illustrated; others may have important introductions or critical material. A library user might want to know not only whether a library has *The Adventures of Huckleberry Finn*, but also whether it has the Norton critical edition.

Another objective of descriptive cataloging is to briefly present information useful to users of the catalog. Date of publication, for example, is a very useful item of information to those who are selecting books on a subject.

The general method used in this chapter will be to proceed from the simple to the complicated. First a basic type of description will be introduced. Then some variations will be noted. Next a brief description of some of the rules from the *Anglo-American Cataloging Rules* (1967) and International Standard Bibliographic Description (ISBD) will be given. At the end of the chapter a few suggestions for typing catalog cards will be made.

Basic Description.

The catalog card illustrated in Figure 42 shows the most basic elements of bibliographic description: author (or other main entry), title, publisher, date, paging, and tracings.

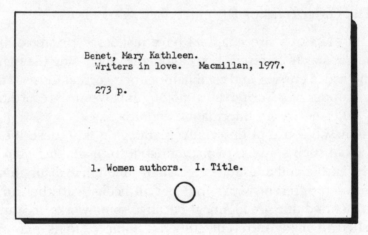

Figure 42.   Basic bibliographic description

Choice and form of main entry have already been amply discussed. The wording of the title is generally that found on the title page. The first word of the title is capitalized, but other words are capitalized only if they would be capitalized in a sentence written in the language of the title. This means that for English language books, proper names are capitalized when used in titles, but most other words are not. In German all nouns and words used as nouns are capitalized because this is the usual practice when writing German. Capitalization of all important words in titles is the rule for bibliographies, footnotes, and other references to titles, so the cataloging rule for recording titles often seems strange to beginners. However, it is consistently given as a rule in cataloging codes and textbooks. Although an adequate justification for the rule has apparently never been given, perhaps there is a difference between *referring* to a title in another work and *recording* a title as in cataloging. In any case, following the rule for capitalization of titles is necessary, if one does not want his work branded as that of an amateur.

The publisher's name need not be given in the complete form used on the title page. Phrases and terms such as "and Company," "and Sons," "Inc.," "Ltd.," "Published by," and initial articles are usually omitted. Forenames and initials of well-known publishers can also be omitted.

If only one date is to be given on a catalog card, the best date to use is generally the latest copyright date given in the work (usually on the reverse side of the title page), because this is the date of the content of the work. The date on the title page may merely be the date of a later printing. A preferable practice, which requires little additional time, is to record the date appearing on the title page whenever there is one and also to give the latest copyright date, if it is different, for example: 1975, c1967. If a library patron requests the 1975 edition of the book, the catalog card shows that the library has this edition.

In basic or simplified description only the paging of the major portion of the book need be given. Roman numerals used for front matter (the parts of the book that precede the text) can be ignored. The paging is the number appearing on the last numbered page, not the total number of pages. Although paging is perhaps not an essential part of simplified description, it is useful because it gives an indication of the extent of the work and helps to distinguish between editions.

The last item appearing on the card shown in Figure 42 is the tracing of subject headings and added entries. The tracings are not actually part of the description of the book itself, but they are necessary as a record of entries made so that if a book is withdrawn, all entries can be removed from the catalog.

One other item appearing on most library catalog cards is the call number. The composition of call numbers will be discussed in Chapter 11.

Why is it necessary to formulate complicated rules for descriptive cataloging when a book can be adequately described as simply as shown above? There are two reasons that a complete set of rules for descriptive cataloging is necessarily complex. The first is that all books are not alike. Many books present other elements, such as subtitles, joint authors, editors, successive editions, illustrations, relationships to other books, and series that may or may not be recorded. The second reason is that some libraries find additional types of information useful. Large libraries may want the place of publication and size recorded. On the other hand, some small libraries want descriptive annotation.

ADDITIONAL INFORMATION NEEDED FOR PARTICULAR BOOKS.

Some, but not all, titles have subtitles. Subtitles should be recorded if they help to identify the nature or subject of the book.
Examples:

> Voltaire; a collection of critical essays.
> To be an invalid; the illness of Charles Darwin.

In simplified description, it is not always necessary or desirable to record all personal or corporate names given on

the title page. However, any name for which an added entry is to be made must be recorded. If the person chosen for the main entry is not the sole author, an author statement should be used to describe the nature of responsibility for the work, whether joint authorship, editorial responsibility, or other relationship. If more than three persons are jointly responsible for a book, only the first is named, and "and others" or "et al." replaces the other names. When a library has many editions of a particular work, editors, illustrators, or translators may be named. If a significantly different form of name for an author is used in the heading, the name as given on the title page should be recorded in the author statement.
Examples:

> All the President's men, by Carl Bernstein and Bob Woodward.
> Contemporary quotations, compiled by James B. Simpson.
> Writing without letters, by Ernst Pulgram and others; edited by W. Haas. (main entry under title)
> The tragedy of Macbeth, edited by Eugene M. Waith. (main entry: Shakespeare, William)
> Letters from the earth, by Mark Twain. (main entry: Clemens, Samuel Langhorne)

If a book is a second edition or any other revised edition, this must be stated. Library users, especially students, frequently have need for particular editions. The customary way of recording successive editions is: 2d ed., 3d ed., 4th ed., 5th ed., etc.

If a book is illustrated, the abbreviation "illus." or "ill." follows the paging of the book. Special types of illustrations such as portraits, maps, music, charts, and colored plates are all covered by "illus." They are not usually named separately in simplified description.

If a series name is prominently displayed on a book, or the

series is one with which patrons of the library are familiar, it is useful to record it. The series name in parentheses follows the paging and illustration statements.

Even in basic description, it may sometimes be desirable to include such notes as the following:

Cover title: The search for justice.
Previous editions have title: An introduction to biochemistry.
Bound with the author's First book of magic.
Sequel to Roses for Mary.

Few, if any, books require all the additions to basic description that have been presented. The card for a fictitious book shown in Figure 43 shows how these elements of description would be displayed on a catalog card if all were required.

```
Jones, Mary Elizabeth.
    Cataloging; a history of cataloging practices
in American libraries, by M. E. Jones and L. A.
Smith.  2d ed.  Watking, 1978, c1975.

    235 p.  illus.  (American library history
series, v.2)

    Cover title: Cataloging in American libraries.

    1. Cataloging. I. Title. II. Title: Cataloging
in American libraries.
```

Figure 43. Basic description with additional elements

Two other frequent variations to basic description are title main entries and descriptions of multivolume sets. A sample card for a title main entry is shown in Figure 44.

A number of variations are usually required for multivolume sets. If the volumes were not all published in one year, the inclusive dates of publication are given. The number of volumes is given instead of paging. If the volumes have individual titles, a contents note is necessary. A sample card is shown in Figure 45.

```
Economic impact of large public programs; the
   NASA Experience, edited by Eli Ginzberg and
   others.    Olympus Pub. Co., 1976.

176 p.


   1. United States. National Aeronautics and
Space Administration.  2. United States. Appro-
priations and expenditures.  3. Aerospace
industries - United States.  I. Ginzberg, Eli,
1911-
                    ◯
```

Figure 44. Title main entry

```
Strode, Hudson, 1893-
   Jefferson Davis.  Harcourt, Brace, 1955-64.

3 v.

Contents. - 1. American patriot, 1808-1861.
- 2. Confederate President. - 3. Tragic hero,
the last twenty-five years, 1864-1889.


   1. Davis, Jefferson, 1808-1889.
                    ◯
```

Figure 45. Multivolume set

Even in a very small library, other problems of description are frequently encountered, but many can be adequately solved merely by the application of reason. If no date is given anywhere in a book, the phrase "no date" can be used, or if the cataloger can make a good guess as to date, "1968?" might be recorded. Either would be better than leaving a blank space because they indicate that the book has been examined with the intent of locating the date of publication.

ADDITIONAL INFORMATION RECORDED BY SOME LIBRARIES.

Two other types of information that appear on all Library of Congress cards, as well as on the cards of most other large libraries, are place of publication and height of the book in centimeters. When a library has books from all over the world, place of publication is a useful piece of information. It also helps to distinguish between publishers with the same or similar names. The height of a book, together with the paging, gives an indication of the extent of the work. Also, it is a part of the description of the book as a physical object and thus may be helpful to the library worker searching for a misplaced book.

A decision must be made at some point on the amount of information that will be given in a library's catalog. In some cases it is simpler always to give a particular item of information than to make a separate decision for each book. For example, it is easier always to give the publisher's name than to decide for each book whether the publisher helps to identify a particular edition or the nature of the work. There are few problems in recording places of publication and heights of books. On the other hand, if users of the library almost never require this information, there is little reason to give it. It has sometimes been conjectured that library patrons are confused when too much information is given on catalog cards, but it is difficult to see how place of publication or a notation such as "27 cm." would confuse any intelligent adult; most library users are more likely to ignore unnecessary information than to be confused by it.

Many libraries also record bibliographies, indexes, and International Standard Book Numbers (ISBNs) for all books that contain them. However, the principal reason that description given on catalog cards in large libraries is more complicated than in small libraries is not because a few additional types of information are consistently given, but because there are more books of the type that require special notes and other elements of description and because the information that is given is given in more detail. Instead of "376 p. illus.," we may have "vii, 376 p., ₁16₁ p. of plates : ill., ports."

An annotation or summary is given on Library of Congress cards for children's books and many types of audiovisual materials. LJ catalog cards contain annotations as shown on the card in Figure 46.

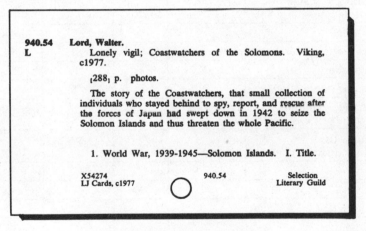

Figure 46. Annotation

Some children's libraries and other small libraries include annotations on all catalog cards, but most libraries that catalog large numbers of books do not find this a practical procedure.

The chart in Figure 47 shows the major types of information included on catalog cards and indicates which are basic for all (or almost all) books, which are basic for only some books, which are used by some libraries for all (or almost all) books, and which are used by some libraries for some books. "Some books" is used to mean either that not all books contain this feature or that it is not always recorded.

INFORMATION ON CATALOG CARDS

Type of Information	Basic: All books	Basic: Some books	Some libraries: All books	Some libraries: Some books
Main entry (usually author)	X		X	
Title	X		X	
Subtitle		X		X
Author statement		X	X	
Editors, translators illustrators, etc.		X		X
Edition		X		X
Place of publication			X	
Publisher	X		X	
Date of publication	X		X	
Paging or volume numbering	X		X	
Illustrative information		X		X
Size			X	
Series		X		X
Bibliography				X
Contents		X		X
Relationship to other works		X		X
Annotation			X	
International Standard Book Number (ISBN)				X
Tracings	X		X	

Figure 47.

The types of information presented on catalog cards are sometimes divided into categories or areas of description and are referred to by special terms. A few important definitions relating to elements on catalog cards are presented below.

Body of the entry. The part of the description that begins with the title and continues through the imprint.

Imprint. Place of publication, name of publisher, and date of publication.

Collation. Paging or volume numbering, illustrations, and size.

Notes. Relationships to other works, variations in title, bibliographies, indexes, contents, and other information which can not easily be incorporated into the preceding parts of the description.

International Standard Book Number (ISBN). A unique number assigned to books published in the United States, Great Britain, and some other countries. It is hoped that in time all books published will contain this number. An International Standard Serial Number (ISSN) is a unique number assigned to a particular series.

DESCRIPTIVE CATALOGING POLICIES.

There is no nationwide standard code for basic or simplified descriptive cataloging. The practices of small libraries are sometimes simplifications of codes used by large libraries, such as the *Anglo-American Cataloging Rules*. Small libraries that buy printed cards or receive cataloging for some of their books often attempt to do their own descriptive cataloging in a manner similar to that used by their primary cataloging sources. Other influences are cataloging textbooks and manuals and the needs expressed by library patrons. It is often useful for a small library to have its own manual of cataloging practices including a collection of sample catalog cards. Catalogers in small libraries need not feel that they must exactly follow the detailed rules used by large research libraries, but it is useful to at least adhere to the basic principles of traditional widespread cataloging practices. This not only helps to keep the library's catalog consistent within itself, but maintains it in general conformity with what patrons observe when they use other libraries.

Descriptive cataloging is not performed in a laissez-faire manner in large academic and research libraries. Every element of the description must be recorded according to exact rules. Not only is the wording used on cards important, but punctuation, capitalization, and spacing must also be used in the prescribed manner. If Library of Congress cataloging is not available for a book, the cataloger must usually attempt to catalog it in the manner of the Library of Congress. There are reasons for this exactitude. In large libraries, which acquire both new and old books from all over the world, many types of cataloging decisions are made. Moreover, many different catalogers are involved in the decision process. A detailed set of rules is necessary in order to maintain consistency. In addition, cooperative cataloging demands that the cataloging of various libraries be acceptable to other libraries. The same code must be used by the participating libraries and be applied consistently.

Is it possible to devise a code for descriptive cataloging so that if 100 different catalogers were to catalog the same book, all of them would catalog it in exactly the same manner? To one who has not worked in the field of cataloging, the compilation of a code that would enable all books to be cataloged by all libraries in a uniform manner might not seem like a difficult task; but to those who have tried to apply the Anglo-American Cataloging Rules or International Standard Bibliographic Description to many different books, it is obvious that no set of rules, no matter how detailed, can be totally unambiguous.

Since most large libraries and many medium-sized libraries follow the descriptive cataloging practices of the Library of Congress, an understanding of how these practices have evolved is useful. A cataloger cannot use the old Library of Congress printed catalogs as a guide for descriptive cataloging, because many of the policies used in the past are no longer observed. For example, in old Library of Congress cataloging, three dots were frequently used to indicate information not transcribed; only the proper names or the first word of a corporate body name were capitalized; the publisher's full name as given in the imprint included terms such as "& Co."; and paging was often described in detail including even unpaged leaves. A sample card is shown in Figure 48.

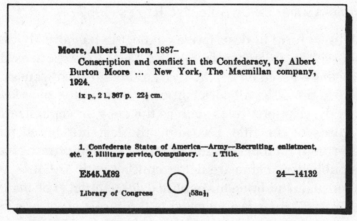

Figure 48. Library of Congress card (old style)

From 1951 to 1963 the Library of Congress practiced "limited cataloging" for some books. It is recognizable by a double dagger (‡) following the LC card number. Author statements were given only when necessary to show a feature such as joint authorship, preliminary pages were not included in the paging statement, "illus." was used for all types of illustrations, and bibliography notes were given only when of special importance. A sample of limited cataloging is shown in Figure 49.

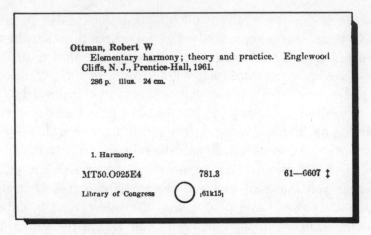

Ottman, Robert W
    Elementary harmony; theory and practice. Englewood
Cliffs, N. J., Prentice-Hall, 1961.
    286 p. Illus. 24 cm.

1. Harmony.

MT50.O925E4   781.3   61—6607 ‡

Library of Congress   [61k15]

Figure 49.   Library of Congress limited cataloging

ANGLO-AMERICAN CATALOGING RULES (1967)

A basic form of descriptive cataloging has already been discussed in this chapter. Almost all of the practices discussed are based on AACR 1967, although the discussions often do not cover all possibilities or contain the niceties of exact description. Rules such as the ones for capitalization of words of the title, recording the last numbered page rather than total pages, and omitting certain phrases from the publisher's name are not in conflict with AACR.

One major addition to simplified description to be made if AACR 1967 rules are followed is the insertion of brackets around information not found in a designated location. According to AACR 1967, the title page is to be used as the basis of description for the body of the entry. Any information located in another part of the book or derived from any other source must be enclosed in brackets. For example, if the place of publication, edition, or date is given only on the verso (reverse side) of the title page, it must be enclosed in brackets.

Another important point to remember when following AACR is that abbreviations should not be used unless specifically permitted. As an example, "edited" is not on the list of words that can be abbreviated, so it must be spelled in full. Appendix III of AACR contains lists of acceptable abbreviations.

Subtitles are always given, but a long subtitle, separable from the title, may be given in a note rather than in the usual position following the title.

The situations in which the author statement can be omitted are listed in AACR. Generally they are those in which form of name in the main entry heading is the same as that that would be given in the author statement. Words such as "by" and "and" are added in brackets when it is necessary to make the author statement more intelligible.

An edition statement given to a work is always included even if the statement is "1st ed."

The place of publication is given. It is followed by its country, state, or similar designation if it is necessary to identify the place or distinquish it from another with the same name. Abbreviations from Appendix III are used for most such designations.

Exact rules for recording the publisher and date are given. In simplified cataloging it is often satisfactory to solve a problem merely by making a reasonable decision, but if a library follows a code strictly, the solution must not only be reasonable but in accordance with the code. An example of a book with no imprint date was given earlier. AACR 1967 has precise recommendations. The last resort, if no date can be established, is "n.d." given within brackets.

The last numbered pages of each section of the book, including short introductory sections, is recorded. An unnumbered group of pages is mentioned if it is one-fifth or more of the entire work. There are special rules for unpaged works, irregular paging, folded leaves, multivolume works, and other variations.

Although the abbreviation "illus." is used to describe all types of illustrative matter, there are particular types such as charts, facsimilies, maps, and portraits that are specifically designated when they are considered important. The height of the book is given in centimeters. The width of the book is also specified if it is less than half the height or greater than the height.

Series are always recorded, usually with the form of title given in the work. Special rules cover multiple series, series with subseries, and other problems in recording series.

Examples of types of notes that are necessary or desirable are given and a general order in which to record them is prescribed.

Punctuation and spacing are not precisely regulated in AACR 1967, although a general recommendation is made to follow standard usage and some examples for the use of particular marks are given in Appendix V. Double punctuation is generally avoided. For example, if the date is in brackets, a comma does not precede it.

A sample card showing the various elements of AACR 1967 and a possible method of punctuation and spacing is shown, together with an actual Library of Congress card, in Figure 50.

INTERNATIONAL STANDARD BIBLIOGRAPHIC DESCRIPTION (ISBD) 1974.

In 1974 descriptive cataloging underwent a major change with the adoption of International Standard Bibliographic Description (ISBD), with guidelines published in the revised Chapter 6 of *Anglo-American Cataloging Rules*.

A complete exposition of ISBD will not be given here, but only some of the principal variations from basic description and AACR 1967. One of the most apparent differences is in punctuation and spacing. The descriptive elements of the catalog entry are divided into seven areas: title and statement of authorship, edition, imprint, collation, series, notes, and ISBN area. Each area that does not begin a new paragraph is separated from the following area by a period - - space - - dash - - space (. —). With the exception of periods

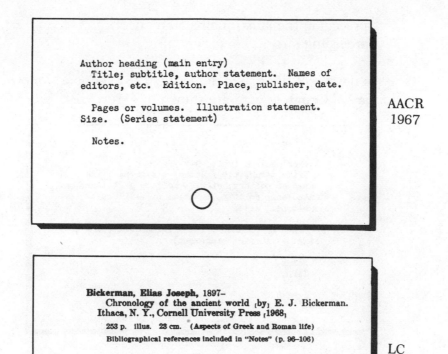

Author heading (main entry)
    Title; subtitle, author statement. Names of
editors, etc. Edition. Place, publisher, date.

    Pages or volumes. Illustration statement.
Size. (Series statement)

    Notes.

AACR
1967

Bickerman, Elias Joseph, 1897–
    Chronology of the ancient world [by] E. J. Bickerman.
Ithaca, N. Y., Cornell University Press [1968]
    253 p. illus. 23 cm. (Aspects of Greek and Roman life)
    Bibliographical references included in "Notes" (p. 96–106)

LC

    1. History, Ancient—Chronology.   I. Title.   (Series)

D54.5.B5 1968   529'.32   68—10758

Library of Congress   [68c3]

Figure 50.   Elements of cataloging and illustrative card

and commas, all prescribed punctuation marks are preceded and followed by one space. The period and comma are
followed by one space. Prescribed punctuation must always
be used even though double punctuation results. Some of
the other major specifications for punctuation are the fol
lowing:

preceding the subtitle :
preceding the author statement /
preceding the publisher :

preceding the illustration statement :
preceding size ;

An outline of the major elements of ISBD and a sample
Library of Congress card are shown in Figure 51.

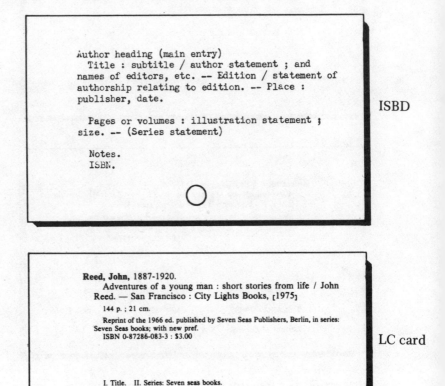

Figure 51. Elements of bibliographic description
and illustrative card

Unlike AACR 1967, which regards the title page as the
primary source of information for the entire body of the
entry, ISBD considers the half title, added title page, verso of

the title page, cover, spine, and colophon to be primary sources of information for the edition and imprint areas. If the information pertaining to edition, place of publication, publisher, or date is given in any of these places, it is not enclosed in brackets in the description. This rule change results in the use of many fewer brackets.

Only a few additions and revisions to the list of abbreviations presented in the appendix of AACR 1967 are made in ISBD, but some of these occur frequently. The abbreviation for "illustrations" and "illustrator" is changed from "illus." to "ill." When no date of publication is given, "n.d." can no longer be used. A date of publication must be estimated. If no place of publication is given, "s.l." for *sine loco* is used instead of "n.p." In ISBD "et al." is used to indicate the omission of names in the author statement even when the title is in English; "and others" is no longer used.

An author statement given in the work is always recorded in ISBD, even if it repeats exactly the main entry heading. (An authorship statement does not always include the word "by" but may merely be the names of the authors appearing on the title page before or after the title or elsewhere in the work.) "By" and "and" are transcribed if given but are not supplied by the cataloger. An example of the same author statement as it would be given in three types of description is shown below in order to illustrate that each type of description has its advantages.

> Basic: The final days, by Bob Woodward and Carl Bernstein.
> AACR 1967: The final days [by] Bob Woodward [and] Carl Bernstein.
> ISBD: The final days / Bob Woodward, Carl Bernstein.

The first is easily understood. The second, however, is more informative because it shows which information actually appears on the title page. It is probably as easily understood as the first, but is more difficult to type, especially if the typewriter used does not have a key for brackets. The third is even more easily typed than the first but may not be as easily understood by infrequent library users. However, persons not familiar with the English language might comprehend it more easily, and universal comprehension is one of the goals of ISBD.

Three additional elements of description frequently appear in ISBD entries. Indexes, as well as bibliographies, are noted; when a series has been assigned an International Standard Serial Number (ISSN), it follows the title of the series; and for all books having International Standard Book Numbers, the ISBN is recorded following the last item in the notes area. There are, of course, many other less apparent differences between AACR 1967 and ISBD.

In this discussion the comparison has been between the rules published in 1967 and those published in 1974. However, although the adoption of ISBD in 1974 was a major change, minor changes in descriptive cataloging rules are continually made by the Library of Congress and published in *Cataloging Service*, a bulletin published by its Processing Department. In large libraries that follow changes in rules made by the Library of Congress, the rules for descriptive cataloging never remain static for very long.

TYPING CATALOG CARDS.

Most libraries that type some or all of their own catalog cards have formalized rules on how many spaces should be left blank at the top and left margins of cards. (It is not customary to leave right or bottom margins.) Rules on indention and spacing are also commonly prescribed. However, it is important to realize that these are only the rules of particular libraries and are not part of a standard, generally accepted code.

Although it is usually desirable for a library to have its own individualized manual or set of sample cards illustrating how cards are to be typed, a number of cataloging textbooks and manuals that give detailed typing instructions can be used. Typing instructions are given in:

Bidlack, Russell E. *Typewritten Catalog Cards*. 2d ed. (Campus Publishers, 1970)

Piercy, Esther J. *Commonsense Cataloging*. 2d ed. (H. W. Wilson, 1974)

Wynar, Bohdan S. *Introduction to Cataloging and Classification*, 5th ed. (Libraries Unlimited, 1976)

The comparison illustrated in Figure 52, which shows a few of the rules given in these three books, not only illustrates the lack of standardization in typing rules but also gives a general indication of customary spacing and indention.

COMPARISON OF RULES FOR INDENTION AND SPACING

	Bidlack	*Piercy*	*Wynar*
Main entry begins on which line from top of card?	Third	Third	Fourth
Main entry begins on which space from left edge of card (First indention)?	Ninth	Ten spaces from left edge	Nine spaces from left edge
Title begins on which space from left edge of card (Second indention)?	Eleventh	Twelve spaces from left edge	Thirteen spaces from left edge
Position of call number	Second line from top of card; as close as possible to left edge	Third line from top; two spaces from left edge	Fourth line from top; one space from left edge

Figure 52.

When a library decides on rules for spacing and indention, it should be kept in mind that it is desirable to allow for the recording of a maximum amount of data on cards in order to avoid excess use of second cards. This is the reason for single spacing and lack of right and bottom margins. Some libraries permit the recording of tracings on the reverse side of cards, which also reduces the number of second cards needed. In spite of the desire to conserve space, an adequate left margin is necessary so that even long call numbers can be displayed in the customary position. A top margin also is needed so that subject headings and added entries can be typed above the main entry on secondary cards.

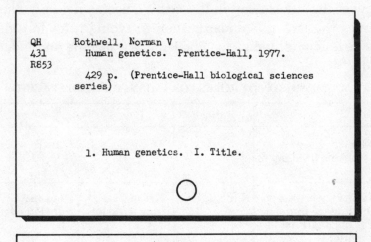

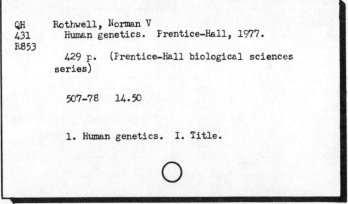

Figure 53.   Complete set of cards

(continued on following page)

152   **INTRODUCTION TO LIBRARY TECHNICAL SERVICES**

```
        HUMAN GENETICS
QH    Rothwell, Norman V
431      Human genetics.  Prentice-Hall, 1977.
R853
         429 p.  (Prentice-Hall biological sciences
      series)


                        ◯
```

```
        Human genetics.
QH    Rothwell, Norman V
431      Human genetics.  Prentice-Hall, 1977.
R853
         429 p.  (Prentice-Hall biological sciences
      series)


                        ◯
```

Figure 53 (continued)

If all cards are individually typed, considerable time can be saved by not including complete information on subject and added entry cards. Tracings are often given only on main entry and shelf list cards and in some libraries only on main entry cards. When contents are listed, they are frequently given only for the main entry. In some libraries and library systems where many added copies and replacements are acquired, less information is given on the shelf list card in order to allow more space for the recording of copy information. If the shelf list card is exactly the same as the main entry card, it should be marked in some way so that it will not be filed by mistake in the public catalog.

Many libraries type subject headings all in capital letters. Some type them in red or mark the top edge of subject cards with red ink. Subject headings and added entries are usually indented two spaces from the main entry heading.

A complete set of cards is shown in Figure 53. The shelf list card can be distinquished because it includes an order number and price. Chapter 13 will discuss further the advisability of giving particular types of information on shelf list cards.

CHAPTER 10

The Subject Approach:

Part 1, Subject Headings

IN MOST American libraries, books on a subject can be located either by consulting the library catalog under the name of the subject or by browsing through the books in one section of the classified shelf arrangement. The dual subject approach is advantageous because some books can more easily be located by subject headings and others by classification. A book can only be shelved in one place, but as many subject headings as necessary can be assigned to it. On the other hand, related subjects such as mathematics and algebra will be shelved close together, but the subject headings will be far apart in the alphabetically arranged catalog.

It is fortunate that the entire responsibility for the subject approach to books does not rest upon the fragile structure of subject headings assigned by librarians. Library subject headings have been criticized for lack of consistency, lack of specificity, use of outdated terminology, lack of agreement with common usage, sexism, racism, and general inadequacy. (For examples of criticisms of subject headings see Elizabeth Dickinson's "Of Catalogs, Computers, and Communication," *Wilson Library Bulletin*, Feb. 1976, and Lillian M. Wehmeyer's "Cataloging the School Media Center as a Specialized Collection," *Library Resources & Technical Services*, Fall 1976.) Although library subject headings are far from perfect, some of the criticism results from unreasonable expectations. In this chapter ten subject heading myths will be exposed, the two major lists of library subject headings will be discussed, and advice will be given on how to assign subject headings.

SUBJECT HEADING MYTHS.

Myth 1. Subject headings should reveal all the information in the library about a subject.

Only very inexperienced researchers expect catalog subject headings to lead them to all of the information in the library. Other library users know that they should consult periodical indexes for articles in magazines, newspaper indexes for newspaper articles, and special indexes for various other types of materials, such as government documents. They also know that encyclopedias and other reference works contain general information and facts on almost every subject.

Myth 2. Without subject headings library patrons would have no means of locating books on subjects.

Although most libraries include subject headings in their catalogs, a few do not. How can books on subjects be located if there are no subject headings? One method is to go directly to the shelves in the appropriate area of the classification and browse. To locate the correct section for a subject the index to the classification can be consulted. Alternatively, bibliographies and other reference works can be consulted to locate author and title information about books on a subject. The library catalog can then be consulted to determine whether the books are available. *Subject Guide to Books in Print*, *The Library of Congress Catalog: Subjects*, and the *Public Library Catalog* and other catalogs in the H.W. Wilson Standard Catalog Series list books on all subjects. Subject headings in a library catalog point out books that are not shelved with other books about a subject and provide a direct approach to books without the intermediate step of checking bibliographies, but they are not indispensable.

Myth 3. If a library catalog does not contain a subject heading for a subject, there are probably no books in the library that contain information about the subject.

If a book devoted to a particular subject cannot be located, books that might contain chapters or pages on the subject can be sought. If a library does not have a book on owls, it is reasonable to check the indexes or tables of contents of books about birds. If a library does not have a book on oak trees, books on trees can be checked. Most library users use techniques such as this without verbalizing a rule about proceeding from a specific to a more general subject. Analytics for chapters in books and cross-references from a specific to a more general topic may occasionally be worthwhile, but they are not so useful as experience and training in research techniques.

Myth 4. Subject headings such as those of the Library of Congress are or should be based on concepts, ideas, popular topics, and a logical organization of knowledge.

A list of subject headings that is to be used in assigning subjects to books is reasonably based on the topics that are discussed in books. The Library of Congress does not develop new subject headings in advance of books appearing on subjects. If a number of books appear on a subject and one term is consistantly used to refer to the subject, it is then reasonable to expect a new subject heading. Criticisms of subject heading lists should take into account their relationship to published books.

Myth 5. Information about a subject can be efficiently located even if one knows nothing about the subject.

If a library user is looking for information about astral bodies and astral projection without knowing the meanings of the terms and does not find subject headings or cross-references in the library catalog, he is not at a dead end. The next logical step is to consult a dictionary. After the meanings of the terms have been determined, information can be sought in books listed under PSYCHICAL RESEARCH, THEOSOPHY, and related headings. The better one understands a subject the easier it is to locate materials related to the subject. The subject heading network should not be expected to function independently of information that can be easily located in basic reference works.

Myth 6. Libraries are self-service institutions.

Many library patrons prefer to search for information independently and only reluctantly resort to seeking help from the library staff. On the other hand, some patrons, no matter how excellent the organization of the library and how self-explanatory the catalog and other reference tools, will continue to seek assistance. If all or almost all the professional and paraprofessionals were transferred from public service work to technical service work so that better and more complete subject headings could be assigned, in most libraries the public would not be better served. A library has only a certain number of staff members, and time spent on improving the library's catalog may not be as well spent as time spent on assisting the public to use a less than perfect catalog.

Myth 7. Subject headings are the realm of catalogers only.

A list of subject headings is not a secret code. There is no reason why a copy of the list of subject headings used by a library should not be available near the catalog for the use of patrons and staff who are assisting patrons. Moreover, public service personnel have as much need for familiarity with subject headings as technical services personnel. Many reference librarians spend as much time with subject headings as do catalogers; the difference is that they are working from subject to book rather than from book to subject.

Myth 8.   The use of books in libraries depends upon the subject headings assigned to them.

Many library books will be used extensively even if no subject headings are assigned to them. In a public library, the demand for works of fiction and nonfiction best-sellers is seldom the result of the books being located in the catalog under subject. In a school or academic library, the inclusion of a book on a teacher's list of recommended reading will usually produce more demand for the book than any subject heading. In specialized and research libraries, scholars and scientists locate books on the basis of their knowledge of others working in their field and by reading current journals and reviews. However, public library users do sometimes seek information on particular subjects, students writing term papers approach the catalog by means of subjects, scholars sometimes seek information on subjects with which they are not familiar, and some books would seldom be used if subject headings did not bring them to the attention of users. All use of books in libraries does not result from their being listed under subject, but properly assigned subject headings do increase the use of some books.

Myth 9.   Subject headings bear little relationship to the terminology used by authors and scholars.

Since subject headings are intended to bring together books on particular subjects regardless of the terminology used by the authors, it is not surprising that one can easily find subject headings using different words than those in the titles. Moreover, many subject headings fail to reflect changing word usage. However, discussions of subject headings that use only inappropriate words or problem subject headings as examples give a misleading impression of the generality of library subject headings. The titles and Library of Congress (LC) and Sears subject headings for ten books selected at random are shown in Figure 54. (This is a small sample, and the reader may wish to browse through a library catalog to verify that it is not unrepresentative; also it is important to bear in mind that subject headings are assigned on the basis of contents of books, not just titles.)

The subject headings for these ten books are not beyond criticism, but neither do they widely depart from the usage of terms by authors or the general public. For all books except numbers 7 and 10, the first words of the LC subject headings appear (or appear in closely related forms) in the titles. Cross-references are made in the LC subject heading list from URBAN AREAS to CITIES AND TOWNS, from BLACKS—UNITED STATES to AFRO-AMERICANS, and from SOCIETY, HIGH and HIGH SOCIETY to UPPER CLASSES. Like LC, Sears has a reference from URBAN AREAS to CITIES AND TOWNS and has a reference from SOCIETY, UPPER to UPPER CLASSES. No new headings were used, but the cataloger using Sears might consider adding headings such as MOLECULAR GENETICS, BLACK SOCIETY, and MUSIC INDUSTRIES AND TRADE. A cataloger, especially in a library in Georgia, for instance, might also consider making a cross-reference from GEORGIA—FOLKLORE to FOLKLORE—GEORGIA.

Myth 10. Subjects are static, have clear boundaries, and exist independently of the way in which we refer to them.

It is difficult to assign subject headings to some books. Since nonfiction books are usually written with the intent of making a contribution to the store of knowledge, they often discuss subjects not previously discussed, approach an old subject in a new way, or relate one subject to another. The relationship between subject headings and the subjects themselves is analogous to the relationship between words

SUBJECT HEADINGS FOR TEN BOOKS

Titles and Subtitles	LC Subject Headings	Sears Subject Headings
1. The poet's third eye: a guide to the symbolisms of modern literature.	Symbolism in literature. Poetry, Modern—History and criticism.	Symbolism in literature. Poetry—History and criticism.
2. The Purchaser's guide to the music industries.	Music trade—United States—Directories.	Musical instruments. (most of the book is about instruments)
3. A treasury of Georgia folklore.	Folk-lore—Georgia.	Folklore—Georgia.
4. Encyclopedia of associations	Associations, institutions, etc.—United States—Directories.	Associations—Directories.
5. Concepts of molecular genetics: information flow in genetics and evolution.	Molecular genetics.	Genetics. Molecular biology
6. Understanding photography.	Photography.	Photography.
7. The urban crisis: problems & prospects in America.	Cities and towns—United States	Cities and towns.
8. Successful management by objectives: an action manual.	Management by objectives.	Management.
9. Hume: a re-evaluation.	Hume, David, 1711–1776—Addresses, essays, lectures.	Hume, David, 1711–1776
10. Gerri Major's Black society.	Afro-Americans—Biography. Upper Classes—United States.	Blacks. Upper classes.

Figure 54.

and meanings. Meanings do not exist independently of the use of the words, and subjects do not exist independently of the way in which they are defined. When we say a building is a house we are assigning it to a particular category, but we are not implying that it is identical to other houses. When we give a book the Sears subject heading HOUSES, even though it is about cottages or mansions, we are assigning the book to a particular category but not implying that it covers exactly the same material as other books in that category.

LISTS OF SUBJECT HEADINGS: LIBRARY OF CONGRESS AND SEARS.

It would be possible to offer a subject approach to most nonfiction books merely by entering them under key words of the titles. The problem with this method is lack of unity. It would not bring together under one heading all books on a particular subject. When a library uses a standard list of subject headings, the catalog user is referred from words with the same or closely related meanings to one heading that assembles all books related to the subject. Use of a standard list of subject headings assists the cataloger in grouping related books so that the library user does not have to seek each book separately but can find under one heading a number of books that may answer his need.

In a large library with many catalogers, use of a list of subject headings also promotes consistency among catalogers. Even in a small library, over a period of years a number of different people may have responsibility for subject headings; without a standard list each cataloger might assign headings in a different manner.

Many large public libraries, college and university libraries, and some special libraries use Library of Congress subject headings. Sears subject headings are widely used by small public libraries and school libraries. Some special libraries use specialized lists prepared for a particular field. PRECIS, the PREserved Context Index System, developed by Derek Austin at the British Library and used for the

British National Bibliography, is receiving increasing attention by catalogers in the United States as a possible alternative to the Library of Congress subject headings. It is based on the concept of an open-ended vocabulary and a set of working procedures. There is currently much research being done on subject indexing, especially in the area of automated information retrieval systems. It is possible that in the future libraries will use a different type of subject approach, but at present most libraries still assign headings from one of the two major standard lists, making modifications and additions as necessary.

Library of Congress Subject Headings, 8th ed., (1975) is a two-volume work containing over 2,000 pages of subject headings and references. The 72-page introduction discusses the filing arrangement of headings, lists types of headings not included in the list, describes the formation of headings and subdivisions, and gives an annotated list of over 600 commonly used subdivisions. A special list of subject headings for children's literature follows the introduction. The eighth edition of the list is kept current by supplements. It is possible to subscribe to the headings on microform. Each issue on microfiche or microfilm is a total cumulation of the headings.

A portion of a page from *Library of Congress Subject Headings* is shown in Figure 55. The subject headings themselves are in boldface type. Notice the heading SUBJECT HEADINGS. Following it is a suggested Library of Congress classification number, Z695. Below it is a scope note explaining that it can be used for two types of books, English language subject heading lists (such as LC and Sears) and books about subject headings. The symbol "sa" means *see also*. The cataloger should consider making such references as:

SUBJECT HEADINGS
see also
AUTOMATIC INDEXING

Subject headings *(Z695)*

Here are entered general works on subject
headings and lists of subject headings
in the English language.

sa Automatic indexing
Classification—Books
Cross references (Cataloging)
Exclusion lists in automatic indexing
Thesauri

x Headings, Subject
Indexing vocabularies
Subject headings, English
Thesauri, Subject

xx Cataloging
Catalogs, Dictionary
Catalogs, Subject
Indexes
Subject cataloging
Thesauri

— Aeronautics, ₍Education, Law, etc.₎
x Aeronautics ₍Education, Law, etc.₎—
Subject headings

— Photographs
See Subject headings—Pictures

— Pictures
x Photographs—Subject headings
Pictures—Subject headings
Subject headings—Photographs

— Programmed instruction

Subject headings, English
See Subject headings

**Subject headings, French, ₍German, Spanish,
etc.₎**
x French ₍German, Spanish, etc.₎ subject
headings

Figure 55. From *Library of Congress Subject Headings*

The symbol "x" means that a cross-reference from HEAD-
INGS, SUBJECT or any of the following three terms can be
made:

HEADINGS, SUBJECT
see
SUBJECT HEADINGS

The symbol "xx" means that a *see also* reference from
CATALOGING or any of the following five terms might be
made.

CATALOGING
see also
SUBJECT HEADINGS

The word "Aeronautics" preceded by a dash means we can use the heading SUBJECT HEADINGS—AERONAUTICS. The words "Education, Law, etc." in brackets mean we can subdivide also by these subjects or similar subjects. Two other subdivisions listed are PICTURES and PROGRAMMED INSTRUCTION. However, the word "Photographs" should not be used as a subdivision; the heading SUBJECT HEADINGS—PICTURES should be used and a cross-reference made:

SUBJECT HEADINGS—PHOTOGRAPHS
see
SUBJECT HEADINGS—PICTURES

Sears List of Subject Headings, 11th ed. (1977), contains 617 pages of headings. The introduction discusses the principles and practices of subject cataloging and gives important directions for use of the list. Before using any list of subject headings, always read the directions contained in the introduction.

The Sears list is much less extensive than the Library of Congress list since it is intended for smaller libraries. However, Sears headings are generally based on Library of Congress headings; modifications have been kept to a minimum. The LC subject headings for children's literature have been incorporated into the Sears list.

A sample page from the Sears list is shown in Figure 56. Notice that words used as headings are in boldface type as on the LC list. The same symbols, "x" and "xx," are used for terms from which *see* or *see also* references should be made, but "sa" is not used, being replaced by see also. The classification numbers given in the Sears list are Dewey rather than Library of Congress numbers.

Factors other than the size of a library and the nature of its collection also often influence the choice between LC and Sears headings. In the past, the wide distribution of LC printed cards spread the use of LC headings. Today, the

Study, Method of 371.3
> *See also* subjects with the subdivision *Study and teaching*, e.g. **Art—Study and teaching;** etc.
>> *x* Learning, Art of; Method of study
>> *xx* **Education; Teaching**

Study abroad. *See* **Foreign study**

Study overseas. *See* **Foreign study**

Stuttering. *See* **Speech disorders**

Style, Literary 808
> *See also* **Criticism; Letter writing; Literature—History and criticism; Rhetoric**
>> *x* **Literary style**
>> *xx* **Criticism; Literature; Rhetoric**

Style in dress. *See* **Costume; Fashion**

Style manikins. *See* **Models, Fashion**

Style manuals. *See* **Printing—Style manuals**

Subconsciousness 127; 154.2
> *See also*

Consciousness	**Mind and body**
Dreams	**Personality dis-**
Faith healing	**orders**
Hallucinations and	**Psychoanalysis**
illusions	**Sleep**
Hypnotism	**Thought transfer-**
Mental healing	**ence**
Mental suggestion	

>> *xx* **Consciousness; Hypnotism; Mental healing; Mind and body; Psychical research; Psychoanalysis; Psychology; Psychology, Pathological; Therapeutics, Suggestive**

Subgravity state. *See* **Weightlessness**

Subject headings 025.3
> *See also* **Classification—Books**
>> *x* **Thesauri**
>> *xx* **Cataloging; Catalogs, Subject; Indexes**

Submarine boats. *See* **Submersibles; Submarines**

Submarine cables. *See* **Cables, Submarine**

Submarine diving. *See* **Diving, Submarine**

Submarine exploration. *See* **Underwater exploration**

Submarine geology 551.4
> *See also* **Ocean bottom; Plate tectonics**
>> *x* Geology, Submarine; Marine geology; Underwater geology
>> *xx* **Geology; Oceanography; Plate tectonics**

Submarine medicine 616.9
>> *x* Medicine, Submarine; Underwater physiology; Underwater medicine
>> *xx* **Medicine**

Submarine photography. *See* **Photography, Submarine**

Submarine research stations. *See* **Undersea research stations**

Submarine telegraph. *See* **Cables, Submarine**

Submarine vehicles. *See* **Submersibles**

Figure 56.   From *Sears List of Subject Headings*

expanding use of Cataloging in Publication (CIP) on the verso of title pages is making LC subject headings more readily available to catalogers. On the other hand, printed cards with Sears headings can be purchased from various sources. When libraries are part of a system or are served by a cataloging or processing center, the decision on subject headings is seldom made by the individual libraries. Finally, it is often easier to continue past practice than to make major changes; a library may not have developed in the manner expected when the decision on subject headings was made but may nevertheless continue using the selected list.

That the LC list is more comprehensive and detailed than the Sears list can be seen by a comparison of the sample pages shown in this chapter. However, the headings used for many books are similar. Earlier in this chapter, ten titles and the subject headings for them were given. In most cases the LC and Sears headings are similar. A cataloger in a small library that uses Sears can easily convert the LC headings given in CIP or located elsewhere to Sears headings. Many subdivisions used by LC are not necessary in a small library and can be omitted. A relatively small amount of time spent on adjusting headings may result in cataloging more appropriate to a small collection and more useful to the patrons.

For original cataloging in a small library with a general collection, the Sears heading list can be used more easily than the LC list. However, if a library receives many scientific or specialized books, such as the one on molecular genetics included in the sample of ten books, the LC list is more helpful. Many more terms are included, so there is a better chance of finding the specific term needed.

How to Assign Subject Headings.

Subject headings should never be assigned on the basis of titles alone. Although many titles accurately reflect subjects, others do not. To determine the subject of a book, read the title page, the table of contents, and as much of the preface, introduction, and text as is necessary to grasp the substance and intent of the book.

Not all books need subject headings. As was stated earlier, certain types of books, such as fiction, are seldom selected by patrons on the basis of subject headings. The poetry, letters, essays, and general writings of individual authors are also usually sought under the author's name. A reader looking for one of Erma Bombeck's popular books will almost certainly look under author or title rather than try to guess at a subject heading. However, there is no rule that forbids using a subject heading for a novel or any other book if the cataloger considers it useful. Historical and biographical novels often contain considerable information about their subjects and are frequently assigned subject headings.

When subject headings are assigned, they are not always derived from subject heading lists. Names of persons, places, associations, institutions, and government agencies are not included in the LC or Sears list except when necessary to indicate possible subdivisions. Names of persons and corporate bodies are used in the same form as for main and added entries. If all possible proper names were included in a subject heading list, the list would be endless.

After the cataloger has examined the content of a book and has decided that a subject heading of the type given in a subject heading list is to be assigned, the next step is to seek as specific a heading as possible. If a book is about library technical services, the heading LIBRARIES—TECHNICAL SERVICES can be found in the Sears list. But if a book is only about cataloging, the appropriate heading is CATALOGING. If the book is about only one aspect of cataloging, such as subject headings, the specific Sears heading is SUBJECT HEADINGS. One does not use all three headings for the same book. *See also* references are made from LIBRARIES—TECHNICAL SERVICES to CATALOGING and from CATALOGING to SUBJECT HEADINGS. References from SUBJECT HEADINGS to CATALOGING and from CATALOGING to LIBRARIES—TECHNICAL SERVICES are not made because it is assumed that a person looking for information about subject headings will know that they are included in discussions of cataloging and that cataloging is part of library technical services.

Inexperienced catalogers are sometimes tempted to use broad areas of knowledge rather than specific subjects for headings. The subject heading should be as specific as the topic of the book. If a book is an introduction to philosophy, PHILOSOPHY may be the appropriate heading, but if the book is about metaphysics, METAPHYSICS is the correct heading. It is seldom useful to have hundreds or thousands of books listed under broad subjects such as philosophy, religion, or sociology. The library user who wants to know what books are available in an area of knowledge can examine the appropriate section of the classification on the shelves or in the shelf list.

Although catalogers usually select the most specific terms available from their lists of subject headings, all books are not assigned truly specific headings. In the sample of ten books given earlier, specific headings for books 1 and 10 respectively would be SYMBOLISM IN MODERN POETRY and AFRO-AMERICAN UPPER CLASSES. If no specific term is available, it is sometimes necessary to select two or more headings, each of which brings out one aspect of the subject.

When a book covers two or three specific subjects, such as algebra, geometry, and trigonometry, separate headings are made for each subject. However, if many different subjects are included in a book, a broad heading covering all of them should be selected. For example, if almost all parts of the subject mathematics are covered, the heading should be MATHEMATICS. Although more than one subject heading is often necessary, headings should be assigned systematically, not with a shotgun approach. The relationships between subject headings used in the list should be considered. Although one should not be too optimistic, it can at least be hoped that most catalog users will approach their subject in a logical manner and with or without the aid of cross-references will proceed from the specific term they have in mind to related subjects.

One method of obtaining more specific entries for books is by means of subdivisions. Some subdivisions are indicated in the LC and Sears lists under the appropriate subjects, but each list also includes a list of general subdivisions. The subject WOMEN can be subdivided according to the form of the book, as in WOMEN—BIBLIOGRAPHY; by the geographical area covered, as in WOMEN—FRANCE; by a chronological division, as in WOMEN—HISTORY—TO 500; and by a special aspect of the subject, as in WOMEN—EMPLOYMENT.

In Chapter 8 of this book, analytical entries for authors and titles of chapters or sections of books were discussed. If a chapter or group of pages in a book discusses a subject for which the library receives many requests for information, a subject analytical entry such as the one shown in Figure 57 below may be useful.

Figure 57.   Subject analytical entry

In small libraries with few, if any, books wholly on certain subjects, subject analytics are more useful than in large libraries. Subject analytics can be used selectively to point out chapters or parts of books that are of special local interest or are closely related to a school curriculum.

The subjects of many books can be easily located in the lists of subject headings, but there are some books about which the cataloger may be uncertain. The library's catalog should be consulted whenever there is doubt as to the best subject heading. A cataloger working for a particular library is not working in a vacuum. He must determine how a book will fit into the organizational structure already established. Checking subject headings already included in a library's catalog and noticing the types of books listed under them is a very useful procedure. Reference works that give subject headings, such as the *American Book Publishing Record*, *Book Review Digest*, ALA's *Booklist*, and the H. W. Wilson Company's Standard Catalog Series can also be consulted. Perhaps most important of all, the needs of the users of the library should be taken into consideration.

Assigning subject headings to books is not the totality of subject heading work. Appropriate *see* and *see also* references must also be made. When a subject heading is used for the first time, the references shown in the standard list should be made if they are considered appropriate for the work in hand and in accordance with the word usage of the library's users. For example, when the heading SUBJECT HEADINGS is used for the first time in a library using Sears headings, the following suggested references should be evaluated:

> Subject headings
> *See also* Classification—Books
> x Thesauri
> xx Cataloging; Catalogs, Subject; Indexes

In many libraries the most useful reference would be:

> CATALOGING
> see also
> SUBJECT HEADINGS

Whether a cross-reference from THESAURI was made would depend on the type of book being cataloged under SUBJECT HEADINGS and on an opinion as to whether the library's users would be likely to use this term.

If some of the books in the catalog under CLASSIFICATION—BOOKS contain considerable information about subject headings, this *see also* reference should be made. Whether *see also* references from CATALOGS, SUBJECT and INDEXES were made would also depend upon the type of book being assigned the heading SUBJECT HEADINGS. As can be seen from this example, a useful network of *see* and *see also* references cannot be devised independently of knowledge of what books are in a library and how the library is used.

There are three methods of maintaining control over the use of subject headings and references. In one method, headings and references that have been used are checkmarked in a copy of the subject heading list. The names of headings that are not on the list and have been used are written in the proper place along with the references made to them. This method probably works best in a small library in which one person is responsible for assigning subject headings; the list used as the subject authority record can be kept on the cataloger's desk.

A second method, used by many medium-sized and large libraries, entails the maintenance of a subject authority file on cards. A card is made for each heading used, and instructions, scope notes, and references are indicated. If a library makes many departures from the subject heading list used as a basic guide, a separate subject authority file on cards or in another format is usually necessary.

The third subject authority procedure—working without a marked list or card file—is most practical for libraries that do original cataloging for only a small percentage of new acquisitions. If a library is able to obtain LC subject headings from CIP or printed cards for over 90 percent of new acquisitions, it may not be really necessary to check each subject heading used on these cards against an authority file or list. The substitute procedure, however, must be followed with care:

a. Watch for differences in terminology between titles and subject headings on all new card sets, for example "urban" in the title, but "cities and towns" in the subject heading. Also watch for other situations in which cross-references might be needed to lead library patrons to the assigned subject headings. Since no separate subject authority file is kept, the public catalog must be checked if there is doubt as to whether a cross-reference has already been made.

b. When filing subject cards (or revising filing), watch for subject headings not previously used. Resolve conflicts and make references when needed.

c. When performing original cataloging, refer to the public catalog whenever necessary. Since the public catalog in conjunction with the subject heading list serves as an authority file, this method of controlling subject headings is less practical if the catalogers are situated far from the catalog.

Subject heading work does not end with the initial cataloging of books. Each new edition of the LC and Sears subject heading lists contains many additions and changes. Moreover, the Library of Congress changes and adds headings continually, with the new and altered headings appearing on new LC cataloging copy. Changes in the terminology used for headings necessitate either changing headings already in library catalogs or making see also references.

Blind references are references that lead nowhere. If a high percentage of references in a catalog are blind references, users will begin to doubt all references. A major cause of blind references is that when books are withdrawn from a collection, the cards for the books are pulled from the catalog, but references to headings used on the cards are not pulled. Tracing each cross-reference on a card for the heading or checking a subject card against the authority file to determine references made if it was the last card under a heading are two methods of controlling this problem.

The following suggestions summarize the basics of assigning subject headings:

1. Do not assess books solely by their titles.
2. Do not feel that it is necessary to assign subject headings to all books. (Example: Fiction)
3. Do not expect to find names of people, places, or corporate bodies in subject heading lists.
4. Try to select headings as specific as the books themselves.
5. Assign multiple headings when necessary.
6. Use subdivisions according to the directions in your subject heading list.
7. Remember that subject headings are intended to serve library patrons; keep in mind their research skills and techniques.
8. Consider making subject analytical entries to meet special demands.
9. Consult your library's catalog whenever necessary to determine past practice; use other aids when expedient.
10. Contribute to a systematic network of headings and references by making needed cross-references, working with the subject authority file, and eliminating blind references.

CHAPTER 11:

The Subject Approach:
Part 2. Classification

How Should the Books in a Library Be Arranged?

The preceding chapters have discussed the preparation of a systematic record, or catalog, of the materials in a library. However, a library catalog is not useful unless there is a connecting link between the record of an item and the item itself. The catalog must provide a location symbol, call number, or other information that will lead the library user to the book he has selected. It is not necessary that the location device be based on the subject matter of the book; the books in a library may be arranged by order of accession, size, author or other characteristics as long as there is some means by which the library user can find a book which is entered in the library's catalog.

Classification numbers as currently used by most American libraries meet the need for a location device, but are also intended to serve other purposes. The classification system is expected to bring together books on a particular subject and place in close proximity books on related subjects. The library user who does not find the particular book he wants on the shelf may find another suitable book on the same subject shelved in the same area. The person who is looking for books about birds will find most of them conveniently located in one section. Subject headings are one means of locating books on subjects; the arrangement of books on the shelves provides an alternate or supplemental approach. The photography enthusiast can determine the area of the classification scheme in which books on photography are placed and peruse the shelves in the corresponding section of the library. This type of use of the classification system assumes that the reader has access to the shelves. In the past it was more common than at present for libraries to have "closed stacks." Library users located the books they wanted in the catalog and filled out "call slips," which they presented to a member of the library staff who then obtained the books. All or most of the library's users were not permitted to enter the area of the library where the books were shelved; in an academic library only faculty members might have had this privilege. Some libraries still have closed stacks or have particular areas that are not open to everyone, such as rare book collections, but the practice is much less prevalent. If library users do not have an opportunity to browse through the books on the shelves, arrangement by subject has fewer advantages. It is not merely coincidental that open shelves and arrangement of books by subject spread in popularity during the same period of time.

Classification numbers provide a location device and assist searchers after information in certain pragmatic ways, but when a classification system is also expected to display all of the books in a library in a completely logical, systematic arrangement, disillusionment may result. But even though the books in a library may never be classified perfectly, an attempt at systematic arrangement by subject will usually help many library users.

Although the books in most American libraries are arranged by subject, there are often exceptions to the basic arrangement. Reference books, children's books, rare books, books in foreign languages, new acquisitions, reserve books in college libraries, paperbacks, and oversize books are some types of books that are sometimes shelved separately with or without arrangement by classification within the particular group. Nonbook materials such as periodicals and audiovisual materials are also usually shelved separately.

When books are shelved by subject, they are usually shelved by one of the established classification systems. Reader interest groups or other homemade arrangements are sometimes used by small libraries, but for the same amount of effort better results can usually be achieved by using a standard system and benefiting from the work of specialists in subject classification.

DEWEY DECIMAL CLASSIFICATION SYSTEM.

In 1873, when Melvil Dewey developed his classification, arrangement of books by subject was not an established practice. In the preface to the first edition of his classification, published in 1876 and reprinted by Forest Press in 1976, he terms his classification as superior to the practice of shelving books in fixed locations on particular shelves. Dewey was a remarkable man. While working as a student at the Amherst College library, he studied hundreds of books and pamphlets on library science, visited many other libraries, and devised a system of classification that was almost immediately adopted by the library in which he worked. Later he founded the Library Bureau, played a major role in establishing the American Library Association, edited and contributed to the *Library Journal*, was librarian of Columbia College, directed the New York State Library, and worked for causes such as simplified spelling. The eighteenth unabridged edition of his classification was published in 1971.

In the Dewey Decimal Classification books are arranged numerically from 000 to 999; the 1,000 possible sections can be subdivided indefinitely by adding numbers to the right of the decimal, creating classifications such as 917.30492. The chief advantages of the system are: it is published in convenient format with instructions for use and index; it contains memory aids that make it easy to learn; it is flexible—the numbers can be expanded or contracted according to the needs of the library; and it proceeds from general to specific in a systematic manner. However, whenever necessary, it departs from logic and philosophical theory to provide a practical arrangement for books. Its disadvantages are that very long numbers must sometimes be used to provide an exact classification for specialized books. All knowledge does not fall naturally into divisions of ten; disciplines and subjects have been forced into a ten-part arrangement rather than a notation designed to fit the more natural but continuously developing divisions of knowledge.

The Dewey Decimal Classification is followed by a majority of American libraries, including nearly all public and school libraries. It is also widely used in other parts of the world and has been translated into many languages.

The abridged edition of Dewey (10th edition) includes an introduction, tables, and an index in one volume. It is designed primarily for small general libraries, especially elementary, secondary school, and small public libraries. The abridged edition is not recommended for libraries that expect to grow much beyond 20,000 titles. Even very small libraries should always use at least three digits in their classification, for example 301 not 300 for sociology. Libraries using the abridged edition will seldom continue more than two places beyond the decimal point. If a number such as 301.29'56'073 is observed on a Library of Congress card, the number can be stopped at any apostrophe; a small library would probably use 301.29.

The latest regular edition of Dewey, the 18th edition, contains three volumes: one for the introduction and tables, one for the schedules, and one for the index. It is intended to provide a shelf arrangement system for libraries of all sizes and is also suitable for use in classified catalogs and bibliographies.

The ten main classes of the Dewey Decimal Classification are shown on the following page.

000 Generalities
100 Philosophy & related disciplines
200 Religion
300 The social sciences
400 Language
500 Pure sciences
600 Technology (Applied sciences)
700 The arts
800 Literature (Belles-lettres)
900 General geography & history

Each of the ten main classes has ten divisions. For all of the classes except 000 and 800 the division is by subject. The first class, 000, is chiefly divided by the form of the materials, and 800 is divided by the nationality of the author. The ten divisions of 000, 500, 800, and 900 will be given below along with some explanatory remarks.

000 Generalities
010 Bibliographies and catalogs
020 Library and information sciences
030 General encyclopedic works
040 Unassigned; most recently used in Edition 16
050 General serial publications
060 General organizations & museums
070 Journalism, publishing, newspapers
080 General collections
090 Manuscripts & book rarities

The Dewey Decimal Classification is noted for its memory aids. Some of the numbers from the 000 divisions reappear in other places, such as the following standard subdivisions, which may be used with any number from the schedules.

——03 Dictionaries, encyclopedias, concordances
——05 Serial publications
——06 Organizations (including administrative reports and proceedings)
——08 Collections

Other frequently used subdivisions are ——016, Bibliographies and catalogs, ——07, Study and teaching, and ——09, Historical and geographical treatment.

500   Pure sciences
510   Mathematics
520   Astronomy & allied sciences
530   Physics
540   Chemistry & allied sciences
550   Sciences of earth & other worlds
560   Paleontology
570   Life sciences
580   Botanical sciences
590   Zoological sciences

It is interesting to note that the above divisions, like most of the other 100 divisions, have remained the same since the first published edition of the classification in 1876. In the first edition, however, the division 550 is called "geology," 570 is called "biology," and the phrase "and allied sciences" is not used.

800   Literature (Belles-lettres)
810   American literature in English
820   English & Anglo-Saxon literatures
830   Literatures of Germanic languages
840   French, Provençal, Catalan
850   Italian, Romanian, Rhaeto-Romanic
860   Spanish & Portuguese literatures
870   Italic languages literatures   Latin
880   Hellenic languages literatures
890   Literatures of other languages

American literature and the other literatures are next divided by form in the following manner:
810   American literature in English
811   Poetry

812 Drama
813 Fiction
814 Essays
815 Speeches
816 Letters
817 Satire & humor
818 Miscellaneous writings

Notice that there is a number for fiction. Since many libraries use the symbol F or Fic for fiction, it is sometimes assumed, incorrectly, that this is a part of the Dewey Decimal Classification. Arranging all English language fiction alphabetically by author, with or without use of a symbol such as F, is a convenient and useful arrangement for school and public libraries; but academic libraries that use Dewey usually place fiction in the 800s.

900 General geography & history
910 General geography   Travel
920 Biography, genealogy, insignia
930 General history of ancient world
940 General history of Europe
950 General history of Asia
960 General history of Africa
970 General history of North America
980 General history of South America
990 General history of other areas

Although 920 is a number for biography, procedures in libraries vary. Some libraries use 92 or B for biography of individuals and arrange the books alphabetically by biographee. If a library prefers to class biography with pertinent subjects, such as musicians with music and engineers with engineering, the standard subdivision ——092 can be added to any number.

The divisions of history are useful to remember because subdivisions for areas of the world use the same numbers.

These area notations can be used with any number from the
schedules. Some of them are:

——4 Europe

——5 Asia Orient Far East

——6 Africa

——7 North America

——8 South America

——9 Other parts of the world and extraterrestrial
worlds

History numbers and the area notations can be expanded
as shown in Figure 58.

Area notation	History	Area
—7	970	North America
—73	973	United States
—75	975	Southeastern United States
—758	975.8	Georgia

Figure 58. Area notations

As an example, a book about the politics and government
of Georgia can be assigned the number 320.9758.

CUTTER NUMBERS AND OTHER BOOK NUMBERS.

The Dewey Decimal Classification does not by itself provide a unique number for each book in a library. In a small
library all books assigned a particular classification may be
arranged alphabetically by author (or other main entry) with
or without the author's name being written or underlined on
the spine. Some libraries use the first three letters of the
author's last name below the classification. For example, a
book by John Brown about Brazil would have the call
number:

981 or 981

B   BRO

In medium-sized and large libraries, and especially in academic libraries, it is usually assumed that each book needs a unique call number. The call number is composed of a classification number and a book number. Book numbers are sometimes called Cutter numbers because Charles Ammi Cutter originated the most widely used author table. (Like Melvil Dewey, Cutter was a pioneer of the American library profession. His *Rules for a Printed Dictionary Catalogue* was published in 1876, the same year as the first edition of Dewey's classification, and is still frequently quoted. Cutter devised the Cutter Expansive Classification, which influenced the development of the Library of Congress Classification. In light of Cutter's notable contributions to cataloging theory and classification development, it is ironic that his name is now used chiefly in reference to a system of book numbering.)

The *Cutter-Sanborn Three-Figure Author Table* (Swanson-Swift Revision, 1969) is a revised and expanded version of Cutter's original table. A sample from the table is shown below.

Andrewe	564
Andrews	565
Andrews E	566
Andrews J	567
Andrews M	568

Suppose a book about the Second World War has the classification 940.54. If an author named Helen Andrews wrote the book, the book number would consist of the first letter of her last name and the number preceding the position of her name in the author table. The complete call number would be:

940.54
A566

If the same author wrote another book on the same subject, a work mark would be used to distinguish between titles, for example if the second book was called *New Insights on World War II*, the number would be:

940.54
A566n

When two authors would share the same number if the table were strictly followed, additional digits are added, so we might have a sequence of numbers such as C685, C6855, C686, and C6862. For shelving purposes, Cutter-Sanborn numbers are treated as decimal numbers.

One advantage of using both a classification number and a Cutter number (or other book number) is that the books themselves and files such as the shelf list can be arranged in exact order by call number. Locating a particular book within a class is expedited. A call number devised with the use of an author table is a shorthand notation; when libraries find it necessary to add the author's names and sometimes parts of titles below classification numbers in order to properly arrange books within a class, more work is being done than would be required by routine use of an author table. A unique number for each book is also useful in many circulation systems although in some libraries this need is met by accession numbers.

THE LIBRARY OF CONGRESS CLASSIFICATION.

The early classifications used by the Library of Congress were based on the size of books, on a system that had been used by Benjamin Franklin's Library Company in Philadelphia, and on Thomas Jefferson's classification. By the 1890s the collection had grown to nearly a million volumes and a new method of classification was needed. The Dewey Decimal Classification was not adopted partly because Dewey did not want the Library of Congress to make any adjustments in his system. Cutter's Expansive Classification served as a basis for the general development of the system, but subject specialists at the Library of Congress developed each of the individual schedules.

The Library of Congress Classification is contained in about 30 volumes edited by different specialists and published and revised at different times. It is more difficult for the beginning cataloger to use than the Dewey Decimal Classification because there is no introduction, set of instructions, or index covering the entire set; there is little uniformity between the way in which individual schedules are developed; the many auxiliary tables are difficult to master; and the classification does not contain the mnemonic features of Dewey. However, the Library of Congress Classification is used by most large American university and research libraries, as well as by some special libraries, because it provides for the exactness of classification needed by large and specialized libraries. It is also used by many medium-sized and small libraries because LC classification numbers are provided on LC cards and in other sources. Can a classification used by a library of 15 million volumes also adequately serve libraries of 150,000 or 15,000 volumes? Obviously the call numbers will be longer than needed for small libraries, but an arrangement of books by discipline and subject will result. The arrangement of books in a small library by LC classification is more useful than arrangement by accession number, size, or specially created classification numbers (which were probably inconsistently assigned by inexperienced catalogers).

In a library arranged by the LC system, the books are arranged from A to Z rather than from 000 to 999 as in the Dewey system. Each main class is identified by a letter of the alphabet, subclasses by combinations of letters, and subtopics within classes and subclasses by a numerical notation. The main classes are

    A   General works

B   Philosophy. Religion
C   Auxiliary Sciences of History
D   History: General and Old World
E–F History of America
G   Geography, Anthropology, Folklore, Etc.
H   Social Sciences
J   Political Science
K   Law
L   Education
M   Music
N   Fine Arts
P   Language and Literature
Q   Science
R   Medicine
S   Agriculture
T   Technology
U   Military Science
V   Naval Science
Z   Bibliography and Library Science

An example of the division of a class into subclasses
follows:

Q   Science
      QA Mathematics
      QB Astronomy
      QC Physics
      QD Chemistry
      QE Geology
      QH Natural History
      QK Botany
      QL Zoology
      QM Human Anatomy
      QP Physiology
      QR Bacteriology

It can be seen that the subclasses of science are very
similar to the divisions of the Dewey number 500, which

were given earlier. However, all LC subclasses are not this similar to Dewey divisions.

The Library of Congress classes and subclasses are not divided into any certain number of subtopics as are the Dewey divisions. The classification is based on a subject grouping of the books in the Library of Congress collection; the notation was composed to fit the collection rather than books being separated into preconceived catagories.

Library of Congress classification numbers include an author number and sometimes added symbols describing a particular work and its edition. Most libraries use the complete LC number, which gives them a distinctive number for each book. All LC numbers are not composed in like manner. The examples in Figure 59 illustrate a few common types of numbers and the meaning added by each part of the number.

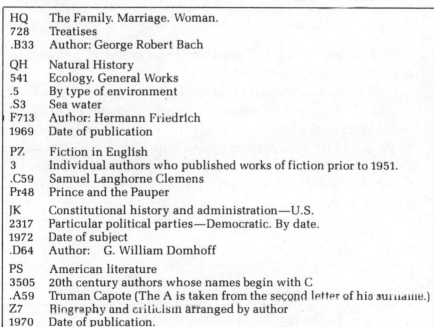

HQ	The Family. Marriage. Woman.
728	Treatises
.B33	Author: George Robert Bach
QH	Natural History
541	Ecology. General Works
.5	By type of environment
.S3	Sea water
F713	Author: Hermann Friedrich
1969	Date of publication
PZ	Fiction in English
3	Individual authors who published works of fiction prior to 1951.
.C59	Samuel Langhorne Clemens
Pr48	Prince and the Pauper
JK	Constitutional history and administration—U.S.
2317	Particular political parties—Democratic. By date.
1972	Date of subject
.D64	Author: G. William Domhoff
PS	American literature
3505	20th century authors whose names begin with C
.A59	Truman Capote (The A is taken from the second letter of his surname.)
Z7	Biography and criticism arranged by author
1970	Date of publication.

Figure 59.   LC call numbers

The LC classification is complex and cannot be easily

summarized. However, the answers to two frequently asked questions follow.

How does LC derive its author number?

Although there is a table, part of which is illustrated in Figure 60, author numbers are assigned in a manner to preserve the alphabetical order of names within a class and are not always in accordance with the table. The numbers are used decimally and can be extended as far as necessary to distinguish between authors and between different books by the same author.

After initial consonants (except S and Qu)							
for the second letter: a	e	i	o	r	u	y	
use number: 3	4	5	6	7	8	9	
After initial vowels							
for the second letter: b	d	l,m	n	p	r	s,t	u,y
use number: 2	3	4	·5	6	7	8	9

Figure 60.   LC author number table

How should an LC call number be arranged on a catalog card or on the spine of a book?

Different libraries use different formats. Some prefer to arrange the entire notation on two lines. Others prefer to use more lines so that each line is shorter and the number will more easily fit in a narrow space. Some libraries copy all decimals; others omit decimals before author numbers. When the number given on a card is PS3505.A59Z7 1970, any one of the formats in Figure 61 might be used.

PS3505	PS	PS
.A59Z7 1970	3505	3505
	.A59	A59
	Z7	Z7
	1970	1970

Figure 61.   LC call number formats

FIVE OTHER CLASSIFICATION SYSTEMS.

Other classification schemes have been developed over

the years for special subject collections. An example is the classification prepared by the National Library of Medicine and used by many medical collections. There are also a number of classifications systems intended to cover all subjects that are of interest to anyone concerned with the efficient organization of knowledge; these, however, are not widely used as methods of arranging books in American libraries. Summaries of five such systems follow.

1. *Expansive Classification.*

Charles Ammi Cutter's Expansive Classification has already been mentioned. It consists of tables of classification of progressive fullness. The first classification outline has eight main classes.

A   Works of reference and general works
B   Philosophy and Religion
E   Biography
F   History and Geography and Travels
H   Social Sciences
L   Natural Sciences and Arts
Y   Language and Literature
YF Fiction

Very few American libraries still classify by Cutter; most of those that do are located in Cutter's native state, Massachusetts.

2. *Bibliographic Classification.*

Henry Evelyn Bliss worked for 30 years developing this classification. It was published in four volumes between 1940 and 1953. A revised edition is currently in progress. Bliss believed that a classification should be based on scientific and educational consensus in order to be satisfactory to the expert scholars in various disciplines. The notation uses all 26 letters of the alphabet; arabic numerals are used for considerations of form.

3. *International Classification.*

Fremont Rider's International Classification appeared in 1961. Rider attempted to correct the American bias in Dewey and LC by making better provisions for other countries and cultures. Call numbers are composed of three letters of the alphabet.

4. *Colon Classification.*

Developed by S. R. Ranganathan of India, this classification divides fields of knowledge into subclasses by facets or catagories of classification. For example, literature has four facets: the language, the form, the author, and the work. The notation uses capital letters, arabic numerals, lower case letters, and various other symbols. The Colon Classification has not been widely used even in India because it is a difficult system to understand and apply, but Ranganathan's ideas are frequently studied by students of classification theory.

5. *Universal Decimal Classification.*

UDC is an authorized expansion of the Dewey Decimal Classification intended for the subject indexing of literature, not merely the arrangement of books on shelves. It follows the basic arrangement of Dewey but attempts to be international in approach. It is widely used for the classification of knowledge.

DEWEY OR LC?

The advantages of using either Dewey or LC are that the classification numbers for books added to the library collection can often be located in various sources, most catalogers have had training in the systems, the classifications are familiar to library patrons, and the schedules are kept up to date. The choice between Dewey and LC is usually based not only on how well the classification will serve the needs of the users of the library, but also on how efficiently new books can be classified by the system. Some advantages of each system follow:

Advantages of Dewey.

1. It is more easily learned and understood by library patrons, especially children and persons not academically inclined.
2. The notations can be shortened by small libraries or extended by large libraries. It is not easy (and probably not advisable) to shorten or adapt Library of Congress classification numbers.
3. The schedules are available in either an abridged or regular edition. The instructions for use and index are included with the schedules.
4. If a library does original cataloging for most books, it is easier to classify by Dewey than by LC due to the complexity of the LC system.

Advantages of LC

1. It is a comprehensive detailed scheme permitting exact classification of very specific subjects and is considered to be superior to Dewey for some scientific and scholarly subjects.
2. Because it uses both letters and numbers, a shorter notation will render the same specificity as a longer Dewer number. This is possible because there are 26 letters but only 10 numerals.
3. Library of Congress classification numbers as indicated on LC cards and in other sources are complete call numbers providing a distinctive call number for each book. Dewey numbers as suggested by various sources often require adaptation to fit a library's classification policies, and a Cutter

number or other author number must be added if each book is to have a distinctive call number.

4. The trend in academic and research libraries has been toward LC. Libraries participating in cooperative endeavors in which the majority of libraries use LC may benefit by using the same system as most of the other libraries.

How to Classify

The first step in classifying a book is often an attempt to locate a ready-made classification number. Library of Congress cards, Cataloging in Publication, the *National Union Catalog*, and *American Book Publishing Record* are some of the sources for LC and Dewey classification numbers. The H. W. Wilson Company's Standard Catalog Series and ALA's *Booklist* also provide Dewey numbers. Classification numbers located in these sources must often be evaluated for agreement with the classification policies of the library.

If no classification number can be located, the cataloger must examine the book and make a judgment as to its subject content as well as the author's intent. As with the assignment of subject headings, which may be based on the same subject evaluation of the book, the title of the book should not be the sole basis for determining the subject. After an opinion as to the nature of the book has been reached, the cataloger may consult the classification index, a subject heading list that suggests classification numbers, or subject headings in the public catalog to obtain suggestions as to possible classifications. The classification of other books in the library on the same subject or similar subjects is always a relevant factor.

Both the Dewey and LC classifications are arranged in classes that are subdivided into subclasses and subtopics. Even if an approximate or tentative classification number has been derived from consulting the index or from another source, the classification schedule itself should always be checked to determine if the number is really an appropriate classification. Not only do the schedules include directions for use of numbers, but the manner in which a subject fits into the organization of a broader subject can be observed. It is also possible to derive classification numbers directly without use of the index by starting with a broad area of knowledge and working down to the specific subject. If the classification is derived in this manner, it is usually desirable to confirm its correctness by checking the shelf list to determine if similar books are shelved in the same area or by looking under the appropriate subject headings in the library's catalog to observe if the classification number has previously been used for the subject. In relating subject headings to classification numbers, it is useful to know that if a book has more than one subject heading, the first subject heading is the one that usually corresponds to the classification.

Beginning users of either the Dewey or LC classification may be surprised to discover that books on a subject are often not grouped together in one location. Subjects such as "alcoholism" and "animals" have various aspects. Both Dewey and LC organize knowledge into disciplines, which are then broken down into particular subjects covered by the disciplines. Psychology is a discipline; alcoholism is a subject that can be treated from a psychological viewpoint. To illustrate how subjects are sometimes located in several places in the classification arrangement, the references given in the index of the abridged edition of Dewey for "alcoholism" and "animals" are shown in Figure 62.

Alcoholism		Animals	
med. sci	616.8	art representation	704.94
psychology	157	cruelty to	
soc. path	362.2	ethics	179
		husbandry	636
		zoological sciences	590

Figure 62. Dewey index entries

The Dewey and LC classifications are not static. As new subjects develop, spaces are found for them. The following types of changes may appear in any new edition of Dewey: expansions and reductions, relocations, reused numbers, and completely reworked schedules for particular disciplines. Most libraries do not find it possible to reclassify all books covered by changes in the classifications schedules, but they do use the new classification numbers for new additions and reclassify when the need is urgent.

CHAPTER 12:

Streamlining the Cataloging Process

RAPID CHANGES are taking place in cataloging methods. Participants in the cataloging process must deal with future shock in their work lives as well as in their daily lives. Even as more efficient methods of producing library catalog cards have been developed, the future of the card catalog has become uncertain. Only recently, computer printed book catalogs were considered a new development, and they are now being replaced by computer-output microform and on-line terminals.

The basics of cataloging as formulated in the *Anglo-American Cataloging Rules* and followed in the assignment of subject headings and classification still survive, but technical services organization and procedures have been drastically changed over the years in many libraries.

Technical services personnel should maintain open minds, survey new developments for possible applications to local situations, and continue to fulfill their objectives in the most efficient manner possible. Small improvements as well as complete new methods of operation should be considered. In this chapter, methods of obtaining catalog cards, problems of cataloging with copy, and alternatives to the card catalog will be discussed.

METHODS OF OBTAINING CATALOG CARDS.

The day of handwritten catalog cards is past, but all or

some cards are still individually typed in many libraries. In very small libraries where cataloging copy is brief, where most sets contain less than five cards, and where the total number of cards needed is not great, there may be little need for advanced methods of card reproduction.

One step up from typing all cards is the use of a small postcard-size stencil duplicator. Prices range from about $45.00 for a basic model manual duplicator to about $500.00 for an automatic model. These duplicators provide relief from tiresome, repetitious typing, but they are not efficient if large numbers of cards must be produced. Card production is comparatively slow and the ink is slow-drying, so the cards often need to be spread out to dry.

Large libraries use full-size stencil duplication equipment, offset duplication, or automatic typewriters for production of catalog cards. Xerographic copiers can be used by either large or small libraries. Small libraries that have such equipment available for the use of their patrons can also use it for card reproduction.

Another method of obtaining cards is to order printed cards. If a library uses the methods of card reproduction discussed in the previous paragraphs, the book must first be cataloged or cataloging copy must be located in a source such as the *National Union Catalog*. By ordering printed cards the library obtains cataloging copy and full sets of catalog cards in one step. The Library of Congress sells printed cards for the books it catalogs. The price is 45¢ per set if the card order number is given on the order form. An additional charge of 60¢ is added for sets sold in response to an order without the LC card order number. A copy of an LC card order form is shown in Figure 63.

If Library of Congress cards are ordered at the same time that the books are ordered, card sets will often be waiting when the books arrive. However, some unnecessary card sets will probably be purchased because some book ordered may be out of print or the orders may be canceled for other reasons.

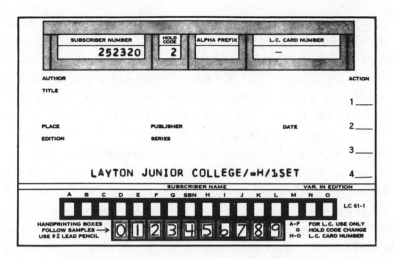

Figure 63. LC card order form

The advantages of ordering LC cards are that they contain cataloging performed by skilled professionals, they are attractive in appearance, and they are available for most books. The chief disadvantage is that waiting for cards to arrive may delay the cataloging of books. Some card sets arrive promptly; others do not. It is not possible to claim sets that are not received. Card sets not received after six months, and there usually will be some of these, may be reordered, but six months plus the time required for a response to a reorder is a lengthy delay. Some libraries classify books and insert temporary cards in the catalog while waiting for LC cards. This is useful to patrons but requires additional staff time.

Library of Congress cards are available for most, but not all books. They are usually not available for laboratory manuals, elementary and secondary textbooks, pamphlets, workbooks, programmed learning, or documents of an administrative or procedural nature. They are not as likely to be available for foreign books, noncopyrighted material, or books of limited distribution as they are for books of major American publishers.

Because of delays in receiving cards, the need to sometimes change information such as imprint and collation on each card individually, and the cost of obtaining large numbers of card sets, some libraries obtain Library of Congress cataloging information from proofsheets, Cataloging in Publication, the *National Union Catalog*, or other sources but produce their own cards. Proofsheets are copies of LC cards issued on strips of paper. Cataloging in Publication (CIP) is prepared by Library of Congress catalogers prior to the publication of many new books and appears on the verso of the title page. An example can be seen on the reverse side of the title page of this book; notice that the imprint and collation are not given. Some libraries that obtain cataloging copy from the *National Union Catalog* use catalogers' cameras instead of copying the information by hand.

Many book jobbers will supply catalog cards with some or all books. Receiving catalog cards with the books is more convenient than having to place a separate card order to the Library of Congress and later having to match cards with books. The cost of cards is usually the same or less. However, libraries should take into consideration the exact nature of the cataloging services offered by book vendors. If there is a substantial delay in delivery of books because of cataloging or processing, another source or another cataloging method may be preferable.

The nature of the cataloging offered by the book jobber is also an important consideration. Small libraries that use abridged Dewey, Sears headings, and simplified description may be able to obtain cards more similar to their own typed cards from a book jobber than from the Library of Congress. Libraries that base their cataloging on that of the Library of Congress may select to receive cards produced by a book jobber from MARC tapes. MARC means Machine-Readable Cataloging. Magnetic tapes in the MARC format have been prepared and distributed by the Library of Congress since 1969. A sample of a dealer-produced MARC card is shown in Figure 64.

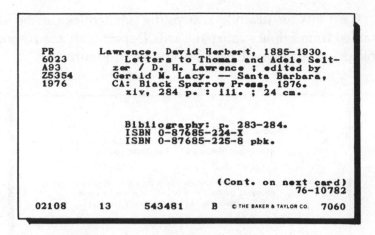

```
PR          Lawrence, David Herbert, 1885-1930.
6023             Letters to Thomas and Adele Seit-
A93          zer / D. H. Lawrence ; edited by
Z5354        Gerald M. Lacy. -- Santa Barbara,
1976         CA: Black Sparrow Press, 1976.
                 xiv, 284 p. : ill. ; 24 cm.


             Bibliography: p. 283-284.
             ISBN 0-87685-224-X
             ISBN 0-87685-225-8 pbk.



                                  (Cont. on next card)
                                           76-10782
02108       13        543481      B   © THE BAKER & TAYLOR CO.   7060
```

Figure 64.   Dealer-produced MARC card

More space is required for the same information on a MARC card than on a regular LC card. Cards can be obtained from jobbers with call numbers already printed in the upper left-hand corner and headings printed above the main entry on secondary cards. Obtaining such cards is a useful option if a library makes few exceptions to LC classification and headings.

Obtaining cards with books from a book jobber seldom solves a library's entire cataloging problem. Some jobbers send cards only for books for which they already have cataloging copy in their data base. Other jobbers supply cards for all books but charge extra for original cataloging. For example, a library that selects to receive MARC cards with books, typically at a cost of about 40¢ per book, will probably receive cards for only about two thirds of books ordered. The exact percentage will vary according to the type of books ordered. Moreover, few libraries receive all of their books from one source. Some books must be ordered directly from publishers; others are received as gifts. Most book jobbers that supply catalog cards sell them only for books that they supply.

Card kits for juvenile and young adult titles can be obtained from Library Journal Cards Department at a resonable price. A sample LJ card is shown in Figure 65.

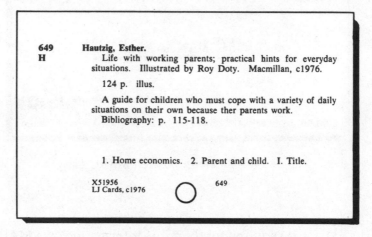

Figure 65. LJ card

Many libraries acquire catalog cards in more than one way. Some printed cards may be ordered or some books may arrive from a book jobber with cards, but cards will also be produced locally.

One of the chief current sources of catalog cards has not yet been mentioned. Unlike the methods of obtaining catalog cards previously described, participation in a library network such as OCLC, Inc. is usually envisioned as a comprehensive cataloging system. Cataloging data from MARC tapes and contributed copy from member libraries is viewed on computer display terminals, corrections and changes are made, and cards are ordered. If a book is not yet in the system, the cataloger can input original cataloging and obtain cards.

OCLC began its on-line cataloging operations in 1971 as the Ohio College Library Center. It is now a nationwide organization. There are other similar operations, but OCLC is the largest and best known. A number of regional networks such as the New England Library Information Network (NELINET) and the Southeastern Library Network (SOLINET) have contractual agreements with OCLC. Not all libraries participating in the system use it in exactly the same manner. One problem with using a display terminal is that while cataloging copy can be compared with the book in hand, the classification, series, subject headings, and form of names cannot easily be checked against authority files, the library's catalog, or shelf list unless a handwritten or print copy is made of the information shown. One solution is to have a printer attached to the terminal so that print copies for checking can be made for some or all items. Another method is the use of computerized authority files concurrently with the use of the OCLC terminal. If there are few problems in integrating OCLC cards into the catalog, a library may decide to wait until the cards arrive to do whatever checking is needed. The disadvantage of this method is that changes will have to be made individually on all cards affected.

PROBLEMS OF CATALOGING WITH COPY.

To the uninitiated it may seem that when a library receives printed cards for books, or participates in cooperative cataloging through a network such as OCLC, little or no cataloging has to be done by the library. This is not true for a number of reasons. With any of the above methods, a residue of books will require original cataloging; these are often foreign books, books issued by obscure associations and publishers, and other books of higher than average cataloging difficulty. Also, most libraries today acquire audiovisual materials and other nonbook materials for which cataloging copy is not so frequently available and which may present special cataloging problems. But perhaps the principal error of those who too readily assume that the burden of cataloging can be eliminated or greatly reduced by using cataloging copy from various sources is that they overlook the problems involved in cataloging with copy.

Even though cataloging copy is available and a method of acquiring or producing cards based on the copy has been arranged, work still remains to be done. First there are the changes, additions, and supplemental activities that could be considered as housekeeping in nature. For example, if a book is to be shelved in the reference section, a symbol such as REF must be added to the call number. If a library shelves oversize books separately, a symbol or statement must be added to the cards for these books. Libraries often have other special collections or have multiple locations; location symbols for these are sometimes added to cards and additional card sets produced for special catalogs. Sets of cards may contain second and third cards when the description of a book is lengthy. The cards for each entry are usually taped or tied together. If the library does not use second and third cards for secondary entries, the extra cards must be discarded and "continued on next card" crossed off where not needed. Whatever information the library customarily records on shelf list cards must be recorded. If a library uses LC card sets or other sets consisting only of unit cards, call numbers must be typed on all cards and headings on secondary cards. Since sources of cards and the requirements of libraries vary, these routine chores vary between libraries, but it would be difficult for any library using printed catalog cards to eliminate all such activities.

Another type of activity supplemental to the use of printed catalog cards or other cataloging copy is the comparison of the book in hand with the copy. After it has been ascertained that the best possible match between available cataloging copy and a particular book has been achieved, the remaining differences between the two must be reconciled. If only the place of publication and name of publisher vary, as frequently happens with books published both in England and in the United States, the incorrect information is usually lined out or erased and the correct information added. Paperback editions frequently vary from the original editions in place, publisher, paging, and date of publication. Cataloging copy is more often available for hardbound editions than for paperbound; when paperbound books are cataloged, a high percentage of changes must be made on copy. If copy is not available for a reprint edition, the additional imprint information may be added to the data for the original edition. However, if a book is a revised edition or an edition with different editors, translators, or illustrators, cataloging copy for the particular edition is usually sought. If it is not found, the available copy may be used as a basis for cataloging, but new cards or copy are usually prepared. The line between cataloging with copy and original cataloging is not always distinct.

Samples of LC catalog cards that have been changed to describe particular books are shown in Figure 66. In addition to observing the changes made, notice that the Library of Congress did not make a title added entry for the first book and that an LC classification number was not printed on the cards for the second book.

One type of catalog entry that always requires adjustment before cards or cataloging copy will adequately describe the volumes owned by the library is the open entry. An open entry is a catalog entry that allows for the addition of information as additional volumes are added. Open entries are most frequently used for serial publications, which will be discussed in a later chapter, but they are also sometimes used for terminal sets and for books published in frequent editions. The sample open entry card in Figure 67 illustrates one of various methods of indicating holdings. Notice that some of the added entries not applicable to the volume in hand have been eliminated. Also notice that this particular card does not contain a recommended Dewey classification number.

The greatest challenge of cataloging with copy, however,

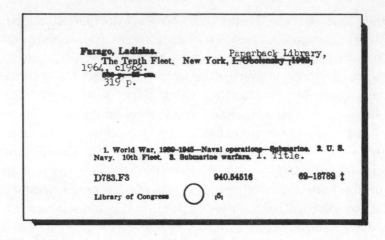

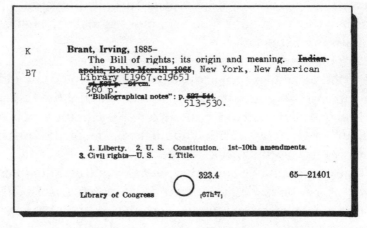

Figure 66. LC cards altered by library

is not the efficient management of clerical routines or the matching of books with cards, but rather the integration of cataloging copy into the local catalog in such a way as to maintain the consistency and usefulness of the catalog. Frances Ohmes and J. F. Jones consider this problem so important that they refer to it as "The Other Half of Cataloging" in their article in *Library Resources and Technical Services* (Summer 1973, pp. 320–329). Arlene Taylor Dowell has also written on the subject—*Cataloging with Copy: A Decision-Maker's Handbook* (Libraries Unlimited, 1976). In the preceding chapters of this book there have been intimations of the problem: the need to establish a uniform form of name for persons and corporate bodies, the fact that cross-references to be made are not indicated on printed catalog cards, the question of when to make series and title entries, the possible need for name, series, and subject authority files, the discussion of the adequacy of standard library subject headings, the need to adjust suggested Dewey classification numbers, and the necessity of adding author numbers to Dewey numbers if distinctive call numbers are to be given to books.

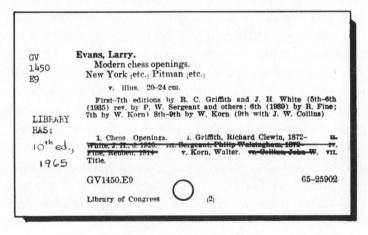

Figure 67. Open entry

Some cataloging copy is not complete. The fact that Cataloging in Publication does not include the imprint and collation has already been mentioned. If a library classifies by Dewey, it will soon be noticed that some LC cards, especially those for foreign books and older books, do not contain

Dewey classifications. Some LC cards do not contain LC classifications, usually because the books fall into the K classification (Law), which is still incomplete. Some catalog cards give a choice of LC classifications, such as an alternate classification for the use of libraries that prefer to place books of fiction with the works of an author rather than in PZ. Alternative classifications are also sometimes given for parts of a set, which some libraries may prefer to classify separately.

In addition to supplying missing information and making choices between alternatives, catalogers must sometimes make changes in cataloging copy. Although many libraries do not make a special effort to locate misspellings, errors in birth dates, and other typographical errors, the errors are usually corrected if noticed. Cataloging from the past, which still appears in the LC catalogs and on printed cards, follows different rules and practices. It is possible to ignore differences in punctuation and capitalization, but if the cards suggest obsolete subject headings and classifications and entries under forms of name from which references have since been made to other forms of name, consistency cannot be maintained in a library's catalog unless the cataloging is updated.

As was previously observed, following exactly the practice of the Library of Congress in making series and title added entries often does not serve the best interests of a library. Most libraries can obtain better results by establishing their own policies on series and title entries.

At one extreme are libraries that check every entry point on LC cataloging against their authority files or catalogs and every classification against their shelf lists. At the other extreme are libraries that file cards exactly as received. However, most libraries fall somewhere in between; changes are made, but only when necessary to maintain the consistency of the library's catalog.

A library that accepts LC cataloging and uses it extensively will probably also have to decide whether to accept cataloging from other sources. The *National Union Catalog* and the data base of OCLC both contain cataloging contributed by many different libraries. The non-LC cataloging in the *National Union Catalog* seldom includes a classification number. Even if classifications are given on contributed copy to NUC or network data bases, most libraries cannot accept without prior checking the classifications assigned by other libraries. In an ideal world, the cataloging of one library might be interchangeable with that of another, but this situation does not exist today even among major research libraries. Cataloging varies not only because of local preferences, but also because catalogers in different libraries must fit books into different preexisting frameworks. The problem of cooperative cataloging is double-edged. Catalogers inputing original cataloging into a system must often follow rules stricter than those they normally follow; it is no longer sufficient merely to catalog in such a way as to meet the needs of their own libraries, but the requirements of other libraries must also be considered. On the other hand, large libraries that follow strict rules will probably still find that the cataloging contributed by most other libraries must be given careful consideration prior to acceptance.

Commercial cataloging is often based on LC cataloging, although it is sometimes simplified to meet the needs of other libraries. Whatever source a library uses for the greatest part of its cataloging usually sets the standard for other cataloging. If a library does original cataloging for most books, cataloging from outside sources is adjusted to conform with the policies used for original cataloging; but if most cataloging copy is obtained from an outside source such as the Library of Congress, original cataloging and cataloging from other sources is brought into conformity with LC practices, at least to the extent that there are not major conflicts of entry in the catalog.

Different types of libraries have different problems with the use of any outside cataloging copy. Large research libraries with long-established catalogs have special problems in integrating new cataloging copy into the catalog in such a way as to keep together works of particular authors and books on particular subjects. On the other hand, they may have little concern over the appropriateness of LC cataloging as a means of serving their users, since the cataloging of a large research library is usually useful for the users of another similar library. Small libraries and most public libraries that use LC cataloging, however, may be more concerned about usefulness than consistency. In a small catalog there will be fewer conflicts of entry, but LC cataloging will often contain excessive detail, may be confusing to some users, and may not always provide a useful subject approach. Evaluating every name entry, subject heading, and classification from the viewpoint of usefulness to a library's patrons lessens the labor-saving benefits of cooperative cataloging but increases the usefulness of the catalog. A catalog must be consistent in order to be useful, but consistency alone does not guarantee that the needs of the library's patrons will be met.

How easily a library can accept outside cataloging copy depends upon the adequacy and appropriateness of the copy and upon the age, size, and nature of the library's catalog. The method used for acquiring and producing cards is also revelant. When printed cards obtained from the Library of Congress, a book jobber, or another source must be changed, each card must be corrected separately. However, if a stencil for the reproduction of cards is prepared after cataloging copy is located and adjusted, changes need be made only once. As was previously mentioned, libraries participating in cataloging networks can adjust cataloging copy before ordering card sets. Since it is advantageous to be able to change only a master copy rather than each catalog card individually, libraries that make many changes can benefit by reproducing their own cards or ordering them through a computerized system that produces cards tailored to a library's specifications. Libraries that purchase ready-made printed cards should try to keep to a minimum the number of exceptions that they make to the policies of the cataloging source.

ALTERNATIVES TO THE CARD CATALOG.

Card catalogs are convenient because new entries can be added at any time, cards for discarded items can be removed, and changes can be made on particular cards when necessary. A card catalog can be kept continually current so that it always reflects a library's holdings. Author, title, and subject cards prepared over a span of years from the beginning of the library to the present can be filed in one alphabetical sequence. Another advantage is that purchased cards from various sources can be interfiled with a library's own cards. Before card catalogs became popular, many libraries had book catalogs, which were much more difficult to update. Often there were separate volumes for different time spans in a library's history, so that library users had to search many different alphabetical sequences for each book.

Although the card catalog is flexible, useful, and convenient, its weaknesses have caused a decline in its popularity and may lead to its eventual demise. A card catalog does not lend itself to easy duplication. It is more satisfactory when used by an independent library with one location than when used by library systems or large libraries with books housed at many locations. A large municipal public library that processes books for itself and its numerous branches must not only maintain a central record of all holdings, but must also provide a catalog record for each branch library. The technical services divisions of some university libraries have an analogous problem in maintaining catalogs for the main research library as well as various departmental libraries. In these types of systems a library user will often want to know not only whether a book is available in a particular library, but also whether it is available in the system. (Most public school library systems present a different situation in that students at one school do not usually obtain books from the libraries of other schools, so there is less need for a central catalog at each location.) When there is need for a complete catalog at many different locations, book catalogs, microform catalogs, and on-line computer terminals have advantages over card catalogs.

Another weakness of the card catalog is that cards must be filed manually. If a filer files 100 cards an hour and is paid $3.00 an hour, filing costs 3¢ per card. (A librarian revising the filing will handle more cards per hour but will be paid at a higher rate.) If each book has five cards, the cost per book is 15¢. If we allow another 15¢ per book for revision of filing and general maintenance of the catalog and 5¢ to 10¢ for alphabetizing cards preliminary to filing, it can be seen that the total cost of inserting a set of cards into a catalog may be similar to the purchase price of the cards, about 35¢ to 40¢. However, the monetary cost is not the only cost. Since filing is often considered to be tedious work, there may also be a cost in loss of staff morale. Since no one has yet invented a machine that can file cards into a card catalog, the alternative is to change the format of the catalog. With computer-printed book catalogs, catalogs on computer-output microfilm (COM), or data bases accessed by on-line terminals, manual alphabetizing and filing can be eliminated.

Two other drawbacks of the card catalog are that it takes up considerable space and is not portable. However, catalogs in other formats also have disadvantages. The principal disadvantage of a book catalog is that it quickly becomes outdated. Frequent new cumulations of a large catalog printed in many copies can be very expensive, but if numerous supplements must be used with the basic catalog the user is inconvenienced. Even with computer-printed book catalogs the difficult choice between expensive reprinting and patron inconvenience must be made.

Catalogs on computer-output microfiche or microfilm are much less expensive than book catalogs. Therefore it is less expensive to produce frequent new cumulations. They do have the disadvantage of requiring equipment, microfiche or microfilm readers. The use of on-line terminals likewise requires adequate equipment so that library users do not have to wait in line to consult the catalog. The time required for catalog users to locate the information they need should be one of the principal bases of comparison of types of catalogs.

In comparing catalog formats, irrelevant cataloging policies and decisions should not be used as factors in the comparison. Regardless of catalog format, the cataloging of a library can be simplified or detailed, consistent or inconsistent, and relevant or irrelevant to patron needs. The use of cooperative cataloging and library networks is not tied to one catalog format. Computers can produce catalog cards, book catalogs, or computer-output microform. A library catalog can be closed whether or not a new cataloging format is undertaken. Author, title, and subject entries can be interfiled or filed separately in card catalogs, book catalogs, and COM catalogs. Specific locations for particular books, such as branches or departmental libraries, may or may not be indicated regardless of catalog format. Computers afford new techniques for coping with changes in entries and in cataloging rules, but computerization by itself will not create consistency. S. Michael Malinconico's article "The Library Catalog in a Computerized Environment" (*Wilson Library Bulletin*, Sept. 1976, pp. 53-64) is a thought-provoking discussion of the problems and potentialities of cataloging automation.

The format in which cataloging is presented is not as important as the cataloging itself. A new edition of Dewey, changes and additions to the LC classification, a new edition of the *Anglo-American Cataloging Rules*, and revised Sears and LC subject headings all present challenges to catalogers attempting to keep an old catalog alive and useful. The Library of Congress plans to close its main card catalog in 1981, and some other libraries may do likewise, but the newly created catalogs will in turn increase in size, absorb changes, and become more complex as they age in years. In the future as in the past there may be optimists who predict an end to cataloging problems but for the foreseeable future, at least, catalogers will continue to catalog.

CHAPTER 13

Maintaining the Public Catalog and Shelf List

CARD CATALOGS, book catalogs, and microform catalogs may be arranged in a number of different ways. Author, title, and subject entries may be arranged together in one alphabet (dictionary catalog), or entries of different types may be arranged separately (divided catalog). Book and microform catalogs may also be arranged with a sequence of main entries in order of accession followed by author, title, and/or subject indexes; the indexes can be frequently cumulated and republished without reissuing the fixed number sequence of main entries. (An example of this type of arrangement is 3M's Bibliographic Control System: the National Union Catalog on Microfiche). Another system is a classified arrangement with an index, as used in the volumes of the H. W. Wilson Company's Standard Catalog Series. The location of particular entries in catalogs or indexes is also affected by the choice of filing rules. The one type of catalog that does not require a linear arrangement of entries is the computerized catalog accessed by on-line terminals.

The decision between a dictionary and a divided catalog has been a perennial library debate subject. A summary of some of the arguments on each side will be given in this chapter preliminary to a discussion of library filing rules and other aspects of catalog maintenance. The reasons for maintaining a shelf list and some of the types of information included on shelf list cards will then be discussed.

Dictionary versus Divided Catalog.

One obvious advantage of a dictionary catalog is that since all entries are filed in one alphabet, no decision is required as to which catalog to consult. If the division in a divided catalog is between subject and author/title entries, the library patron looking for information about an author may not understand that he must look in the subject section rather than the author/title section. Also, no matter how clearly the division of the catalog is indicated, there will always be some people who will absentmindedly consult the wrong catalog.

Perhaps the most frequently cited advantage of a divided catalog is that filing is less complex. Patrons can supposedly locate entries more quickly and cards can be filed more rapidly, thus reducing the cost of catalog maintenance. It is also sometimes claimed that dividing the catalog lessens congestion in the catalog area, but whether this is true is probably dependent upon the relative usage of the author/title and subject approaches by library patrons.

Maintaining a divided catalog does mean that some entries and cross-references must be duplicated. Autobiographies, diaries, letters, and critical editions of literary works will often need both author and subject entries under the name of the person involved. Art books will frequently require both author and subject entries for the artist. Title entries should be made even if they are identical with subject entries. Cross-references for names of persons and corporate bodies will often be needed for both catalogs.

A divided catalog eliminates the opportunity of locating books under title while searching under an incorrect subject term. On the other hand, divided catalog advocates claim that patrons are misled when they locate the word or phrase they are seeking on a title card and assume that they have found a subject heading.

A further problem with dividing a catalog is deciding how

to divide it. If the primary purpose of dividing the catalog is to simplify filing, a separate catalog with names only has some advantages; it eliminates problems in arranging personal names and titles that begin with the same word. If personal names used as subjects are also filed in this catalog, books by and about an author are brought together. The catalog can be split in three sections—names, titles, and subjects; or titles and subjects can be interfiled. However, no possible arrangement of a catalog can eliminate such filing problems as compound names, names with prefixes, forenames used as entry elements, uniform titles, corporate names, acronyms, and all of the other departures from the usual that perplex filers. Whether a catalog is divided or dictionary, rules for filing will still be needed.

Library Filing Rules.

Library filing, like a number of other technical services skills, has a reverse side, the ability to locate information in alphabetical files. Locating an item in a bibliography or a library catalog requires more than a knowledge of alphabetical order. Three requisites of skill in bibliographic searching are:

1. An understanding of the principles of main and added entry. This is particularly important if one is searching a tool such as the *National Union Catalog*, which is arranged by main entry. In searching any catalog or bibliography one should be aware of what types of entry are included.
2. A knowledge of proper forms of names. It is useful to know what part of a personal or corporate name will probably be the entry element, but it is even more important to know when one should look in more than one place for a name.
3. An awareness of possible filing arrangements. The preceding two skills have been covered in previous

chapters. Perhaps the most important fact one should know about filing rules is that all catalogs and bibliographies are not arranged according to the same rules.

If one is interested in filing chiefly from the viewpoint of a user of library catalogs and bibliographies, it is especially important to be aware of alternative approaches to particular filing problems. Many libraries follow the suggestions in the *ALA Rules for Filing Catalog Cards* (2nd ed., American Library Association, 1968), but some libraries make exceptions to particular rules and other libraries use an entirely different set of rules. John C. Rather's "Filing Arrangement in the Library of Congress Catalogs," (*Library Resources & Technical Services*, Spring 1972) presents a different set of rules and also discusses the relationship of filing to cataloging and reasons why filing rules for a large research library cannot be simple. The first edition of the ALA rules, published in 1942, contained many options, including a rule for filing subject entries that resulted in their being arranged in a manner similar to that suggested by Rather:

1. The subject alone: MAN
2. The subject followed by a dash: MAN— INFLUENCE ON NATURE
3. The subject followed by a comma: MAN, PREHISTORIC
4. The subject followed by a word or words in parentheses: MAN (BUDDHISM)

Many university and research libraries still use portions of the 1942 rules because they believe that grouping entries by kind of entry or form of heading will facilitate systematic subject searching better than a straight alphabetical arrangement.

Although different libraries use different filing rules, the filing in any one library should consistently follow the set of rules it has selected. The advantage of using an established set of rules is that almost every filing problem is covered by the rules. Different staff members who encounter special filing problems can consult the same set of rules and arrive at the same decisions. On the other hand, if filers, or revisers of filing, resolve filing problems according to their own opinions, filing will not be consistent.

The American Library Association also publishes an abridged edition of its 1968 rules, which presents the same basic rules but omits most of the specialized and explanatory material. Small libraries may prefer to use the abridged edition.

The 1968 ALA rules recommend a straight, word-by-word alphabetical arrangement disregarding punctuation. The major exception is that surname entries are always arranged before other entries beginning with the same word or combination of words. Because the straight alphabetical arrangement is simpler than grouping headings into particular catagories, many small and medium-sized libraries prefer the ALA rules to the more complex rules used by large research libraries. To illustrate the difference, the example in Figure 68 shows how a particular set of headings would

ALA Rules	Rather's Rules
Art, Robert J.	Art, Robert J.
Art [serial title]	ART—TURKEY
ART, AFRICAN	ART, AFRICAN
Art and action	ART, DECORATIVE
ART AND STATE	Art [serial title]
ART, DECORATIVE	Art and action
Art et action, Paris	ART AND STATE
ART—TURKEY	Art et action, Paris
Arthur, Joseph Charles	Arthur, Joseph Charles

Figure 68.   Rules for filing catalog cards

be arranged by ALA rules and by the rules recommended in Rather's article.

A brief selection of filing rules based on the ALA rules is given below. In general it can be assumed that rules are formulated only when there is a decision to be made, and that therefore there is an alternative possibility. When searching for a difficult-to-locate entry in an unfamiliar catalog or when seeking to find a misfiled card in one's own catalog, the alternative filing possibilities should be kept in mind.

1. Disregard modifications of letters—umlauts, accents, and other diacritical marks.
   Mull, John
   Müllen, Gustav
   Muller, Arnold
   Münch, Amalie
   (This is an example of an ALA rule that differs from the policy followed in many bibliographies and catalogs, including the *National Union Catalog*.)

2. Disregard initial articles, but not articles within an entry. Prepositions and pronouns are considered in filing. Remember that this rule applies to articles in all languages.
   Man and state
   The man of his time
   A man of the better class
   Les misérables
   To live is to love

3. Arrange initials as one-letter words before longer words beginning with the same letter. Disregard variations in spelling and punctuation.
   AAAS Conference on Science Teaching
   The ABC of collecting
   A.B.C. programs

A is for apple
A.M.
Aaron, John

4. Arrange acronyms that are commonly written and spoken as words as they are spelled.
Ford, Mary
FORTRAN
Unemployed
Unesco manuals

5. Arrange abbreviations as if spelled in full, including geographical abbreviations.
Mr. Jones tells a story
Montana skies
The United States and Canada
U.S. Dept. of State
United States departments

6. Arrange names beginning with the prefixes M' and Mc as if written Mac.
McHale
Machen
McHenry
M'Laren

7. Arrange elisions, contractions, and possessives as written.
Dont, Jacob
Don't be afraid
Don'ts
Dony, Yvonne

8. Arrange numbers as if spelled in the language of the entry.
100 American poems [One hundred American poems]
115 homes for living [One hundred fifteen homes for living]
100 to dinner [One hundred to dinner]
One summer in Hawaii

9. Arrange hyphenated words as separate words when each part is a complete word. Arrange as one word hyphenated words that consist of a prefix added to a regular word.
Epoch-making papers
The epoch of reform
Posted missing
Post-war British cards
Postwar British fiction

10. Arrange compound names as separate words.
Hall of fame
Hall-Quest
Hallan

11. Arrange proper names with prefixes as one word.
Defoe
De la Ramee
Delmar, Dora
Del Mar, Eugene
De Morgan

12. Arrange entries under one author alphabetically by title regardless of whether his name is a main entry or an added entry. File subject cards for books about an individual after all of the works by him.

13. If there are several books with the same title or subject heading, arrange alphabetically by main entry.

14. Arrange different editions of the same title chronologically by imprint date.

15. The order of subject headings is as follows:
    a. Subject without subdivision.
    b. Period divisions arranged chronologically.
    c. Alphabetical extensions of the main subject heading interfiled word by word in one alphabet with titles and other headings.

U. S.—HISTORY
U. S.—HISTORY—COLONIAL PERIOD
U. S.—HISTORY—REVOLUTION
U. S.—HISTORY—REVOLUTION—CAUSES
U. S.—HISTORY—1783–1865
U. S.—HISTORY—1815–1861
U. S.—HISTORY—CIVIL WAR
U. S.—HISTORY—20TH CENTURY
U. S.—HISTORY—BIBLIOGRAPHY
U.S. history bonus book
U. S.—HISTORY—DRAMA
United States history in rhyme
U. S.—HISTORY, LOCAL

The ALA rules are intended for dictionary card catalogs but can also be used in divided catalogs, book catalogs, and indexes. They are designed primarily for manual filing rather than filing by computer.

Because accurate and consistent filing are essential to the maintenance of a useful card catalog, cards should be filed by skilled personnel, or the filing should be reexamined for accuracy. In many libraries, cards are filed into the card catalog by clerical employees or student assistants, but the filing is revised by catalog librarians. Librarians who revise filing often watch for conflicts of entry, duplicate books, needed cross-references, and other problems as well as checking for filing accuracy. If one person is solely responsible for filing, it may still be desirable to first file the cards above the drawer rod and then double-check for accuracy and problems before removing the rod and dropping the cards.

CATALOG MAINTENANCE.

Card catalogs grow rapidly. It is useful to keep in mind a few approximate figures when planning for catalog growth. Approximately 100 cards can be filed per inch; a card catalog tray that contains 10 inches of cards will probably contain about 1,000 cards. Although a tray may be advertised as holding 1,300 cards, it is usually impractical to plan for more than 1,000 cards per tray because constant shifting between trays will be required when the average number of cards per tray is higher. Also, if the trays are more than two-thirds full, they are awkward to handle and consult.

If a library contains 10,000 titles and there are an average of four cards per title, a card catalog with 40 trays will be needed. However, this does not allow for growth. If the library adds 2,000 titles per year, in five years at least 80 trays will be needed. If cards are also inserted for nonbook materials, if many reference and guide cards are made, if there are an average of more than four cards per book, if the cards are unusually thick, or if an average of ten inches of cards per tray is considered too full, more trays will be needed. The important point to remember is that it is possible to plan systematically for catalog growth.

When a card catalog cabinet is purchased at the opening of a library or when new cabinets are added at a later date, the cards can be divided between the trays in the following manner. Measure the number of inches of cards to be filed. Divide by the number of trays. The answer will be the number of inches to be filed in each tray. The number can be varied slightly to allow for natural breaks in the alphabetical arrangement. Each tray should be labeled with its contents, and guide cards should be used to show the placement of particular names or subjects within trays as well as to give guidance in the filing arrangement.

The Shelf List.

The cards in a shelf list are arranged in the same order as the books on the shelves. When an inventory of books is taken, the cards can be checked against the books on the shelves and against the circulation files.

Most libraries record holdings of copies of books only in the shelf list. In the sample holdings record shown in Figure

69, the copy numbers, order numbers, and prices are given.

~~c. 1 405—72 6.00~~	withdrawn 6/77
c.2 408–73 7.50	
c.3 gift	

Figure 69.   Holdings record

When a missing copy is replaced, a new copy number is usually used for the replacement since the missing copy may reappear. If books are marked with accession numbers, accession numbers can be used instead of copy numbers (see Figure 70).

14687	SW
16930	CEN
17625	CEN (Avon)

Figure 70.   Accession numbers

In Figure 70, neither prices nor order numbers are given, but the locations of the copies are shown, and a variant publisher is indicated for one copy. It is difficult to generalize about shelf list practices because the needs and practices of libraries and library systems vary. Prices are sometimes given so that borrowers can be charged an appropriate amount when they lose books. However, the time involved in recording prices for all books should be weighed against the time that would be required to search bibliographic tools for the prices of books actually lost. Also to be considered is whether the borrower should be charged the purchase price of the book or the replacement cost.

For multiple-volume sets or books published in annual editions, holdings may be shown in one of the ways indicated in Figure 71.

In addition to its importance for inventory purposes and as a record of exact holdings, the shelf list can be used to

v.1	34567		1974	16.50
v.2	34568		1975	17.00
v.1	46723		1976, v.1	12.00
v.3	54321		1976, v.2	12.00

Figure 71. Holdings records: sets and annual editions

evaluate library holdings within an area of knowledge and can be consulted by catalogers classifying new books. If prices are given, it can also be used for insurance purposes.

Filing in the shelf list involves the same problems as correctly arranging books on the shelves. Both the Dewey and LC classifications use decimal numbers. Cutter numbers and LC author numbers are also decimal numbers. Samples of correct arrangements are shown in Figure 72.

Dewey classification numbers

621	621.3	621.38	621.4

Call numbers with the same Dewey classification but different Cutter numbers.

621	621	621
B382	B3825	B383

LC classification numbers.

PZ	PZ	Z	Z
3	3	693	1035
C2562	C257	P54	W77
Sh	An	1974	1972

Figure 72.

In LC call numbers the first numbers following the class letters are whole numbers, but numbers following a decimal point or other letters are decimal numbers.

Keeping the public card catalog and shelf list accurate, up-to-date, and in good order is an important responsibility. An excellent catalog reflects well upon the present and past technical services staff.

CHAPTER 14

Physical Preparation of Books and Book Repair

STEPS IN PHYSICAL PREPARATION OF BOOKS.

A surprising number of different things can be done to books in order to prepare them for circulation and shelving. Not all libraries perform all of the following steps and not all books require all procedures, but nevertheless in most libraries the physical preparation of books includes a number of different steps.

1. Open the book by taking a few pages at the front and back alternately and pressing them gently against the covers. (This will help pages lie flat and may keep the spine from breaking.)
2. Cut pages if necessary.
3. Secure loosely attached plates; glue in errata sheets; make pockets for folded maps or similar material.
4. Write the date, cost, and source in the inner margin of the page following the title page.
5. Stamp the book with an accession number. ?
6. Mark the book with ownership stamp and/or attach a book plate.
7. If the book is not already bound, make a decision on binding. Prepare books that are to be sent to the bindery. Insert pamphlets in pamphlet covers.

8. Insert special tape or marker for the library's book detection system.
9. After the book has been classified, write the call number in pencil on the page following the title page.
10. Underline the main entry on the title page or put a dot under it.
11. Type the call number, author, and title on a book card and pocket.
12. Attach the pocket.
13. Attach a date due slip.
14. Mark the spine with a call number.
15. Cover the paper book jacket with a transparent cover and attach it to the book.

The first eight steps can be performed prior to cataloging. If technical services work is divided into separate acquisitions and cataloging sections, these steps are sometimes considered part of acquisitions rather than cataloging. In Chapter 4 of this book, which covered acquisitions procedures, accessioning and marking books with property stamps (Steps 5 and 6) were discussed.

Steps 1, 4, 9, and 10 are frequently eliminated if time is tight. Step 1 may be performed only for books that seem to particularly require careful opening. Recording order information in books is seldom justified by the amount of use later made of this information. Writing the call number in the book and underlining the main entry are probably necessary only if the person who types the book card does not have access to the catalog cards or if the call number and main entry are not indicated on the book card, pocket, or elsewhere in the book.

Steps 2, 3, and 7 are necessary only for particular books. Foreign books and older books are the most likely to arrive with pages uncut; the pages can be cut with a letter opener. Loosely attached plates can be secured more firmly with paste or with double-coated tape. Errata sheets and other loose pages can be tipped in with paste or liquid adhesive. Supplementary material that is too thick to be placed in a pocket can be bound and shelved separately. Pamphlets of less than about 150 pages that are to be cataloged separately can be inserted in pamphlet covers of the type sold by most library supply houses. Pamphlet covers are not as satisfactory for thicker pamphlets and paperbound books, which should be sent to a bindery if it is expected that they will be used heavily.

Step 8 is a recent addition to the customary procedure of preparing books for circulation. Different book detection systems require different types of inserts to be placed in books.

Usually the most time consuming of the physical processing steps are the preparation of the book card and pocket, the labeling of the spine with a call number, and the attachment of a transparent book jacket cover. These procedures will be discussed individually.

Book Cards and Pockets.

Procedures for book cards and pockets vary with circulation procedures. The traditional procedure is to type the call number, author's last name, and title on a book card and pocket. The reason for typing the information on the pocket as well as the card is to facilitate the accurate matching of book cards and books when books are returned from circulation. If accession numbers are used, the accession number is stamped or typed on the book card and pocket, and no further information is needed on the pocket since accession numbers are good matching devices. Some libraries prefer to type sheets or strips of pressure-sensitive labels and attach them to the cards and pockets rather than inserting cards and pockets individually into a typewriter. Labels for book cards and pockets may also be computer printed.

Using a paste brush and a jar of paste to paste pockets into books is often a messy, time-consuming procedure. Pregummed pockets, which only need to be moistened before attaching, can be purchased, but they do not hold as fast as pasted or glued pockets. Another type of pocket is the self-stick, pressure-sensitive book pocket; the backing is peeled off before the pocket is applied to the book. If plain ungummed pockets are used, they can be attached by using squeeze-bottles of glue, spray adhesives, or glue sticks. Special gluing machines for pockets are also sold.

Some libraries attach book pockets to the inside back covers of books; others prefer the front or back flyleaf. If the book jacket is covered and attached to the book, it is usually necessary to use one of the flyleaves for the pocket since the book jacket will cover most of the inside back cover. Although it is desirable to consistently use one position for pockets, it is not always possible because some books have maps, charts, indexes, or other important material on the inside covers and flyleaves.

Pockets can be purchased imprinted with the library's name and address. They can also be obtained with a preprinted grid for recording date-due information, which eliminates the need for separate date-due slips. If separate date-due slips are used, they are usually pasted on the page opposite the pocket.

Call Number Identification.

Whatever procedure is used for labeling spines, it is desirable to place the call numbers in a uniform position on each book; the top of each call number may be one and a half to three inches from the bottom of the spine, depending upon the policy of the library. The standard position may be occasionally varied in order to leave uncovered important information such as volume numbers. Although it is easier to shelve books that have call numbers on their spines, some books and pamphlets are so thin that call numbers must be placed elsewhere, such as in the upper left corner of the front cover.

One simple method of marking books with call numbers is with pen and ink. The numbers are lettered in white ink on most books, but in black ink if the book has a light-colored spine. Another method is to use an electric stylus and white or black transfer paper. A disadvantage of either of these methods is that a certain amount of skill is required in order to achieve neat, legible markings. Another popular method is to type the call numbers on pressure-sensitive labels. This method works particularly well if book jacket covers are used. The label is applied to the paper book jacket before the transparent cover is attached. The cover protects the label and helps to hold it in place. When pressure-sensitive labels are attached directly to cloth book spines, there are often problems with the labels coming loose or corners peeling. Labels used for this purpose should be carefully selected; it may be necessary to experiment in order to determine which labels work best. The labels may be protected with special label protectors, transparent tape, or a coating of transparent liquid adhesive. Some types of labels can be heat-sealed with an electric sealing iron. Plastic spray coating will also give protection to either spine markings or call number labels.

Another method of labeling book spines is the Gaylord Se-lin Book Labeling System, which uses a special labeler assembly attached to the platen of a typewriter. After the call number is typed on a strip of base tape with backing, it is automatically covered by a strip of clear tape. A special cutter is then used to cut through the protective tape and typed label tape so that each call number can be separately removed from the backing strip. After the label is positioned on the spine, a heating plate or iron is used to seal the label to the spine. The fact that such a complicated system is used by some libraries is indicative of the problems encountered when simpler, less expensive systems of spine labeling are used.

Book Jacket Covers.

The principal advantage of covering book jackets with transparent covers and attaching them to the books is that preserving the colorful book jackets makes the library more attractive. Also, book jackets sometimes contain information not given in the book, such as biographical information on authors, plot summaries of fiction, and brief descriptions of the contents of nonfiction books. When covered with a transparent cover, the book jacket also gives protection to the book itself and helps it to survive more circulations.

Keeping book jackets on books is a very common practice in public and school libraries but less common in academic and research libraries, where books are less likely to be chosen for their attractiveness or because of information given on the book jackets. Covering and attaching book jackets is one of the more time-consuming of physical preparation procedures, and book jackets cost about ten cents each, so some libraries use them only for fiction or for books with particularly attractive jackets.

Most transparent book jacket covers are made of Mylar or polyester. They can be purchased in sheets or rolls. Covers which are adjustable are the most practical for small libraries as fewer sizes must be ordered.

After the book jacket is covered with a transparent cover, it is attached to the book with tape or glue.

Cutting Processing Costs.

Two elements of physical processing cost are supplies and staff time. Even in a small library, it is interesting and useful to study the costs of processing rather than to depend upon conjecture. An example of an informal study of processing costs is shown in Figure 73.

Twenty books were stamped in four places with a property stamp. (The three edges of the book and the inside front cover were stamped.) Book cards and pockets were typed. The pockets were attached with paste. Se-lin labels were typed and attached. The length of time, cost in time, and cost of supplies are given for each step. An estimate of $3.00 per hour for staff time is used; this type of work is usually performed by student assistants or minimum-wage personnel.

COST OF PROCESSING TWENTY BOOKS

	Time	Salary cost	Supply cost
Stamping with property stamp	5 min.	.25	
Typing book cards and pockets	40 min.	2.00	book cards .10 pockets .24
Pasting pockets	16 min.	.80	paste .03 (est.)
Typing and attaching Se-Lin labels	30 min.	1.50	Se-lin tape .40
Total	91 min.	4.55	.77
Cost per book	4.55 min.	.23	.04

Figure 73.

The total cost for supplies and labor is about 27 cents per book. Alternate procedures were also studied. Typing labels for book cards and pockets and attaching them to the cards and pockets for twenty books required 55 minutes of staff time, so it was not considered an economical procedure. On the other hand, attaching 20 pregummed pockets took only 10 minutes, a saving of about 1.5 cents per book. Since the extra cost of pregummed pockets is only about a fifth of a cent per book, using them would be economical. This example is intended only as an illustration showing that it is not difficult to determine approximate costs and to compare the costs of different procedures. More serious studies of book processing costs would include a larger sample and a variety of library workers.

One reason for knowing the approximate cost of processing books in the library is that book jobbers offer this service along with the sale of catalog cards. However, factors other than cost, such as speed, convenience, and the availability of staff time for processing, may enter into the decision as to whether a library will purchase processing services.

BOOK REPAIR.

In some libraries technical services personnel have no responsibility for books after they have been processed and sent on to the circulation or public services staff. However, in many libraries it is convenient for the technical services section to handle book repair and rebinding, because the procedures are closely related to those used in the initial preparation of books for the shelves. The same work area and some of the same supplies can be used for both types of work.

Book repair can usually be done more successfully and efficiently if books needing repair are set aside and a definite assignment of responsibility for repair work is made. Although immediate, temporary repairs may occasionally be needed, if speedy repairs are made by whichever staff member observes the need, sloppy repair work with excessive use of transparent tape will probably result. If a particular work area is used for book repair, if all of the necessary supplies are conveniently available, and if one or more staff member has practiced and learned book repair techniques, better results can be obtained.

First, it is necessary to decide if repair is the proper procedure. Badly worn copies can often be withdrawn if there are enough other copies, if the edition has been superseded, or if the content is no longer of interest. If a book is still needed, but pages are missing or the book is damaged beyond repair, purchasing another copy is often the proper procedure. If a book is expensive, heavily used, and not easily repaired, the book should probably be professionally rebound. Spending three to four dollars on rebinding a twenty dollar book is likely to be a worthwhile expenditure. Moreover, the new binding may be more durable than the original binding. It is not usually worthwhile to make temporary repairs if rebinding will soon be necessary. The choice between repairing, rebinding, and purchasing another copy also depends on whether the problem is torn pages, loose pages and signatures, missing pages, or one of a variety of other problems.

Books to be repaired should be sorted by type of problem. If torn pages have a feathered tear, they can often be more neatly mended with liquid adhesive than with transparent tape. Loose pages should almost always be "tipped in" with liquid adhesive rather than tape; tape may interfere with later rebinding. Special cloth tape or transparent book tape can be used to cover worn or torn spines. Special tapes are also available for repairing weak or loose book hinges and loose covers. Demco, Brodart, and Gaylord, three library suppliers, have published book repair guides that give detailed instructions for handling specific problems. Their addresses are included in a list at the end of this chapter.

A particularly annoying problem is the discovery that pages have been torn out of bound periodicals. Usually it is possible to obtain photocopies of the missing pages from another library and then tip them in as with other loose pages.

Repairing rare books and archival material requires special knowledge and skills. Rare books are often more impressive and valuable in their original bindings, even if worn, than if rebound in more durable bindings. It should also be kept in mind that labeling or marking spines of rare books may detract from their value. Often a premium is placed on rare books with uncut pages, but the value of a book with uncut pages to a library is questionable. Ordinary transparent tape should never be used to mend the pages of rare books or archival material. Special supplies are necessary when working with these materials.

ORDERING LIBRARY SUPPLIES.

Technical service procedures require many types of library supplies, such as:

Book request cards
Book order forms
Catalog cards
Book cards
Book pockets
Paste
Mending tape and other book repair supplies
Pamphlet covers
Transparent book jacket covers
Call number labels
Special labels for audiovisual materials
Periodical record cards

Some library supplies can be purchased from local stationery stores, but specialized library products must often be ordered from one of the major library suppliers.

Not all library supplies can be kept on hand indefinitely. Some tapes and pregummed products will deteriorate if stored at high temperatures or for long periods of time.

One of the best ways to become familiar with book processing and book repair techniques is to examine the catalogs of library suppliers. Often the description of an item in a catalog will suggest a new method of handling a particular procedure. The names and addresses of some library suppliers who issue catalogs are given below. Inclusion on this list indicates only that a supplier publishes an interesting catalog and does not constitute an endorsement of the products sold. The names of other suppliers can be found in the annual buying guide issue of *Library Journal* and in advertisements in library periodicals.

Library suppliers:
Brodart, Inc., 1609 Memorial Avenue, Williamsport, PA 17701
Demco Educational Corp., Box 7488, Madison, WI 53707
Gaylord Bros., Inc., Syracuse, NY 13201

The Highsmith Co., Inc., P.O. Box 25, Highway 106 East, Fort Atkinson, WI 53538 (Catalog includes a section on audiovisual equipment and supplies.)

University Products, Inc., P.O. Box 101, So. Canal St., Holyoke, MA 01040 (Catalog includes a section on museum and archival supplies.)

CHAPTER 15

Audiovisual Materials:
General Principles and Acquisition

WHAT'S IN A NAME?

THE TERMS *audiovisual materials*, *nonbook materials*, *nonprint materials*, and *media* have all been used to refer to some or all of the materials other than books that are collected by libraries. None of these terms is free of problems.

According to some definitions, unless an item is both audible and visible, it is not a true audiovisual; slides and filmstrips would therefore not be included with audiovisuals unless they were accompanied by sound. On the other hand, if we say that audiovisual materials are materials that can be seen and/or heard, books are not excluded since they are visual materials.

Our problem with the term *nonbook* is that it is a very broad term. Serials, documents, and pamphlets are very important to many libraries, but are given little attention in some discussions of nonbook materials. To illustrate the different connotations that the term *nonbook* has to different types of librarians, school and public librarians are usually surprised to discover that in *Anglo-American Cataloging Rules* (1967 edition) the first type of nonbook material discussed is manuscripts. To a librarian working with a rare-book collection or archival material, on the other hand, manuscripts are a very important category of nonbook material.

Another problem with the term *nonbook* is that it is sometimes considered to be derogatory since it may imply that the chief attribute of these types of materials is that they are not books.

Nonprint, like *nonbook*, may also have a disparaging connotation to some people. In addition, there is a problem if art prints, charts, and maps are considered nonprint materials since they are printed. It seems contradictory to say that an art print is a type of nonprint material. If *nonprint* is conceived as meaning "not containing the printed word," there is the problem of transparencies, filmstrips, and other supposedly nonprint materials which do contain the printed word.

Media is probably the most problematic of these words. It is the plural of "medium," which is a word with a variety of meanings, none of which specifically implies a type of material such as a motion picture, filmstrip, or set of slides. If a medium is taken to be a medium or means of communication, books are also media. Indeed the term *media* is used in both ways, including and excluding books. If the type of medium is specified, as in "educational media," "instructional media," "mass media," "art media," or "nonbook media," a clearer meaning is conveyed. Unless modified, *media* is a very vague term.

One of the features that distinguishes many of the materials most commonly designated as audiovisual materials is that they are used with equipment. In this category are phonograph records, audiotapes, filmstrips, motion pictures, slides, transparencies, videorecordings, and combinations of the above. The materials themselves are referred to as *software*; the equipment is the *hardware*. However, other types of materials sometimes included with the above do not require equipment. In this category are art prints, charts, games, globes, maps, models, pictures, realia, specimens, and pamphlets.

Instead of attempting to divide the contents of libraries

into two categories, book and nonbook, it may be simpler to use more categories, as in the following division:

1. Books
2. Serials
3. Audiovisual materials
4. All other materials: pamphlets, documents, maps, charts, pictures, college catalogs, manuscripts, etc.

In the discussion of audiovisual materials in this chapter and in the following chapter, only the types of audiovisual materials requiring equipment will be considered. Serials will be discussed in a separate chapter because they are a major part of the collection in many libraries and present many special problems. All other types of nonbook materials will be covered in the last chapter of the book.

No method of categorizing library materials is without problems. Although microform materials require equipment, their chief use is as a substitute for printed materials. If a library decides to purchase periodical backfiles on microform rather than binding paper copies, does the collection of serials on microfilm become part of the audiovisual collection rather than the serials collection? Because microform materials serve different purposes, they will not be included with audiovisuals in this discussion.

Although we have eliminated many of the types of materials sometimes included in discussions of audiovisual or nonbook materials, the materials considered in this and the following chapter—audiorecordings (disc and tape), filmstrips, motion pictures, slides, transparencies, videorecordings, and multimedia kits—have in recent years been increasingly acquired by libraries and have presented many special problems to technical services personnel. Serials, pamphlets, government documents, pictures, maps, manuscripts, and similar materials have, on the other hand, been of concern to libraries for a longer period of time, and grouping them with audiovisual materials does not necessarily illuminate the complexities involved in acquiring and organizing them.

USE OF AUDIOVISUAL MATERIALS IN LIBRARIES.

In addition to knowing exactly what types of materials are encompassed by the term "audiovisual materials," it is useful to know how these materials are used in libraries before considering procedures for acquiring and organizing them. Audiovisual materials should not be purchased because adding them to library collections is a current trend, but because they may be useful to patrons. Although there are published cataloging rules and policies for these materials, some organizational decisions will need to be made on the basis of the way the materials are actually used in a given situation.

Audiovisual materials are most often used in the following ways:

1. They are circulated to teachers or group leaders for use with classes or groups.
2. They are used by students to meet particular assignments.
3. They arc used for recreational or cultural purposes.
4. They are used by students or other library patrons who are seeking information on a subject.

The first type of use is very common in school situations. Materials that are purchased chiefly for classroom use are sometimes referred to as instructional materials. When school systems purchase 16mm motion pictures, it is usually with this type of use in mind. Transparencies are another type of audiovisual primarily intended for group use. All of the other types of audiovisual materials are also frequently used by teachers with their classes. Instructional materials are almost always handled by the school library, which is now commonly called a media center to emphasize its handling of many types of materials. In junior and community colleges, the library may be called a learning resources center for the same reason.

Public libraries frequently circulate materials such as motion pictures to group leaders for use with clubs, societies, or special meetings. This type of use is similar to classroom use.

Media centers and learning resources centers commonly provide for direct use of audiovisual materials by students as well as circulation to teachers. Often this use is in conjunction with a planned course of study or learning program. Students studying a language may need to listen to language tapes, shorthand students may use dictation tapes, and in any subject the instructor may have selected or prepared slide-tape sets, videocassettes, or other materials that the students can use independently when they reach the proper point in the course of study.

In public libraries particularly, audiovisual materials are frequently used for noninformational purposes. Patrons who use phonograph records or audiotapes are usually seeking enjoyment rather than information.

Some discussions of the organization of audiovisual materials in libraries assume that they are used chiefly by people seeking information on subjects, but this is not usually true. The type of use envisioned is that of a person seeking information about Norway for instance, and wanting to view filmstrips, motion pictures, and slides and listen to music in addition to reading the books on the subject. Encouraging this type of use is one of the major reasons for including cards for audiovisual materials in the card catalog and integrating them with books on the shelves. Although this type of use does occur and is certainly desirable, in most school and academic libraries materials are more often used by teachers with classes or by students in response to direct assignments. In public libraries, many audiovisuals are more frequently used for pleasure than for information, and group use is also frequent. Purchase decisions as well as cataloging policies should take into consideration the various types of uses.

SELECTION AIDS AND BIBLIOGRAPHIC TOOLS.

Audiovisual materials are not so widely reviewed or so systematically listed in bibliographies as books, but nevertheless there are a number of useful sources of information. *Previews* is published monthly from September to May by R.R. Bowker Company. Although the fact that it is published only from September to May indicates the principal intended audience, it reviews materials of interest to many types of libraries. It includes news items related to both audiovisual software and hardware. All types of audiovisual materials are covered. *Booklist* reviews audiovisual materials as well as books. All types and age-levels of materials are included, but not always in each issue. The reviews in both *Previews* and *Booklist* frequently comment on technical qualities as well as content.

The NICEM indexes are a major source of information on audiovisual materials, particularly those with an educational purpose. NICEM stands for the National Information Center for Education Media located at the University of Southern California. Separate indexes are published for each major type of educational media, such as films, filmstrips, audiotapes, videotapes, educational records, 8mm motion picture cartridges, overhead transparencies, and slide sets. All indexes contain a subject index, an alphabetical title arrangement of entries, and a list of producers and distributors. However, prices are not given, so it is usually necessary to check the producer's catalog or correspond with the producer or a distributor before placing a purchase order. Another drawback of the NICEM indexes is that they are expensive.

Libraries with small audiovisual budgets that wish to borrow motion pictures free of charge can use the *Educators' Guide to Free Films* (Randolph, WI, Educators'

Progress Service). *Audiovisual Market Place*, published annually by R. R. Bowker Company is a useful guide to companies active in the production and distribution of audiovisual software and hardware. The *National Union Catalog* has separate sections for music and audio materials and for motion pictures and other visual materials. Libraries that purchase many phonograph records will probably want to have a recent issue of the *Schwann Record and Tape Guide*. This guide is strongest on classical music, although it also lists popular music, folk music, and spoken-word records. It does not include educational records, which are produced chiefly for sale to schools and libraries. Schwann guides can sometimes be obtained free of charge from one's purchase source for records.

One of the most important sources of information on audiovisual materials in most libraries is the collection of producers' and distributors' catalogs. As with book catalogs, it is not always clear whether the company issuing a catalog is itself the publisher or is merely a distributor. These catalogs can almost always be obtained free of charge. Most libraries that order audiovisual materials receive a bountiful supply of catalogs and advertisements, but it may sometimes be necessary to request particular catalogs when seeking information about specific materials.

PREVIEWS AND ON-APPROVAL ORDERS.

Although the terms *preview* and *on approval* are sometimes used interchangeably, there are two different types of procedures and it is useful to refer to them separately using the appropriate term for each.

The decision to purchase a 16mm motion picture is a major one for most libraries since it may involve the expenditure of as much money as the purchase of fifty books. Libraries usually preview films before issuing a purchase order. A request for preview specifying desired dates is sent to the producer or distributor. A preview copy is sent by the supplier and is returned after a purchase decision has been made. A purchase order is issued if the decision was positive and the supplier sends a new copy of the film. Preview procedures of this type are common for motion pictures, but special preview copies are less often available for other audiovisual materials.

Other audiovisual materials are frequently ordered on approval. Ordering material on approval may be as simple as placing a check mark on an order form sent with an advertisement, but evaluating the material, packing and shipping it back to the vendor, and handling the invoices and statements of account may not be so simple. The difference between previewing and ordering on approval is that when ordering on approval one receives a new copy, which must be either purchased or returned within a certain length of time. Some vendors send invoices even before the evaluation period is over, with the understanding that payment need not be made if the material is found to be unsatisfactory and is returned within the specified period of time.

If a number of people in an institution request materials on approval and adequate records are not kept, it may be difficult to identify subsequent requests for payment. In addition, as with books, it should be kept in mind that there may be a tendency to retain on-approval items of marginal value because it is easier to keep them than to return them. Some libraries issue regular purchase orders with an on approval note when they wish to evaluate items before purchase. Either this method or another method of control should be used.

When ordering audiovisual materials, it is often helpful to read the ordering information in the producer's catalog, because previewing or approval policies will usually be described. Phonograph records, individual audiotapes, and inexpensive audiovisual items are not usually ordered on approval; most vendors of these materials do not anticipate return unless the material is defective or there is another very good reason for rejection.

The opportunity to evaluate audiovisual materials before making purchase decisions is particularly useful for expensive items and materials for which no reviews can be found, but materials should not be ordered on approval unless there is a reasonable expectation that they might be approved for purchase, and previewing should never be used as a substitute for rental. Distributors' policies have become less liberal as abuses have occurred. Some vendors require a purchase order or an authorized signature before materials will be sent on approval, and some film suppliers charge for previews.

OTHER ACQUISITION PROCEDURES AND PROBLEMS.

The responsibility for purchasing audiovisual materials is sometimes delegated to a separate audiovisual department that handles all aspects of work with audiovisual material. However, ordering audiovisuals involves few departures from procedures used for ordering books and other materials. If the materials are ordered from the same budget, cataloged in a similar manner, and added to the same collection, there is usually less duplication of effort if the ordering of audiovisuals is integrated with book ordering. Even procedures for ordering materials on approval are not unique to audiovisual materials, since expensive books and reference sets are also sometimes ordered on approval. However, the ordering and scheduling of rental films, like the ordering of office supplies, is a different sort of procedure and often involves a different budget, so it is usually kept separate from the purchasing of library materials.

Special forms are not needed for ordering audiovisual materials. The same request cards and order forms can be used as for books; the type of material can be given in parentheses after the title. When a library first begins ordering audiovisual materials it may not be necessary to check requests against the catalog and order files, but collections quickly grow beyond the point where it is possible to remember which materials are already in the collection. As with books, the acquisitions staff must often seek missing information such as prices and producer's addresses.

Audiovisual materials are more often ordered directly from producers or publishers than are books. Usually fewer AV items are ordered at any one time, so there is less benefit in assembling orders to be sent to a jobber. Moreover, audiovisual materials are produced and distributed in such a variety of ways that one jobber can seldom supply a major part of a library's needs. An increasing number of publishers, associations, and institutions publish both books and audiovisual materials, and thus the two types of materials can sometimes be purchased on one order.

The ordering of phonograph records is in some ways more similar to book ordering than to the ordering of materials such as motion pictures and multimedia kits. Frequently, a large number of records issued by many different companies are ordered at the same time. A number of dealers specialize in selling records to schools and libraries and offer discounts of up to 40%. Local record shops are another possible source, especially if discounts can be obtained.

Another situation in which audiovisual materials are often not ordered directly from the producers is when a group of materials have been selected from a dealer's catalog. Some catalogs of this type include materials related to a particular subject, such as Spanish language instruction, but others are general in nature and describe a wide variety of materials of interest to school, public, or academic libraries. It is usually simpler to order from the company advertising the materials than to determine the actual producers.

Another source of materials for many media centers and learning resource centers is local production. Audiotapes, slides, sound and slide sets, transparencies, and most other types of audiovisuals are frequently produced locally. Although these materials are usually cataloged in the same manner as purchased materials and may add greatly to the cataloging work load, they have little impact on acquisitions work. Occasionally, decisions such as whether to purchase transparencies or transparency masters, or whether to purchase slides of trees or prepare one's own may involve coordination between the media production and acquisitions sections. Another type of decision involving both sections may be the question of duplication rights. A few companies permit unlimited duplication for use within an institution, others sell duplication rights, and some do not permit any duplication but sell copies at reduced prices. Many companies offer replacements at less than the original price, especially if the damaged copies are returned.

Although the ordering of audiovisual materials does not differ greatly from book ordering, there are more differences in handling required when the materials arrive. Those ordered on approval must be evaluated before purchase. It is also desirable to check other materials to be certain there are no defects. The procedures for accessioning, marking with a property stamp, and forwarding for cataloging may also be different.

The next chapter will discuss the cataloging of audiovisual materials.

CHAPTER 16

Audiovisual Materials: Cataloging

THE CATALOGING of phonograph records, audiotapes, motion pictures, filmstrips, videorecordings, slides, transparencies, and multimedia kits should not be approached with fear and trepidation. Nevertheless, there are complications. A book can be easily opened and read, but more time is required to place audiovisual materials on the proper equipment so that subject matter and other information needed for cataloging can be determined. Moreover, LC cards and other commercial or cooperative cataloging are less frequently available for audiovisuals than for books. Finally, the shorter history of audiovisual cataloging means that standardization has not been achieved to the extent that is has been for book cataloging. The beginning cataloger of audiovisuals who consults a number of different sources may be confused by the variety of methods suggested.

The publication of revisions of Chapters 12 and 14 of the *Anglo-American Cataloging Rules* in 1975 and 1976 and the fourth edition of the Association for Educational Communications and Technology's *Standards for Cataloging Nonprint Materials* (by Alma Tillin and William J. Quinly) in 1976 has finally resolved a number of differences of opinion. It is now generally agreed that although many audiovisual items should be entered under title because they are collaborative works, it is appropriate to enter other works under their authors. It is also agreed that the type of medium should be stated after the title. Previously the medium designation was sometimes enclosed in parentheses or brackets; this issue has been resolved in favor of brackets.

There is also general agreement on the terms to be used as medium designators. The revised AACR rules specify the following terms. Notice that they are all given in the singular.

Sound recording (Includes discs, cassettes, and reels)
Motion picture (Includes 8mm and 16mm reels, loops, and cartridges)
Filmstrip
Videorecording
Slide
Transparency
Kit

Medium designators are broad terms. The Library of Congress previously used "Phonodisc" for phonograph records and "Phonotape" for tapes, but now has switched to the generic term "Sound recording." The number of items and the specific type of material are indicated in the collation, for example: 1 disc. 33⅓rpm. stereo. 12 in. The AECT code uses "Audiorecording" instead of "Sound recording," but concurs with AACR on the other six terms.

Libraries that follow Library of Congress cataloging policies can receive guidance by observing the cataloging in two LC catalog series: *Films and Other Materials for Projection* and *Music, Books on Music and Sound Recordings.* Even if a library uses simplified cataloging, recent issues of these publications provide many useful illustrations of methods of handling problems in audiovisual cataloging.

CLASSIFICATION AND ARRANGEMENT.

Intershelving audiovisual materials with books is an attractive idea because it eliminates artificial distinctions between the various types of media, grouping them instead by subject content. However, the way in which audiovisual materials are used in libraries, which was discussed in the preceding chapter, and special storage problems should also be considered. Large numbers of filmstrips, tape cassettes, or slides can be shelved in cabinets which occupy only a small amount of space; intershelving usually makes less efficient use of space available. Also, it may not be possible to shelve expensive items such as motion pictures on open shelves because of the danger of theft.

A compromise between intershelving of individual audiovisual items and complete separation is the placement of groups of audiovisual materials in the appropriate general area of the collection. For example, music recordings could be shelved in a browsing bin near the music books instead of intershelving them one by one with the books.

The shelving or housing of audiovisual materials should be determined prior to a decision on classification because one of the purposes of classification is to provide a shelving arrangement. If it has been decided that certain materials will be shelved separately in an area closed to the public, classification by subject has fewer advantages; shelving by accession numbers is an alternative to a classified arrangement. However, since classification by subject facilities the preparation of subject lists of audiovisual materials, it is sometimes useful even when audiovisuals are housed in separate collections by type of material. Even if there is limited access to the audiovisual collections, arrangement by subject may help the staff members or faculty who do have access to locate the materials they need. If audiovisuals are classified, they should generally be classified by the same system that the library uses for books.

Many libraries use a medium code above the call number, such as FS for filmstrip and MP for motion picture. The use of such a code can probably not be justified as a method of informing library users of the type of material because this is the function of the medium designator that appears after the title. However, libraries have often used symbols such as

REF to indicate that an item is shelved in a special collection. Therefore, the use of a location code above or preceding the call number is a legitimate means of notifying the catalog user that a particular item is housed in a special audiovisual collection. There need not be a one-to-one relationship between location codes and medium designators. If ordinary filmstrips and sound filmstrips (filmstrips accompanied by records or cassettes) are shelved in separate collections, different symbols might be used. If some or all audiovisual materials are intershelved with books in the general collection, there is no need for a location code for these materials. Catalogers who have worked with location codes for books in special collections and departmental libraries are aware of the difficulties created by relocation of materials; a location code should be used only when it appears that materials will be permanently housed in a special collection.

GENERAL CATALOGING POLICIES.

The question of dictionary versus divided catalogs was discussed in Chapter 13. Another way to divide a library catalog is by type of material: books, serials, motion pictures, phonograph records, and so forth. The question of whether to divide is relevant to card catalogs, book catalogs, and microform catalogs. If time and money are available, libraries sometimes try to have the best worlds by having an omnimedia catalog and special catalogs or lists for various types of materials. The anticipated use of the materials and the promotion of their use are the principal factors to be considered.

Another cataloging decision is whether or not to color-code AV materials. Using a rainbow of colors on catalog cards, one for each specific type of medium is no longer being recommended because media categories multiply faster than colors can be shaded. However, if a colored band across the top of all catalog cards for audiovisual materials helps to bring them to the attention of persons who are particularly seeking AV resources, it should not be ruled out merely because it conflicts with a theory that no distinction should be made between book and nonbook materials.

If materials in two or more media are issued together, for example a set of slides accompanied by a sound recording and teacher's guide, the combination is cataloged according to the principal medium with the other media noted or described subordinately. In practice, this usually means that combinations of visual and audio materials are cataloged from the visual portion (filmstrips, slides, transparencies, etc.) with the accompanying sound recording described in the collation. A collection of independent media is cataloged as a kit.

If the title on a container is different from the title on the work itself, the title on the material or closest to the contents is used in the descriptions. The title on the title frame of a filmstrip is chosen in preference to the title on the container or box. Titles for phonograph records are recorded from the record label rather than the album cover in most cases.

The physical description or collation includes number of items, running time, sound and color characteristics, dimensions, and description of accompanying material in that order. All of these elements of description are not needed for every medium. Enough information should be given in the collation or notes area to enable the user to select the proper type of AV hardware.

Subject headings should be assigned to audiovisual materials in the same manner as for books. It is not necessary to use special headings or subdivisions to reveal the type of material; the catalog user can ascertain the format of an item by reading the catalog card. Whether or not added entries are made for the companies producing or distributing the materials and for producers' series depends upon the polices of individual libraries.

In many media centers and learning resource centers,

half or more of the audiovisual items being added to the collection may be locally produced rather than purchased materials. Slides, tape cassettes, and transparencies are among the most frequently produced, but many media departments also produce motion pictures, videorecordings, filmstrips, and multimedia kits. There is little justification for declining to catalog slides, sound recordings, or other items merely because they are locally produced when purchased items of similar value are cataloged. The chief criteria for deciding whether to catalog locally produced material is whether they will be useful as permanent additions to the library collection. On this basis, tape recordings of instructors' lectures intended for use by currently enrolled students and student projects with no lasting value need not be cataloged.

Library of Congress cards or commercial cataloging can sometimes be obtained for purchased AV materials, but never for locally produced works. Rules and instructions for cataloging AV materials also pay less attention to these materials and give fewer cataloging samples. The AACR rules (Chapter 12) do state that notes should be used to give information on the source and date of production of materials that are not released, published, or issued in multiple copies rather than attempting to indicate a place, publisher, and date in the imprint area. Chapter 14 of AACR suggests a format such as that shown in Figure 74 for a locally recorded tape.

In the remaining portion of this chapter, attention will be given to seven types of audiovisual materials. Some questions of a general nature, such as choice of main entry and whether items in sets should be cataloged individually, will receive attention in the discussion of particular types of materials.

SOUND RECORDINGS.

Sound recordings include phonograph records (discs),

```
Hanson, John James.
     Lecture on Ernest Hemingway. [Sound recording]

     1 reel. 7 1/2 ips. 1-track. mono. 7 in.

     Recorded at John Jones College, Aug. 1977.




     1. Hemingway, Ernest, 1899-1961.
```

Figure 74.   Locally recorded tape

cartridges, cassettes, reels, cylinder recordings, player-piano rolls, and a variety of experimental media. Recordings include musical performances, prose and poetry readings, interviews, lectures, sound effects, and the aural presentation of information on all subjects. Because of the variety of formats and types of presentation, cataloging rules are complex.

The main entry for sound recordings is less likely to be under title than it is for visual materials. Music has traditionally been entered under composer. A collection of two or more works by different composers is entered under title; if there is no collective title, each work is cataloged separately. Lectures are entered under the lecturer, and readings of a literary work are entered under the author of the work. As with other audiovisual materials, works whose authorship is diffuse, indeterminate, or unknown are entered under title.

The cataloging for a phonograph record entered under title is shown in Figure 75. An added entry is made for the performing quintet. When a publisher is principally a publisher of recordings, the imprint consists of the trade name of the publisher and the serial identification of the record (BCP 6020). The year of copyright is preceded by a "p" rather than a "c." The collation for phonograph records includes the number of discs, the speed in revolutions per minute, an abbreviation indicating whether it is monophonic, stereophonic, or quadraphonic, and the disc diameter. The notes give further information about the recording.

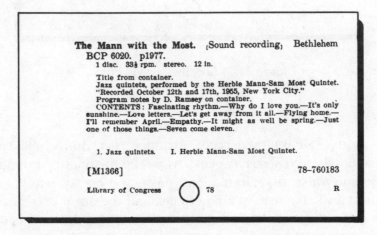

Figure 75.   Phonograph record

The catalog card shown in Figure 76 illustrates a musical work entered under composer. It also shows the use of a uniform title. Uniform titles are used to bring together various printed editions and recordings of a musical work regardless of the language and wording of the titles. (Uniform titles may also be used to bring together editions of nonmusical publications.) Small libraries that do not expect to ever have more than ten or fifteen items entered under any composer may not need to use uniform titles. For libraries using uniform titles even on original cataloging, *Music, Books on Music and Sound Recordings* (issued by the Library of Congress) is the best source of guidance. The *Schwann Record and Tape Guide*, which was described in the last chapter, also uses uniform titles. Notice that the uniform title is bracketed and given on the line between the composer and the title. The medium designator, "Sound recording," follows the uniform title rather than the title of the work itself. This example also illustrates the cataloging of a work that appears on only one side of a disc; notice the note beginning with "With." Added entries are made for the clarinetist and the ensemble.

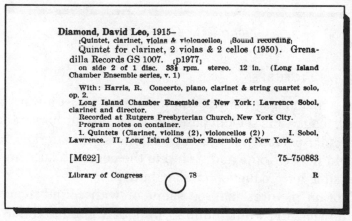

Diamond, David Leo, 1915–
    ₁Quintet, clarinet, violas & violoncellos, ₁Sound recording₁
    Quintet for clarinet, 2 violas & 2 cellos (1950). Grena-
dilla Records GS 1007. ₁p1977₁
    on side 2 of 1 disc. 33⅓ rpm. stereo. 12 in. (Long Island
Chamber Ensemble series, v. 1)

    With: Harris, R. Concerto, piano, clarinet & string quartet solo,
op. 2.
    Long Island Chamber Ensemble of New York; Lawrence Sobol,
clarinet and director.
    Recorded at Rutgers Presbyterian Church, New York City.
    Program notes on container.
    1. Quintets (Clarinet, violins (2), violoncellos (2))   I. Sobol,
Lawrence. II. Long Island Chamber Ensemble of New York.

[M622]   75–750883

Library of Congress   78   R

Figure 76.   Musical work

Musical recordings, which are among the most frequently acquired of audiovisual materials, are also, in the opinion of many, the most difficult to catalog. Anyone who has mastered the art of cataloging recorded music will probably find the rest of audiovisual cataloging relatively easy.

The cataloging for a cassette tape of a lecture is illustrated in Figure 77. For tape in cassettes, the collation includes the number of cassettes, the number of tracks, the dimensions of the cassette (if other than 3⅞ × 2½) and one of the three terms—"mono.," "stereo.," or "quad." The duration of sound recordings is given if stated on the work or easily ascertainable.

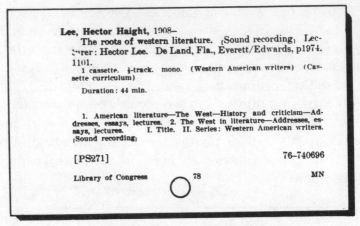

Figure 77.   Cassette tape

Motion Pictures.

The main entry for motion pictures is almost always the title because it is seldom possible to ascribe authorship to a particular person. As with other audiovisual materials, one should not attribute authorship to the commercial firm responsible for production or distribution.

Motion pictures may be silent or with sound, in color or in black and white, 8mm, 16mm, or 35mm, and may be accompanied by a teacher's guide or other material. All of these facts are given in the collation, as shown on the two cards in Figure 78. AACR rules specify that place of publication and a summary of the contents be given, but not all libraries follow these practices.

Filmstrips.

Most filmstrips are entered under title, but a decision must often be made as to whether a filmstrip that is part of a set should be entered under its own title or cataloged as part of the set. The decision depends upon such factors as how closely the subjects of the filmstrips in the set are related to each other, whether each filmstrip has an independent,

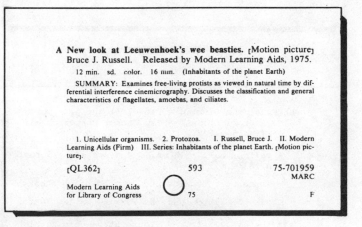

A Study of density. [Motion picture] / Rand McNally and Co. ; made by Science Software Systems. -- Chicago : Rand McNally, 1973.

1 cartridge, ca. 4 min. : si., col. ; super 8 mm. & teacher's guide. -- (Interaction filmloops --inquiry in physical science)

Correlated with the textbook, Interaction of matter and energy, by Abraham, et al.

1. Specific gravity. I. Interaction of matter and energy.

A New look at Leeuwenhoek's wee beasties. [Motion picture] Bruce J. Russell. Released by Modern Learning Aids, 1975.

12 min. sd. color. 16 mm. (Inhabitants of the planet Earth)

SUMMARY: Examines free-living protists as viewed in natural time by differential interference cinemicrography. Discusses the classification and general characteristics of flagellates, amoebas, and ciliates.

1. Unicellular organisms. 2. Protozoa. I. Russell, Bruce J. II. Modern Learning Aids (Firm) III. Series: Inhabitants of the planet Earth. [Motion picture].

[QL362]   593   75-701959
                                                      MARC
Modern Learning Aids
for Library of Congress   75   F

Figure 78.   Motion pictures

self-sufficient title, and whether the filmstrips are sold individually or as a set.

Examples of a filmstrip entered under its own title and a set of four filmstrips cataloged as a unit are shown in Figures 79 and 80. Notice that the physical description includes the number of frames, whether in color, and width in millimeters. A filmstrip accompanied by a phonograph record or cassette is cataloged in the same manner as other filmstrips with the accompanying materials noted in the collation.

```
Environmental awareness--signs of change.
  [Filmstrip] / Joseph L. Becker ; made by
  Films Inc. -- Boston : Allyn and Bacon, c1976.
  82 fr. : col. ; 35 mm. & 1 cassette. --
(Ecology--the living web ; 6)

With teacher's guide and student activity book.


1. Environmental protection. 2. Conservation
of natural resources. I. Becker, Joseph L.
II. Series: Ecology--the living web ;
[Filmstrip] ; 6.
```

Figure 79. Filmstrip

```
Entering the working world. [Filmstrip] / Gordon
  Glyn Productions. -- New York : Butterick
  Publishing, 1975.

  4 rolls : col. ; 35 mm. & 4 discs (33 1/3 rpm.
12 in. 42 min.)

With teacher's guide and 30 student workbooks.

CONTENTS: 1. You and the working world. 74 fr.
--2. Landing a job. 77 fr.--3. Lifestyle--on and
off the job. 75 fr.--4. Your future--aiming high.
66 fr.
1. Personnel service in education. 2. Vocational
guidance.
```

Figure 80. Set of four filmstrips

VIDEORECORDINGS.

Videorecordings are designed for playback on television equipment. The term includes videocassettes, videodiscs, and videotapes. The cataloging of videorecordings is similar to that for motion pictures. The collation includes the number and type of units, the running time in minutes, sound and color statements, and dimensions (width of tape, diameter of disc, etc.). The type of machine needed for playback can be specified in a note. A sample card for a videorecording is shown in Figure 81.

```
Stroke rehabilitation. [Videorecording] /
Washington/Alaska Regional Medical Program.
-- Seattle : The Program ; Washington :
distributed by National Audiovisual Center,
1970.

3 cassettes, 69 min. : sd., col. ; 3/4 in.

U standard.

1. Stroke patients - Rehabilitation.
I. Washington/Alaska Regional Medical Program.
```

Figure 81.   Videorecording

SLIDES.

Slides include stereoscope slides, glass slides, and audio-slides (a strip attached to the mount contains recorded sound). However, 35mm color slides in two-by-two-inch mounts are the ones most frequently added to library collections.

The problem of cataloging slides in many libraries is that there are vast quantities of slides and many do not fit neatly into sets. The most stable kind of slide set is the purchased set of slides that is accompanied by a sound recording; slides will probably not be pulled from the set and used individually. A purchased set of slides accompanied by a teacher's guide or script is also usually used as one unit. However, many groups of slides have little in common except that they were purchased or produced at the same time. It is better to organize a collection of slides by classification number, subject, or artist (for art slides) than by an artificial grouping based chiefly on the date of accession. Teachers or other library users will often compose their own sets of slides by selecting individual slides from various parts of the collection. Sometimes an instructor will even pull a group of slides from a collection and record a tape to accompany them, thus creating his own slide-sound set.

When a library has tens of thousands of slides, it is usually not practical to catalog individual slides separately. In addition to cataloging slide-sound sets and other sets that will be used as units, it is also possible to create open-ended sets of slides on particular subjects. For example, slides about American Indians might be cataloged as shown in Figure 82. Any slides purchased or produced about American Indians that were not part of sound-slide sets or other stable sets could be added to this set. Slides added to the open-ended set would be numbered consecutively; it would not be necessary to change the catalog cards each time a slide was added.

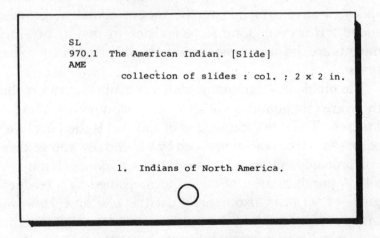

Figure 82. Collection of slides

The cataloging for two slide-sound sets is shown in Figure 83. Notice that although these sets were cataloged as recently as 1974, and 1978, there are variations from present cataloging practices. The medium designator would now be "Slide" in both cases.

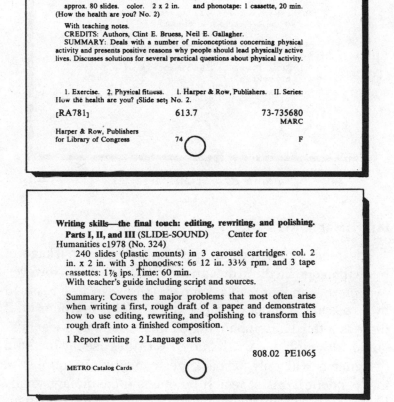

Run, do not walk. ₁Slide set₎ Harper & Row, Publishers, 1974.

approx. 80 slides. color. 2 x 2 in. and phonotape: 1 cassette, 20 min. (How the health are you? No. 2)

With teaching notes.
CREDITS: Authors, Clint E. Bruess, Neil E. Gallagher.
SUMMARY: Deals with a number of misconceptions concerning physical activity and presents positive reasons why people should lead physically active lives. Discusses solutions for several practical questions about physical activity.

1. Exercise. 2. Physical fitness. I. Harper & Row, Publishers. II. Series: How the health are you? ₁Slide set₎ No. 2.

₁RA781₎   613.7   73-735680
                                                    MARC

Harper & Row, Publishers
for Library of Congress   74   F

Writing skills—the final touch: editing, rewriting, and polishing.
Parts I, II, and III (SLIDE-SOUND)   Center for
Humanities c1978 (No. 324)
       240 slides (plastic mounts) in 3 carousel cartridges. col. 2 in. x 2 in. with 3 phonodiscs: 6s 12 in. 33⅓ rpm. and 3 tape cassettes: 1⅞ ips. Time: 60 min.
With teacher's guide including script and sources.

Summary: Covers the major problems that most often arise when writing a first, rough draft of a paper and demonstrates how to use editing, rewriting, and polishing to transform this rough draft into a finished composition.

1 Report writing   2 Language arts

                                        808.02 PE1065

METRO Catalog Cards

Figure 83.   Slide-sound sets

TRANSPARENCIES.

Transparencies, designed to be used with overhead projectors, present some of the same problems as slides in that they can also be purchased or produced individually or in sets. The cataloging for a transparency set is shown in Figure 84.

```
Drafting techniques. [Transparency]. -- Redwood
    City, Calif. : Visual Materials Incorporated,
    1967.
    40 transparencies (127 overlays) : col. ;
25 x 30 cm & teacher's manual.

    CREDITS: Educational consultant, Herbert A.
Lewis.
    SUMMARY: Presents fundamentals of a basic
drafting course.
```

Figure 84. Transparencies

MULTIMEDIA KITS.

The medium designator "Kit" is used for a package of more than one medium designed for use as a unit. However, two interdependent media, such as a filmstrip accompanied by a cassette, are not considered a kit. This is true even if there is a third accompanying element, such as a teacher's guide. Although the AACR and AECT rules use the medium designator "Kit" only for packages containing a number of independent items of which no one is predominant, many libraries have found it convenient to group sound filmstrips and slide-sound sets with kits; one reason for this practice is that it is often not convenient to intershelve sound filmstrips with filmstrips and sound-slide sets with individual slides, but both can be conveniently intershelved with kits. Now that medium designators have become standardized as broad generic terms, however, they should no longer be interpreted as location devices. (Sound recordings in the form of phonograph records, tape cassettes, and reel tapes cannot be intershelved or housed together any more conveniently than can filmstrips and sound filmstrips.) It is, therefore, possible to use the designator "filmstrip" for a sound filmstrip even though it will be shelved with kits.

A sample card illustrating how a kit might be cataloged is shown in Figure 85. The component media are described in alphabetical order with an indication of number of items; the dimensions of the container are also given. The various media can be individually described within parentheses if necessary.

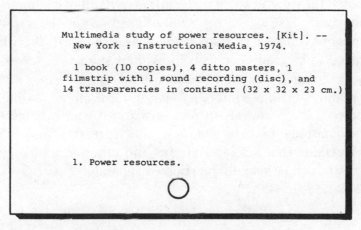

Figure 85. Multimedia kit

PHYSICAL PROCESSING.

Decisions on classification, shelving or housing, and physical processing are closely related. The type of label used and its placement are obviously influenced by the way in which an item will be stored. Circulation policies also affect physical processing; book cards may or may not be typed. Probably the only universal principle of AV processing is that all items, including all components of sets, should be marked with some type of property identification. A classification number or other location device must also usually be affixed. Most library supply catalogs offer many types of AV labels, storage boxes, and storage cabinets, thus suggesting various methods of handling AV materials.

Some audiovisual materials are packaged by the producers in attractive boxes that can be conveniently placed on the shelves. However, a common problem is the tendency of producers to package materials in unnecessarily large boxes, perhaps with the hope that the materials will thus appear more impressive. Most libraries, on the other hand, are perennially short of space and must repackage these materials in smaller boxes. In addition, when original boxes are too flimsy, and some materials arrive unboxed, libraries must purchase boxes especially designed for the various types of AV materials. With some types of materials there is a choice to be made between individual storage in boxes or mass storage in cabinets. Boxes, binders, and other small containers facilitate intershelving, but it is often possible to shelve more materials in less space by using cabinets. A disadvantage of cabinets, such as filmstrip and slide cabinets, is that teacher's guides and other accompanying materials must usually be shelved separately.

CHAPTER 17

Serials: A Challenge to Libraries

IN MEDIUM-SIZED and large libraries all over the country, there are librarians, library assistants, and clerks who work almost entirely with serials. Acquisitions, cataloging, circulation, and reference aspects of serials work may be centralized in one department, but more often different kinds of serials work are handled by different departments. Even when a library has a serials department, it seldom handles all technical service and public service functions related to serials.

The vast number of serials published, the many different types of serials, the variety of sources from which they must be acquired, and the constant changing of titles, formats, publishers, and frequency all contribute to the complexity of serials handling. Even school and small public libraries with only a few hundred titles are not immune to problems with serials.

DEFINITION AND TYPES OF SERIALS.

A serial is a publication issued in successive parts and intended to be continued indefinitely. Serials include magazines, journals, newspapers, bulletins, quarterlies, proceedings, monographic series, periodical indexes, abstracting services, newsletters, yearbooks, reviews, business services, and a variety of other publications. Among the most familiar of serials are popular magazines such as *Time*,

Reader's Digest, and *National Geographic*. While the term "magazine" is most frequently used to refer to popular publications of the type seen on newsstands, the term "journal" is usually used in reference to academic, professional, and specialized publications.

The term "periodical" includes both magazines and journals, but its exact meaning varies from library to library. Publications issued once a year or less frequently, the proceedings, papers, and other publications of corporate bodies, irregular publications, and newspapers are not usually considered periodicals. Each issue of a periodical usually contains separate articles, stories, or other writings. Most, but not all, periodicals have distinctive titles. In actual practice, whether or not a publication is shelved in the periodical collection of a library may determine whether or not it is counted as a periodical.

Two types of publications that are sometimes handled as serials, although they are not true serials, are pseudoserials and terminal sets. A pseudoserial is a frequently reissued and revised publication such as *Ulrich's International Periodical Directory*. A terminal set is a multivolume work that is intended to be completed in a certain number of volumes, such as an edition of the complete works of an author. In defining a publication as a serial, the intention of the publisher is an important factor; some magazines and journals unexpectedly cease after publication of one or two issues, and some terminal sets continue for decades. Standing orders are not synonymous with serials since libraries frequently have standing orders for pseudoserials and terminal sets. On the other hand, a library may individually order one volume of a yearbook or review series.

BIBLIOGRAPHIC TOOLS.

Knowledge of a few basic sources of information is helpful to the beginner in serials work. The *Union List of Serials in Libraries of the United States and Canada* (3d ed., H. W.

Wilson, 1965, 5 vols.) lists 156,499 titles that began publication before 1950. In addition to serving as a basic source of information on beginning dates, title changes, and other publication data, it lists holdings of 956 libraries, which is useful for interlibrary loan purposes.

The current issues and cumulations of *New Serial Titles*, published by the Library of Congress, give publication information and holdings for serials that began publication in 1950 and succeeding years.

Ulrich's International Periodicals Directory (R.R. Bowker, biennial) provides publication data on about 60,000 periodicals from all over the world. If critical and evaluative information is needed, *Magazines for Libraries*, edited by Bill Katz and Berry Gargal is a useful guide (3d ed. Bowker, 1978). Although the guide covers only about 6,500 periodicals, it does include the titles most likely to be of interest to public, school, and small college libraries.

ORDERING AND PAYING FOR SERIALS.

The decision to subscribe to a $10.00 periodical is more important than the decision to purchase a $10.00 book. New subscriptions should always be carefully evaluated because once begun they are often continued indefinitely. Frequent subscription changes are not desirable, because scattered holdings are less useful than unbroken runs of basic, frequently used periodicals. Over a ten-year period, allowing for a 10 percent annual increase, a journal with an original subscription price of $10.00 will cost a library about $159.00. (Actual estimates of periodical price increases due to inflation vary from 10 to 22 percent.)

In recent years subscription prices have generally increased at a faster pace than library materials budgets. Even if no subscriptions are added, the cost of subscriptions is likely to require each year a higher proportion of a library's budget. Binding costs and the costs of replacing missing issues are related expenses incurred by many libraries. In spite of the cost and the problems in handling them, serials are an essential part of most library collections. Periodicals frequently contain more current information on popular subjects than books. Special interest serial publications are available on almost every sport, hobby, and personal interest. Scientific, technical, and medical journals contain the latest developments and are often a more important part of library collections in these areas than are books. Students and research workers can approach almost any subject by using indexing and abstracting services as guides to the periodical literature. Although it is necessary to evaluate the need for each new subscription carefully, serials holdings can be as important as book and audiovisual collections in determining whether library objectives are met.

Serial subscriptions are placed directly with publishers or with subscription agents. In addition, almost all libraries receive some serials free, and some libraries receive serials through exchange arrangements with other libraries or institutions. The advantage of using a subscription agent is that there are fewer individual purchase orders and invoice payments. However, one should not assume that by using a subscription agent, all serial subscriptions will be covered by one annual invoice. Some serial publishers do not work through agents, and direct subscriptions must be placed. Moreover, subscription agents send additional invoices to cover price increases and new subscriptions and bill separately for volumes published on an irregular basis.

Although it would be desirable to set up serial subscriptions so that all would expire at the same time, this is not possible. The first issue of a periodical volume is not always published in January. Many educational journals and school-related magazines are published from September to May or June; the beginning date of the volume for some periodicals depends upon the date that publication first began. Subscription agents will attempt to have as many subscriptions as possible expire on the same date (such as the end of the year), but must work with publisher policies, library requests to begin new subscriptions as soon as possible or with the beginning of volumes, and extensions of subscriptions because of missed issues or delayed publication.

Some periodical publishers offer lower rates for multiple-year subscriptions. Although it is desirable to take advantage of these discounts, the problem of estimating annual subscription costs becomes more complicated because not all subscriptions are paid every year.

The selection of an agent and changes in the subscription list are decisions that should be carefully made. A new subscription will usually not begin arriving for two to three months. If the publication is issued infrequently or if the publisher will only begin subscriptions with the first issue of a volume, a longer period of time may be required. Address changes do not usually take effect for four to eight weeks. Some subscriptions can be canceled only at the end of a subscription period, and many publishers will send several issues beyond the end of a subscription. Frequent changes in a library's subscription list and in subscription agents further complicate the problems involved in arranging for the regular arrival and payment of subscriptions.

RECEIVING CURRENT ISSUES.

Recording the receipt of current issues of newspapers, periodicals, and other serials is a daily routine in many libraries. In a library with 500 subscriptions it may require only an hour or two; in a library with 5,000 subscriptions it is a full-time job. The process usually begins with the sorting of the mail. Serial publications are separated from publishers' advertising, dealers' catalogs, book shipments, and miscellaneous correspondence. In a typical procedure, the serials are stamped with a property stamp, dated, alphabetized, and carried to a card file where receipt is recorded. As they are checked in, shelving or routine instructions are observed so that the materials can then be shelved in the correct spot or sent to the appropriate person or department.

There are many variations in check-in procedures. Some libraries do not stamp materials with a property stamp until they are recorded on a check-in record. The first letter of the title or other entry may be underlined to prevent misshelving. The addresses on mailing labels and wrappers are usually observed for correctness; it is sometimes desirable to preserve wrappers and mailing envelopes until check-in problems are resolved.

Small libraries with less than 100 subscriptions and gift serials may use a drawer, tray, or box to hold their periodical record cards. Visible indexing units are used by many larger libraries. The cards are housed in flat, sliding trays; when a tray is pulled out, a sequence of titles can be observed. Automation of check-in procedures will be discussed later in this chapter.

Periodical record cards can be ordered from library supply houses or designed and printed locally. An example of a locally designed card showing the receipt of one periodical issue is shown in Figure 86.

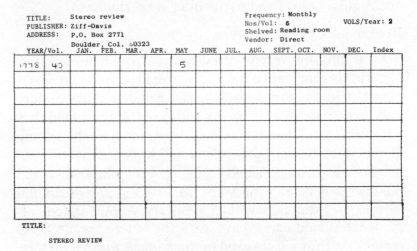

TITLE: Stereo review
PUBLISHER: Ziff-Davis
ADDRESS: P.O. Box 2771
Boulder, Col. 80323

Frequency: Monthly
Nos/Vol: 6
Shelved: Reading room
Vendor: Direct
VOLS/Year: 2

YEAR/Vol.	JAN.	FEB.	MAR.	APR.	MAY	JUNE	JUL.	AUG.	SEPT.	OCT.	NOV.	DEC.	Index
1978	40				5								

TITLE:

STEREO REVIEW

Figure 86. Periodical record card

The amount of information included on periodical record cards varies from library to library. Consulting the latest available issue of a magazine for the publisher's address when necessary may be more efficient than recording it on the card because addresses change frequently and many magazines have different addresses for different purposes. It is important to record volume and issue numbers as well as dates so that missing issues can be more easily spotted. The date indicated on the card in Figure 86 (May 1978) is the date of the issue rather than the date of receipt. Some libraries also stamp or write dates of receipt on cards; this is particularly useful for irregular publications. Payment information is usually recorded on a separate card.

CLAIMING.

The person who records the receipt of serials usually also watches for missing issues. The same person is also sometimes responsible for claiming.

There are two types of situations in which claims are necessary. The first type is the individual missing issue. When the receipt of an issue is recorded, it is sometimes observed that the previous issue has not yet arrived. It may be desirable to check the shelves to be certain the issue did not slip through or, in the case of a daily publication, to wait a few days, but there is usually little doubt that a claim will be required. The other type of situation is the case in which a serial stops coming or, if a new subscription, never starts arriving. The routine checking-in procedure will not reveal this type of problem because only cards for actual arrivals are examined. Catching the ones that stop coming completely requires special procedures such as examining every card in the file once every three or four months, examining racks of current newspapers and periodicals to determine if recent issues have been received, using a special system of colored tabs or other signals to indicate expected arrival dates, or a combination of the above. Routine follow-up on new subscriptions and observing whether serials have been arriving regularly before approving invoices for payment are also useful procedures.

Although discovering that the issue preceding one just received has not yet arrived is almost always a good reason for a claim, the proper claiming of other late arrivals requires knowledge of serial receipt patterns. April issues of some magazines will arrive in March, others in April, and some in May or even June. Quarterly publications, especially those issued by small associations and university departments, frequently arrive far behind schedule. If dates of receipt are not indicated on the check-in record, the dates stamped on the previous issues received should be observed in order to establish a pattern of receipt.

Most subscription agents will handle all types of claims but also permit direct claims to publishers. There is little advantage in placing claims for individual issues and replacements for copies received in badly damaged condition through the agent, but if a serial has stopped arriving altogether, it may mean that the subscription was not properly renewed; therefore, it is useful to place the claim through the agent. An agent is not responsible for the actual safe, prompt arrival of each issue, but he is responsible for entering a subscription so that the library is on the mailing list properly.

Before sending claims to a subscription agent, it is advisable to read the agent's instructions for claiming. Most agents also supply claim forms. An example of the type of form that can be used for direct claims to publishers is shown in Figure 87.

If the subscription was placed directly with the publisher, the payment information might be given as "on your invoice no. 602, dated April 24, 1978." If the subscription was placed through an agent "through our agent, J. Jones Co." would be given as payment information. Although a form such as this can be used for most problems with direct subscriptions,

ELMTOWN PUBLIC LIBRARY
ELMTOWN, GA.

Date_____

To:

Title_____

We have a subscription to the above publication which was paid_____

_____

_____We have not received any issues or volumes.

_____We did not receive_____. Please send us a copy.

_____We have received no issues since_____. Please send or explain.

_____Damaged copy received. Send replacement for_____

_____Imperfect copy received. Send replacement for_____

_____Two copies received. Mailing labels attached. We want only one

subscription. Please correct your records.

Signature_____

Figure 87. Claim form

problems with subscriptions placed through an agency should usually be referred to the agency when no issues or duplicate copies are being received.

A record of claims must, of course, be kept. A notation on the periodical record such as "cl. 4/1/78" will advise other staff members that claiming has not been neglected. Colored tabs on the record cards of items claimed or a separate claims file can be used for follow-up procedures.

Renewal notices and renewal invoices will be received even for subscriptions handled through an agency. Since most libraries also have some direct subscriptions, all such notices cannot be automatically disregarded, nor is it advisable to depend upon personal memory except in a very small library. Payment records or a file or list indicating subscription sources and renewal dates should be consulted.

Mass circulation magazines present different problems to libraries than small circulation specialized journals. Library subscriptions account for only a small percentage of the circulation of popular magazines; distribution policies are not formulated with libraries in mind. Publishers of these magazines are seldom directly involved with circulation, which is often handled by a separate fulfillment agency. Missing issues must be claimed immediately because back issues are seldom kept in stock. On the other hand, large subscription discounts are frequently available. A library whose subscription list consists mostly of popular magazines will probably receive a discount from an agent rather than having to pay a service charge as do libraries subscribing to more specialized, esoteric journals.

At the other extreme are highly specialized periodicals with small audiences. Many of the subscribers may be libraries. When dealing with these journals one may be communicating with a real person rather than a computer. Some, but not all, of these publishers are interested in helping libraries with their problems. However, publication of journals of this type is often delayed and irregular, and billing and other transactions may not be handled in a systematic manner. Back issues and volumes of such serials are frequently available from the publisher. Because of the difference in publishing methods between popular magazines, specialized journals, and other serials, it is useful to specify the type of serial one has in mind when discussing subscription problems.

AUTOMATION.

Serials automation seldom handles the most time-consuming clerical procedures or the more difficult professional decisions related to serials. It does not open the mail, decide which items are serials whose receipt must be recorded, scan covers and title pages for entry words, arrange a pile of materials in alphabetical order, stamp them with property stamps and dates, locate volume numberings hidden deep within issues, or transport materials to the proper shelf location. It does not insert loose-leaf pages in volumes or look through a pile of issues to see if all numbers of a volume are present. Likewise it does not make a selection between two good journals or two reputable subscription agencies. It cannot tell you whether a gift serial will continue coming or whether anyone will ever read it. Nor will it locate the source for an important missing issue. The computer cannot decide whether a serial should be shelved in the classified book collection or in the periodical section or whether it is better to catalog volumes separately or as a set.

Nevertheless, automation has been used successfully in handling some aspects of serials work in some libraries. Some of the principal developments have been the use of computer-printed arrival cards to replace manual check-in records; computerization of payment, claim, and renewal records; use of computer-printed lists of serials received; and the development of data bases that list serial titles or index articles within serials. With the arrival card system, the computer prepares an arrival card for each serial of which an issue is expected during a particular period of time. The frequency of publication and past receipt record are taken into consideration. Obviously, a system of this type solves some claiming problems. Computerization can also assist with financial accounting, for instance by determining the amount spent for serials in particular subject areas. Computer-printed holdings lists are a well-established means of distributing holdings information frequently and efficiently. Countless acronyms abound in the language of data bases, among the ones that will probably be most important in future years is CONSER(Conversion of Serials), a cooperative project for building and maintaining an on-line data base of authenticated serial records.

Obtaining Missing Issues and Volumes.

Even when claiming is conducted efficiently, some issues will be missed; one reason is that publishers sometimes extend subscriptions rather than supply missing issues. In most libraries, however, the principal reason that individual numbers of serials are sought is that the original copies have disappeared from the library. Obtaining replacements for missing issues is usually a preliminary step to preparing volumes for binding, although there may be times when a library wishes to obtain a particular issue to complete an unbound file or because it has been requested by a patron.

Before purchasing missing issues, many libraries seek to obtain them free of charge. Replacement issues for popular magazines can sometimes be obtained from individual subscribers. Aside from missing issues, many libraries have a collection of unneeded and duplicate issues, so a common practice is for libraries to circulate exchange lists. If each library in a large group regularly issues a list of unneeded periodicals, many libraries will eventually be able to replace a high percentage of their missing issues free of charge. Although there is no cash expenditure except for postage, participating in an exchange system of this type does require considerable staff time.

Universal Serials and Book Exchange (3335 V St. NW, Washington, DC 20018) has over the years distributed millions of serial issues. There is an annual membership fee and also a handling charge for each periodical issue obtained. The handling charge in some cases is equal to or higher than the cost for which the item could be purchased from another source. Nevertheless, because of the number and variety of titles available, membership in USBE is worthwhile for libraries that must obtain many missing issues.

Missing issues and volumes can be purchased from a variety of commercial firms that advertise in library magazines. At some point in the procurement procedure for missing issues and volumes, it is useful to determine whether or not the items needed are still available from the publishers. In some cases this information can be located in a recent issue of the journal; if not, an inquiry can be sent. It may be more desirable to obtain missing issues free of charge through exchange arrangements or to purchase a large number of issues of various titles from one source, but availability from the publisher should be determined before much time or money is spent in trying to obtain volumes or issues elsewhere.

Preparation for Binding.

Any library that spends a considerable portion of its budget on subscriptions should consider binding at least some of the serials received. If it is worth $26.00 a year to subscribe to a quarterly or bimonthly journal, it is probably also worth $6.00 to have it bound. On the other hand, newsletters and other materials that are chiefly of current interest may not be worthy of binding. The decision on whether or not to bind particular serials is based on such factors as whether they are of ephemeral or permanent interest, whether they are covered by periodical indexes, and anticipated use. Even small libraries, such as school libraries, should consider binding at least a few of their periodicals. The use of periodical indexes is an important approach to information that is best encouraged by convenient access to at least some of the periodicals indexed. Even if only a few periodicals are regularly bound, at the end of a ten-year period a collection that will answer many questions on recent events and topics of interest will be available.

The choice does not lie entirely between commercial binding and discarding. As long as space is available, issues can be kept in hanging folders, boxes, or on the shelves. Library supply catalogs offer various kinds of binders and filing boxes.

Some commercial binders will pick up volumes to be

bound; in other cases the volumes must be packed and shipped. All binders will supply directions for preparation for binding and most supply forms to be used by the library. Some of the factors complicating bindery preparation work are missing issues, irregular volume numbering, changes in title, frequency, and format, and uncertainty as to how long to wait for a title page and index.

Serials on Microform.

Obtaining serials on microfilm is an alternative to having them bound. It is not usually an alternative to periodical subscriptions, because microfilm is seldom available until volumes are complete, which is not soon enough to meet library needs. Moreover, there may be a requirement that the library subscribe to the paper edition in order to be eligible to purchase recent volumes on microfilm. Simultaneous publication of journals in paper copy and microfiche is a growing trend, but only a small fraction of most library subscription lists can presently be obtained directly on microfiche.

Most libraries have a mixture of bound periodicals and microfilm. Many libraries accumulated large collections of bound volumes before microfilm was available. Although the list of serials available on microfilm (or microfiche) is increasingly extensive, there are still many serials available only in paper copies. On the other hand, even libraries that usually prefer to bind their periodicals rather than purchase them on microfilm will occasionally purchase backfiles on microfilm when the paper copies are expensive or unavailable.

The actual cost of binding a volume and purchasing a microfilm copy is similar. A weekly periodical will usually need to be bound four times a year, but the microfilm is comparatively expensive. When the costs of microfilm and bound volumes are compared, other factors are usually considered. The cost of maintaining the space needed to shelve bound volumes is an important factor, especially when a library is filled to capacity and the cost of acquiring new space must be computed. The cost of obtaining missing issues and later repairing worn or mutilated bound volumes must also be considered.

On the other hand, satisfactory service cannot be provided with serials on microfilm unless an adequate number of readers and reader/printers are purchased and maintained in good operating condition. This is particularly important in academic libraries; even in a small college library a dozen or more students may be using periodical backfiles at the same time. Microfilm reader/printers are much more expensive than simple readers, but students of today expect to be able to make copies. (The librarian who suggests to a student that he can take notes rather than make copies is not likely to receive an enthusiastic response.)

Traditionally microforms have been obtained for infrequently used or research materials. If they are used in this way, there is less need for equipment, but problems with missing issues and mutilated volumes are not alleviated because frequently used periodicals are the principal source of these problems. The real problem in many libraries is heavy usage, conflicting demands, and unreasonable patron expectations. A library user should not expect to find every serial issue and volume on the shelf in its proper place and every item of equipment available and ready for use unless he is the sole user of the collection.

In addition to the decision as to whether to bind serials or obtain them on microfilm, there is the question of the relative merits of microfilm and microfiche. In the past few years serials on microfiche have become more widely available and have gained in popularity, particularly with special libraries that already have collections of documents and reports on microfiche. A particular journal article can usually be located more quickly on microfiche than on microfilm, and microfiche readers are less expensive than micro-film readers. However, if a microfiche collection is used extensively, keeping the file in correct order may require considerable staff time.

Newspapers are one type of serial about which there is no binding versus microfilm debate. Backfiles of newspapers can almost always best be kept on microfilm.

CLASSIFICATION AND ARRANGEMENT.

Different types of serials are usually handled differently. In most libraries, current unbound periodicals are shelved in one location and bound periodicals and serials on micro-film in another. Materials such as corporation annual reports, newspapers, and governmental reports may be shelved in separate collections. Yearbooks, annual reviews, proceedings of conferences, and monograph series are frequently intershelved with books. Many of the books in most reference collections are really serials or pseudoserials.

Most libraries maintain separate periodical collections, although some libraries do classify bound periodicals and intershelve them with books. The decision to shelve a serial in the periodical collection or with books cannot be based solely on whether it arrives bound or unbound. *American Heritage* is an example of a serial that arrives bound, but it is usually shelved with periodicals. Other factors to consider are whether the serial is indexed in periodical indexes, the frequency of publication (some libraries do not consider annual and less frequent publications to be periodicals), and whether or not the library has a subscription. Loose-leaf serials of reference importance, such as *Facts on File*, are usually classified and shelved in the reference collection.

When serials are classified, they are usually broadly classified on the basis of the subjects covered or to be covered in the entire series rather than on the basis of the subject content of a particular volume. An exception to this policy is made for monographic series when the cataloger feels that it would be more useful for each volume to be shelved with other books on the specific subject.

SERIALS CATALOGING.

The general rules for cataloging serials are the same as for books, but exceptions are made to reduce the number of changes needed to cover slight variations between volumes and to allow for recording important information such as frequency, holdings, and relationship to other publications.

Most libraries do not catalog periodicals until a complete volume is available. It is expedient to wait until a number of issues have been published before cataloging them because changes may occur or the publication may not survive. Some libraries catalog only bound periodicals with the reasoning that a publication not worth binding is not worth cataloging.

Although only bound volumes may be cataloged, temporary cards are sometimes inserted in the catalog for unbound issues. Some libraries do not include periodicals in the catalog at all, but instead prepare lists or maintain separate files of holdings. Serials that are classified and shelved in the book collection or in the reference section are almost always cataloged even if periodicals are not.

A serial that changes its title or that is entered under a corporate body that changes its name during the course of publication is normally cataloged with a separate entry for each new title or corporate body name. (An older rule said to catalog all volumes under the latest title and this type of cataloging is still frequently observed.)

A serial publication in several volumes with varying bibliographic information (other than changes in title) is cataloged from the latest volume with variations noted. Terminal sets, on the other hand, are usually cataloged from the first volume published with variations from it noted.

Cataloging is based upon the title page. If there is no title page, the title is taken from the cover, caption, masthead, editorial pages, or other place, in that order of preference. This rule should also be remembered by those who work with serial receipt or bindery preparation procedures, because choice of title must also frequently be made in those situations.

Serials are entered under title with the exception of certain publications issued by corporate bodies such as annual reports, proceedings, and special series and the occasional serial written by a personal author. It has frequently been proposed that all serials be entered under title, but there would then be problems with the many corporate publications with such nondistinctive titles as *Bulletin*, *Report*, or *Proceedings*.

Subtitles are not included unless necessary to identify a publication or to indicate its scope. If a subtitle is given it is usually given in a note.

Changes in place of publication or publisher not warranting specific description can be indicated by "etc." If the name of the publisher is essentially the same as the title of the publication, it is not given.

Editors, compilers, directors, or founders are not named unless they are important to the identification or characterization of a work, nor are added entries made for them.

If a serial has ceased publication and the library has a complete set, holdings can be typed in the body of the entry. For other serials, library practices vary widely. Some libraries use special holdings cards. Others write holdings in pencil on the card itself. Some do not give holdings but instead refer to a special periodicals holding record. Within a particular library, procedures may vary for periodicals and other serials and according to whether or not the library has a current subscription. When holdings are given they are often indicated only on the main entry card.

Even though all volumes of a serial are cataloged and classified together, analytical entries may need to be made for particular volumes or parts of volumes. The analytical may be a unit card with author, title, and subject entry or a single card under an author, title, or other entry. A unit card analyzing one volume of a serial is shown in Figure 88.

```
PA        Studies in Greek historians : in memory of
25          Adam Parry / edited for the Dept. of Classics
.Y3         by Donald Kagan. -- Cambridge ₍Eng.₎ ; New
vol.24      York : Cambridge University Press, 1975.


          xv, 236 p. ; 24 cm. -- (Yale classical studies
          ; v. 24)


          Includes bibliographical references.
          1. Greece - Historiography - Addresses, essays,
          lectures. 2. Parry,     Adam. I. Parry, Adam.
          II. Kagan, Donald.
```

Figure 88.   Unit card analyzing one volume of a serial

Shown in Figures 89 and 90 is the Library of Congress cataloging for four serials. Notice that three of the four have title main entries. Also notice that no mention is made of the editors. A complete set of cards for one serial is shown in Figure 90 to illustrate one library's method of recording holdings.

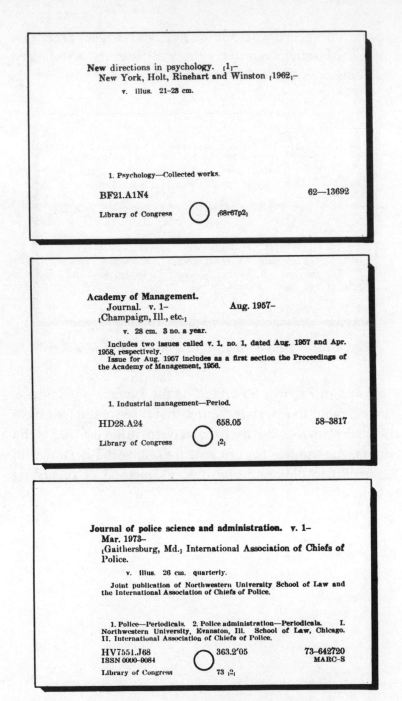

New directions in psychology. [1]–
New York, Holt, Rinehart and Winston [1962]–

    v. illus. 21–23 cm.

    1. Psychology—Collected works.

BF21.A1N4   62—13692

Library of Congress   ◯   [68r67p2]

Academy of Management.
    Journal. v. 1–   Aug. 1957–
  [Champaign, Ill., etc.]

    v. 28 cm. 3 no. a year.

    Includes two issues called v. 1, no. 1, dated Aug. 1957 and Apr. 1958, respectively.
    Issue for Aug. 1957 includes as a first section the Proceedings of the Academy of Management, 1956.

    1. Industrial management—Period.

HD28.A24   658.05   58–3817

Library of Congress   ◯ [2]

Journal of police science and administration. v. 1–
Mar. 1973–
  [Gaithersburg, Md.] International Association of Chiefs of Police.

    v. illus. 26 cm. quarterly.

    Joint publication of Northwestern University School of Law and the International Association of Chiefs of Police.

    1. Police—Periodicals. 2. Police administration—Periodicals. I. Northwestern University, Evanston, Ill. School of Law, Chicago. II. International Association of Chiefs of Police.

HV7551.J68   363.2′05   73–642720
ISSN 0000–9084   MARC-S

Library of Congress   73 [2]

Figure 89. LC cataloging for serials

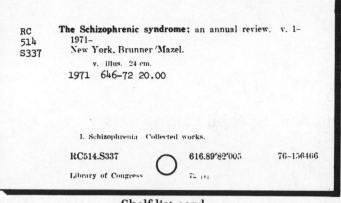

Shelf list card

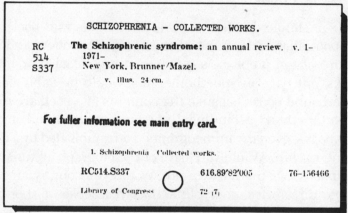

Subject card

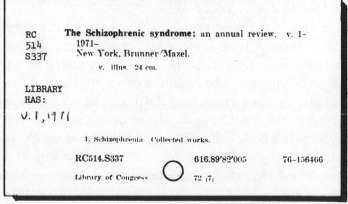

Main entry card

Figure 90. LC cataloging for a serial

CHAPTER 18

The Vertical File
and Other Special Collections

What Is a Book?

Even a simple division of library materials into book and nonbook materials is not always easy. To understand the nature of the problem, suppose you are asked how many books you have in your home. You would probably count paperbound books because the contents of a book are more important than the binding. But would you count all of your cookbooks, even the mimeographed one published by a local women's club? Would you leave out photograph albums and scrapbooks even if hardbound? Would you count your telephone directories, your old school yearbooks, a shopping catalog, a college catalog, a paperbound road atlas, and every copy of the Bible including pocket testaments? Would your encyclopedia count as one book or thirty?

Libraries also have problems in determining what to count as books. The nature of the contents is usually considered more important than the number of pages or type of binding, but judging the contents of an item is a subjective appraisal. In many cases, the definition of a book rests on where it is shelved. Items that have been classified and are shelved in the book collections are counted as books. Items included in special collections, such as collections of pamphlets, bound periodicals, government publications, theses, music scores, college catalogs, or telephone directories, are not counted. If the problem is considered from this viewpoint, whether or not a particular item will be counted as a book depends upon the judgment of the person who decides in which section of the library collection it will be placed.

Although dividing library materials into categories makes it easier to organize them, the physical nature of the material is less important than its anticipated use. One type of material should not be considered intrinsically superior to another type of material. Acquisition and cataloging decisions should not be based on format alone.

In addition to books, audiovisual materials, and serials, many library collections include a variety of other materials, not all of which can be easily categorized. School media centers often acquire many of the types of instructional materials that we did not include with audiovisuals, such as maps, charts, globes, educational games, models, pictures, and posters. Public libraries may serve their patrons by acquiring such informational tools on community resources as church directories, bus schedules, maps, sightseeing guides, local history items, and college catalogs. Academic libraries often include collections of theses, government publications, music scores, maps, and special research materials. In many special libraries, technical reports, corporation publications, reprints of journal articles, government publications, and unpublished materials are an important part of the collection.

Brief attention will be given in this chapter to some of the types of special materials that are collected by many libraries, but an attempt will not be made to cover every type of material of interest to any library.

PAMPHLETS AND OTHER VERTICAL FILE MATERIALS.

Most libraries do not use a definition of *pamphlet* that limits use of the term to publications with fewer than 50, 100, or any other number of pages. Whether or not a particular item is considered a pamphlet and filed in a vertical file or is considered a book and fully cataloged depends upon a number of factors, of which number of pages is only one.

Some of the factors considered are:

1. number of pages
2. size, thickness, and type of binding
3. price paid
4. whether it was specifically requested (in an academic library, if it was included in the book requests of a faculty member this would be considered as a factor, but not necessarily a crucial one)
5. availability of Library of Congress cards or other cataloging copy
6. whether it is cited by author and title in bibliographies and reading lists
7. whether it is of temporary or permanent interest
8. nature and subject of the content
9. anticipated use

A reason for using the term *vertical file* rather than *pamphlet file* is that it carries no implication that all of the materials in the file are pamphlets. Leaflets, brochures, folders, charts, maps, pictures, newspaper clippings, individual issues of magazines, small paperbound books, government documents, and other items can be placed in the file.

Shirley Miller's *The Vertical File and Its Satellites* (Libraries Unlimited, 1971) presents the useful concept of a basic file composed primarily of pamphlets and clippings supplemented by "satellite" collections of such special materials as vocational material, local history, maps, and pictorial material. If a library has few items in a particular category, such as maps or clippings, they can be included in the basic file, but as their number and importance grow, special collections may be needed. Whether it is more useful to consider collections of charts, art prints, pictures, and maps as supplementary to the vertical file or as supplementary to the audiovisual collection depends upon the way in which they are used. In academic libraries, maps would not usually be considered as supplemental to either but would be considered of independent importance. Three-dimensional materials such as models, games, and realia do not fit into the vertical file framework, but files of materials such as college catalogs, annual reports, trade catalogs, and vocational materials may appropriately be considered vertical file satellites.

Vertical file materials are acquired in three principal ways. Many of these materials arrive unsolicited as gifts from individuals or organizations; one advantage of maintaining a vertical file is that a third option is added to the choice between adding an item to the book collection and discarding it. Other materials are selected from lists, such as *Educators' Index of Free Materials* (Randolph, WI, Educators' Progress Service) or *Vertical File Index* (New York, H. W. Wilson Co.) or are directly gathered at meetings or fairs and on visits to institutions and firms. Other materials arrive in response to specific purchase requests; even though the request does not indicate that an item is to be placed in the vertical file, this decision may be made after the material arrives if the vertical file appears to be the best place for it.

Vertical files usually contain both free and inexpensive materials. Acquiring inexpensive materials may be a problem if a library does not have a petty cash fund and if prepayments by check require justification and extensive paperwork. Some vendors accept payment in postage stamps; others do not. Even if coins or bills are available, routine payment in cash is not desirable because there is no proof of payment. On the other hand, issuing a formal purchase order and requesting an invoice in quadruplicate is a cumbersome procedure for obtaining an inexpensive item. Whenever possible it is desirable to select and order a number of items from the same source at the same time. In some cases it may be necessary to evaluate whether an item is worth the time required to acquire it as well as the actual cost.

Building a useful vertical file involves creativity, ingenuity, and common sense. Materials should not be acquired merely because they are available. Whether the materials will be useful is always the primary criterion. In some libraries vertical files are the responsibility of reference personnel rather than technical services personnel since vertical file materials are useful sources of ready-reference information. The materials in a vertical file can also supplement the book collection when there is great demand for information on specific subjects. In addition, pamphlets sometimes contain more up-to-date or specialized information than books.

Vertical files are often contained in metal cabinets with file folders for each subject, but pamphlet boxes can also be used. Each item should be stamped with a property stamp and the date of acquisition. Many pamphlets do not contain copyright or publication dates, so dating them is important. There are two schools of thought on assigning subject headings. One method is to use the same subject headings as used for books (probably either Sears or LC headings). Cards such as the one shown in Figure 91 can then be filed in the catalog for each subject on which there are vertical file materials.

However, some librarians believe that pamphlets require different, usually more specific, subject headings than books. If enough time is devoted to the project, and if a talented individual remains in control of the headings over a long period of time, good results may be achieved by this method; but cataloging methods dependent on the skills of a particular individual are not a good choice for most libraries. This is not to deny that some of the best vertical files are chiefly creations of individual librarians.

Whether ready-made or special headings are used, a list of

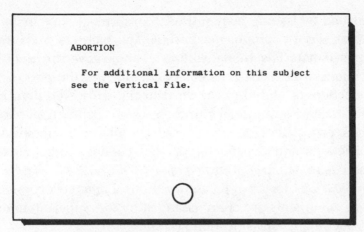

ABORTION

For additional information on this subject
see the Vertical File.

Figure 91. Catalog card referring to vertical file

headings already used should be kept. Adding material to established subject files does not require new folders or new catalog cards. The appropriate subject heading should be written on each item or typed on a label that will be attached to it so that after it circulates or is used in the library, it can be returned to its correct location. Whether or not individual book cards and pockets are prepared depends upon circulation frequency. If pamphlets circulate only occasionally, book cards can be prepared at the time of circulation.

Most vertical files are arranged by subject and contain materials that will be sought after because of their subject content. College catalogs, corporation reports, and society and government publications of an administrative nature are examples of publications that are often approached on the basis of the issuing body. In many libraries they are arranged in separate collections. If the users of a library are most likely to search for a particular publication under author and title, consideration should be given to cataloging it as a book.

GOVERNMENT PUBLICATIONS.

Government publications are a type of material distinguished by issuing body rather than format. They include books, serials, pamphlets, charts, maps, pictures, and other types of materials. In many libraries some government publications are cataloged as books, included in the periodical collection, or placed in the vertical file. However, libraries that receive substantial numbers of government publications, especially U.S. documents, usually maintain special collections and depend on printed catalogs and indexes such as the *Monthly Catalog of United States Government Publications* for an approach to them. Large collections of U.S. documents are often arranged by the Superintendent of Documents classification system.

Libraries that have been designated as depositories receive U.S. documents automatically. In each state at large and within each congressional district, libraries serve as depositories for government publications so that these materials will be widely available to scholars and the general public. Depository libraries receive much valuable reference and research material free of charge, but considerable staff time must be spent in organizing the materials and making them available for use. Depository libraries cannot make item-by-item selections of materials they wish to receive but can select particular categories. When depository publications are discarded, guidelines must be followed.

Even depository libraries must purchase some U.S. Government publications, because not all are available through the depository program. Most U.S. documents are available from the Superintendent of Documents at the Government Printing Office, but some must be ordered directly from particular agencies. Purchasing U.S. Government publications is an exception to routine book ordering procedure because documents can seldom be obtained through book jobbers, special order forms must often be used, and prepayment is required. In the past, document coupons could be purchased in various denominations, but coupons are no longer sold. Opening a deposit account with the Superintendent of Documents simplifies prepayment, because the exact price of publications may not always be known. In many large cities there are Federal Information Centers, which include bookstores that handle U.S. Government publications. Publications of general interest can often be purchased directly from these bookstores, and information on other items can also be obtained.

Price lists of U.S. documents on particular subjects and lists of selected current publications can be obtained free of charge from the Superintendent of Documents. Some publications that are sold by the Government Printing Office can be obtained free by writing or going to other sources, such as a local office of the Cooperative Extension Service or the issuing agency. Another method of attempting to obtain U.S. documents free of charge is to write a letter to a Senator or member of Congress; these officials are usually helpful in other ways to libraries in their districts but are not always able to obtain the particular publications that are needed.

State documents and documents of international organizations also are frequently collected by libraries. The *Monthly Checklist of State Publications* is the basic list covering the publications of state governments. Most states also publish their own lists, which are useful for libraries interested chiefly in the documents of their state. Many research libraries maintain extensive document collections, both current and retrospective. Because of the space required to house large collections and also because of price considerations, documents are frequently acquired in microform.

PRINTED MUSIC.

Most general libraries contain at least some songbooks, hymnals, books of instruction on playing instruments, or other books that contain the words and music of songs. Academic and large public libraries also sometimes acquire collected editions of composers' works, opera scores, and similar materials. When music appears in book format, it can be integrated into the library collection with few problems. However, if sheet music, scores with parts, or an extensive collection of choral, orchestral, or piano music is maintained, special treatment may be necessary. If printed music is bound or reinforced, care must be taken that it can be opened so as to lie flat.

The sale and distribution of printed music has traditionally been separate from that of books. Because of this separation, many libraries have perhaps neglected to acquire collections of folk music and popular songs, books of music instruction, opera scores, musical comedy scores, and similar materials that would be of interest to their patrons. Macmillan, the well-known book publisher, now distributes opera scores and other music published by its subsidiary G. Schirmer, an innovation that may set a trend in the combined sale of books and music that will encourage more libraries to acquire printed music.

As with music recordings, the basic rule is to catalog music scores under the composer. If the words for the music were written by a different person, an added entry is

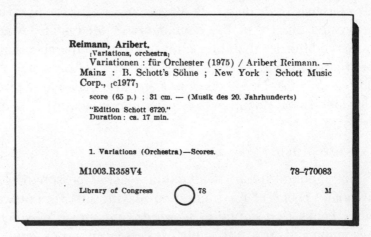

Figure 92.   Music score

needed. Uniform titles are used in the same manner as for musical recordings to bring together all copies of a work regardless of the language or wording of the title on a particular edition. Collections of songs are usually entered directly under title. Paging for collections of songs, hymnals, and similar works is indicated in the same manner as for books, but if a work consists of a score only, and this is not indicated in the uniform title or the body of the entry, it is specified in the collation. An example of Library of Congress cataloging for a music score is shown in Figure 92.

MAPS.

Maps can be purchased from commercial publishers such as Rand McNally, Hammond, and Denoyer-Geppert. Federal and state governmental agencies also produce many maps. Free and inexpensive maps can often be obtained from the same sources as pamphlets and other vertical file materials. Shirley Miller's *The Vertical File and Its Satellites* devotes a chapter to maps that lists many possible sources as well as discussing map care, organization, and cataloging.

If a library has only a few maps and these are of the type that can be conveniently folded, they can be filed under subject or under "Maps" in the vertical file. If a library has a larger, more important collection of maps, they will probably be stored flat in special cabinets. The same type of flat-file cabinet can also be used for art prints, charts, blueprints, posters, and, according to one supplier, church linens.

Anglo-American Cataloging Rules specifies that maps should be entered under the name of the person or corporate body primarily responsible for the contents. The title may be taken from any part of the map. The collation gives the number of maps and a statement of size in centimeters. For example:

3 col. maps 78 × 113 cm.

A statement of the scale of the map is given preceding other notes.

Libraries that do not strictly follow AACR rules for all cataloging often do not follow the AACR rules for main entries of maps, but instead enter them under the area covered or the title. Maps may be classified and arranged by the Dewey Decimal Classification, the Library of Congress Classification, or locally prepared map classifications, which are usually based upon geographic area covered.

MANUSCRIPT MATERIALS AND ARCHIVES.

Manuscripts are works in handwriting or typescript, such as unpublished letters, diaries, journals, reports, or the author's manuscript of a literary work. The term *archives* refers to the organized body of records pertaining to an organization, institution, or governmental unit. Archives usually contain at least some manuscript materials.

Copies of ancient or medieval manuscript books and manuscript copies of important literary works are very valuable items, but few libraries are fortunate enough to own them. Many libraries, however, occasionally acquire such materials as unpublished letters, typed reports, or other archival material.

Manuscript materials can be cataloged either as individual items or as collections. Collections that center on an individual person, family, or corporate body are entered under the appropriate name if they contain material written by or to the person, family, or corporate body. This rule applies even if they also contain related materials. Example:

Beckingham family.
Papers 1857–1910.

Other types of manuscript collections may be entered under the name of the collector or title. See the AACR rules for further explanation of rules of entry and methods of description.

MICROFORMS.

Microform materials include microfilms, microfiche, microcards, and other microformats. Newspapers, periodicals, and documents account for the major part of the microform holdings of many libraries. The fact that the materials copied are newspapers, periodicals, or government documents is usually more important than the fact that they are microforms; therefore, they should be cataloged, indexed, or listed in the same manner as hard copies of the same materials.

Collections of books on particular subjects, usually books that are out-of-print and difficult to obtain, also are available in microform format and are frequently acquired by libraries. Sometimes microform copies of individual books are purchased or produced when a copy of the book itself cannot be located. According to the AACR rules, microform reproductions are described primarily in terms of the original. The reproduction itself is described in a note following any notes that pertain to the original. An example of such a note is:

Microfilm. Ann Arbor, Mich., University Microfilms, 1967, 1 reel. 35 mm. (American culture series, 352:1)

Many other types of materials, such as theses and collections of college catalogs and corporation reports are also available on microform. Some microform materials are original publications rather than reproductions. Microfiche can be used for some of the same purposes as sets of slides, for example to illustrate human anatomy. Moreover, a cassette tape can then be prepared to describe what is seen on the microfiche. A microfiche-cassette set of this type fits in the category of audiovisual materials even if "audiovisual" is as narrowly construed as it is in this book.

MISCELLANEOUS NONBOOK MATERIALS.

Charts, dioramas, flash cards, games, globes, models, and

realia are frequently used for instructional purposes and are therefore included in the collections of school media centers. An example of the cataloging for a globe is given in Figure 93 to show that cataloging these materials is not necessarily difficult. One frequently consulted source for information on cataloging many different types of instructional materials is the fourth edition of *Standards for Cataloging Nonprint Materials* by Alma M. Tillin and William J. Quinly (Washington, D.C., Association for Educational Communications and Technology, 1976.)

Public libraries often have such diverse uncataloged collections as ones comprising comic books, dress patterns, newspaper clippings, postcards, and sales catalogs. The possibilities are endless. Some scholarly libraries collect such materials as comic books and dime novels for their research value. Many different types of materials can contribute to the study of social and cultural history.

```
Rand McNally world portrait globe.  [Globe].
-- Chicago : Rand McNally, 1966.

1 globe : col.; 42 cm. in diameter.

Scale 1:31,680,000; 1 inch equals 500 miles.


  1. Globes, Physical. I. Title: World portrait
globe.
```

Figure 93. Globe

WHAT SHOULD BE CATALOGED.

Although there are rules and instructions covering the cataloging of almost every type of material, this does not necessarily mean that everything in a library except the desks and chairs should be cataloged. It would certainly be possible to catalog the pictures on the wall, a display collection of agates, and the single globe owned by a small public library, but whether this should be done is doubtful. In deciding whether to catalog particular materials, format is less important than anticipated use. If individual items will be sought by author and title, there should be individual author and title entries. If they will be approached by subject, there should be subject entries. If shelving them with books and other materials on the same subject would be useful, they should be classified. However, in many libraries staff time for cataloging is not adequate enough to provide full cataloging for all items for which it might be desirable, and alternative methods, such as using published indexes and catalogs, must be used.

Another factor that sometimes influences decisions on whether particular materials will be cataloged is the nature of the funds from which they were purchased. If a school media center purchases pictures, transparencies, games, and models from funds intended for the purchase of library materials, these materials should not be considered either ephemeral or of interest to only one teacher. In most libraries, materials that are expendable or intended for only one person are not purchased from the library materials budget. There is generally an obligation to organize library materials and make them available for use.

Special Collections versus Intershelving.

Some of the most important and difficult cataloging decisions involve the organization and cataloging of groups or types of materials rather than the choice of entry, classification, or subject heading for an individual item.

The question as to whether audiovisual materials should be intershelved with books was discussed in a previous chapter. Serials, pamphlets (broadly classified), government publications, college catalogs, and physically similar materials can likewise be intershelved with books. Special containers or binding can solve most problems of format. Complete integration is an interesting concept, but not necessarily the best method of organization. Library users are often interested in a particular type of material such as college catalogs. One indication that shelving all or most materials in one classified sequence has disadvantages is that libraries frequently receive suggestions that all books in a certain category, such as books on careers, study-for-examination books, or books of local interest, should be pulled from the collection and shelved separately. Whether or not it is advantageous to maintain separate collections for these materials depends upon the particular situation; in some cases a list of materials held by the library in a certain category will meet most needs.

An example of a type of book that can either be classified by subject and shelved with other books on the same subject or shelved in a separate collection is programmed learning in book format. Although several publishers specialize in programmed learning and offer special collections, many different trade and specialized book publishers issue some books that use a programmed approach to the study of a subject. The Library of Congress does not usually catalog books of programmed learning, regardless of publisher, subject, or importance, but this is not necessarily a sufficient reason for placing them in an uncataloged special collection.

Exercises and Activities for Students
of Library Technical Services

THE FOLLOWING are some general suggestions for activities that may help a student to become acquainted firsthand with the problems and routines of technical services work. The exact details of each project will need to be worked out by the student or instructor.

1. Fill out book request slips (or other three-by-five-inch slips) for all of the books listed in the bibliography of this book. Check the catalog of your library to determine which ones are owned. Check the acquisitions files to see if books that are not held are on order. If not, find the prices and other ordering information in *Books in Print* or another bibliography. Locate LC card order numbers if possible. Resolve any problems of entry. Type book orders for the two books that you consider to be of highest priority. (If your library has all of the books, select some for which you think added copies would be useful.)

2. Make a list of variant forms of names for Feodor M. Dostoyevsky. Check *Books in Print, National Union Catalog*, your library's catalog, encyclopedias, and biographical reference works. When

checking NUC and your library's catalog, notice the author statement as well as the heading.

3. For each of ten books, write on a worksheet the main entry, added entries, proper forms of name for main and added entries, descriptive cataloging, subject headings, Dewey classification, and Cutter number. Also select an LC classification for two of the books. Type complete sets of catalog cards for two of the books.

4. Write on cards or slips of paper all of the headings used in all of the examples of filing arrangement in Chapter 13. Arrange them in one alphabetical sequence according to the ALA filing rules. If your library uses different rules, arrange the cards according to these rules also.

5. Prepare an order for the supplies needed to catalog and process 500 books. Use any library supply catalog and write the order on the form provided in the catalog. Do not order basic equipment such as a typewriter, but do order blank catalog cards. Make your own decision on the method of spine labeling, whether to use book jacket covers for some or all books, etc.

6. Select a broad general subject such as alcoholism, drug abuse, ecology, energy, gardening, or interior decoration. Make a list of the following types of materials available on your subject: two 16mm motion pictures, two other audiovisual items, two periodicals, two pamphlets, two U.S. Government publications, and two state government publications.

7 Consult books and magazine articles about various aspects of library technical services to compose a

list of differences in opinion and differences in recommended practices. Cite a reference for each differing opinion or practice. Some topics you might check are on-approval order plans, the use of pseudonyms as entries, divided versus dictionary catalogs, filing rules, integrating audiovisuals with books, spacing and indention on catalog cards, the future of automation, and the duties of professionals and nonprofessionals.

Appendix: AACR 2

THE SECOND EDITION of *Anglo-American Cataloguing Rules* (AACR 2) was published by the American Library Association in late 1978. The new code will be adopted by the Library of Congress on January 1, 1981. Most large American libraries base their cataloging on Library of Congress practices and will also begin following the code in 1981.

Many small libraries do not follow AACR or attempt to catalog all books in the manner of the Library of Congress. However, they also will eventually be affected by the new code if they use Library of Congress printed cards, Cataloging in Publication, or the cataloging produced by book jobbers or central cataloging agencies that base their practices upon those of the Library of Congress.

Because cataloging in the United States is so greatly influenced by the decisions made by the Library of Congress, when and to what extent LC adopts a new cataloging code is of great importance to American libraries. Although LC did adopt most of AACR 1, a policy called "superimposition" was followed in the selection of the form of name to be used for authors; author headings already in the catalog were not changed, in spite of the recommendations of the 1967 rules. With the adoption of AACR 2 in 1981, LC will follow a policy called "desuperimposition," which means changing author headings to conform with AACR 2. However, LC has already indicated a few exceptions that it will make to AACR 2, such as using the abbreviation "Dept." instead of the full spelling, "Department." In addition, AACR

2 sometimes provides options, and in these cases the option selected by LC will influence the cataloging of many libraries.

Study of the new code does not by itself provide sufficient guidance for the preparation of cataloging cards (or cataloging in other formats) that will conform with LC practices after 1981. Knowing the exact policies of LC in regard to the code and observing LC cataloging based on the code are also necessary. Moreover, AACR 2 is not written in a manner that can be easily understood by the beginning cataloger. Most students preparing to catalog by the new rules will probably need to read explications and interpretations and study sample cards in addition to studying the rules themselves. Familiarity with AACR 1 is helpful to the study of AACR 2, but is not a prerequisite.

The discussion of AACR 2 that follows will focus on the six chapters of this book that are affected by the new rules. It is not a complete exposition of AACR 2, but rather an attempt to relate the new code to material previously presented.

Chapter 7: Choice of Main Entry.

AACR 2 has not abolished the concept of main entry. The rules still assume that one main entry, as well as added entries, is made for each item cataloged. The introduction to the rules mentions the concept of sets of equal entries for each item but states that lack of time did not permit the full exploration of this alternative.

Choice of main entry is discussed in the first chapter of AACR 1. In AACR 2, on the other hand, the rules for bibliographic description are given first, and discussion of main and added entries does not occur until Chapter 21. AACR 2 assumes that in most libraries the selection of main and added entries (access points) is made only after the item has been fully described. Although ISBD description does make description independent of the choice of access points, many libraries will still need to consider the question of main entry and proper form of name during preorder and precataloging searching. Unless one knows the main entry and proper form of name it may not always be possible to determine whether an item is already in the library or on order. Moreover, one of the first steps in many cataloging operations is the determination of whether cataloging copy is available, for example, by searching the *National Union Catalog* to see if a book has been cataloged by LC or other libraries. Whether one searches NUC or a computer data base, knowing the main entry and correct form of the author's name may be necessary, or at least helpful. Therefore, consideration of the main entry does often precede bibliographic description. However, the sequence in which cataloging steps are discussed in AACR 2 does not mean that libraries must perform them in that order.

The definition of "author" is changed in AACR 2. A corporate body, such as an association, institution, business firm, or government agency, can no longer be considered an author. However, main entry under corporate body is still prescribed for certain items, such as works issued by a corporate body that are of an administrative nature or record the collective thought of the body, for some legal and governmental works, and for the reports of the collective activities of conferences, expeditions, and events. The concept of corporate authorship has been abandoned, but works are still entered under the names of corporate bodies if they fit into the categories enumerated in the code.

The ten rules for choice of main entry that were given in Chapter 7 of this book still generally hold true, although in some cases the rules would have been worded differently if they had been derived from AACR 2. Collections of works by different authors and works produced under editorial direction are entered under title rather than editor or compiler as in AACR 1, but this change in rules was already adopted by LC and many other libraries during the period between publication of the editions. As has already been mentioned, AACR 2 limits more strictly the type of works to be entered under the names of corporate bodies than did AACR 1. The rule covering reproductions of the works of artists no longer considers whether the text is a minor part of the publication, but recommends entry under artist unless the writer of the text is represented as the author of the work on the title page or other chief source of information.

Chapter 8: Proper Form of Names and Added Entries.

The changes made by AACR 2 that have received the most attention and that will cause the most problems for libraries are those related to the choice of form of name. The new rules will require the use of different headings for many persons and corporate bodies. Changes requiring the use of different forms of names are more troublesome than changes in bibliographic description, because entries with different types of punctuation in the body of the entry can be easily interfiled, but the use of different headings for one author result in the works of the author not filing together in the catalog. Either all of the old headings must be changed or references must be made. If many headings need to be changed, it may be simpler to close the old catalog and begin anew with a catalog following the new rules. The Library of Congress and some other libraries do plan to close their catalogs when they adopt AACR 2 in 1981.

One important rule change concerns fullness of name for personal authors. AACR 1 recommended that when the forms of name appearing in different works of an author varied in fullness, the fullest form should be used. If most of the title pages of an author's works used initials for his forenames, but one title page gave the full name, the full name was used. Moreover, a first forename was always spelled out if the surname was a common one. Under AACR 2 the most commonly used form of name is always chosen regardless of fullness. If it is necessary to distinguish between different authors with the same surnames and initials, the spelled out forms are added in parentheses, but the names with initials would still file before the full names. For example:

Adams, J. A. (James Albert)
Adams, J. A. (James Allen)
Adams, J. A. (Joyce Amanda)
Adams, James Edgar
Adams, Jill

Another change specifies that if a person using pseudonyms is not predominantly known by one name, each work is entered under the name appearing in it. This rule was given as an alternative in AACR 1 and has been widely followed by public libraries but will be a major change for libraries that have attempted to keep all of the works of each author together under one form of name.

The basic rule for headings for corporate bodies is the same except that it no longer provides for any entries under the names of places where institutions are located. The punctuation used in some headings is different. For example, compare the following headings for conferences.

AACR 1: International Geological Conference, 15th, Pretoria, etc., 1929

AACR 2: Louisiana Cancer Conference (2nd : 1958 : New Orleans)

Uniform titles are substituted for form subheadings by AACR 2 as shown below.

ACCR 1	*AACR 2*
Illinois. Laws, statutes, etc.	Illinois ₁Laws, etc.₁
U. S. Treaties, etc.	United States ₁Treaties, etc.₁
Catholic Church, Liturgy and ritual.	Catholic Church ₁Liturgy of the hours (U.S.)₁

The most significant change between AACR 1 and AACR 2 in regard to added entries is the AACR 2 rule stating that added entries should be made for almost all titles. The chief exceptions occur when a title is the same as the main entry and when, if the library has a dictionary catalog, the title is identical with a subject heading.

Chapter 9: Descriptive Cataloging: From Simple to Complex

The recommendations for bibliographic description contained in AACR 2 are based on International Standard Bibliographic Description (ISBD), which was also used as a basis for the revised Chapter 6 of AACR 1 that was issued in 1974. There are fewer differences between AACR 2 and the revised Chapter 6 than there were between the revised Chapter 6 and AACR 1 as originally published in 1967.

The rules for bibliographic description are presented in a different manner in AACR 2 than in AACR 1. Instead of giving a method for describing books and then covering the variations required for cataloging serials, audiovisual materials, and other nonbook materials, AACR 2 first presents a general form of bibliographic description meant to cover all types of library materials and then in the following chapters covers the variations needed when cataloging particular kinds of media, including books.

Because the general rules of AACR 2 for bibliographic description are meant to cover all types of library materials, the words used sometimes differ from those used in the book-oriented rules of AACR 1. Some examples are:

AACR 1	AACR 2
title page	chief source of information
subtitle	other title information
author statement	statement of responsibility
imprint	publication, distribution, etc., area
collation	physical description area

AACR 2 recognizes that different library catalogs serve

different needs by listing three levels of description. The
first level, which is the briefest, includes:

> title
> statement of responsibility if different from main entry head-
> ing
> edition
> for serials and cartographic materials only: material (or type
> of publication) specific details
> publisher, date of publication, etc.
> extent of item
> notes
> standard number

Apparently, the place of publication and height in centimeters would not be included in the first level of description, but the discussion of levels of description is not suffi-
ciently detailed to enable one to say that the first level
provides a standard code of simplified cataloging.

Cataloging based on AACR 2 will closely resemble that
based on the 1974 revised Chapter 6 of AACR 1. One small
but easily noticed difference is that "2nd ed." and "3rd ed."
replace "2d ed." and "3d ed."

Chapter 16: Audiovisual Materials: Cataloging.

AACR 2 moves in the direction of equal treatment for all
library materials. The use of a general material designation
(GMD), previously called a medium designator, is made
optional. Separate lists of designations are given for British
and North American use. The lists include terms for all
types of materials, including "manuscript," "microform,"
and "text."

The general material designation is not capitalized; there
is no period after the title. Example:

Changing Africa [kit]

Rules for choice of main and added entries for audiovisual
materials are not given separately in AACR 2; the rules
given in Chapter 21 apply to all materials. An exception is

that there are specific rules given for sound recordings. In the past, sound recordings containing the works of two or more composers were entered under title; they are now entered under the heading for the person or body (such as a musical group) represented as the principal performer.

Rules for the description of the types of materials included in Chapter 16 of this book (sound recordings, motion pictures, filmstrips, videorecordings, slides, and transparencies) are divided among three AACR 2 chapters as follows:

Chapter 6   Sound Recordings
Chapter 7   Motion Pictures and Videorecordings
Chapter 8   Graphic Materials

Chapter 8 covers art prints, charts, photographs, and other two-dimensional materials as well as filmstrips, slides, and transparencies. A separate chapter covers three-dimensional artifacts and realia.

Using AACR 2 to catalog a particular audiovisual item such as a filmstrip would not be simple. The chapter on graphic materials is not divided by type of material, so it would be necessary to study the entire chapter picking out the parts related to filmstrips. It would also be necessary to know the general rules of description from Chapter 1 and the rules for choice of access points given in Chapter 21 since these rules apply to all media. Moreover, there are no examples showing the completed cataloging of filmstrips as there were in the revised Chapter 12 of AACR 1. Until explanations and illustrations of the new rules have been published it will not be easy to use them for cataloging audiovisual media.

Chapter 17: Serials: A Challenge to Libraries.

AACR 2 does not contain a separate chapter discussing choice of main and added entries for serials. As with audiovisual materials, the general rules for choice of access points apply. Since one of the principal questions that arise concerning choice of entry for serials is whether certain serials should be entered under the name of a corporate body or under title, the general rules for entry under corporate body are particularly relevant to serials. As with books, under AACR 2 there will be fewer instances in which serials will be entered under the names of corporate bodies.

A separate chapter is devoted to the description of serial publications. It covers the description of serial publications in all media—not just printed serials. A major change from AACR 1 is that the description of a serial will now be based upon the first issue rather than the latest volume. However, as with AACR 1, if the title changes, each title is cataloged as a separate item. Unlike AACR 1, AACR 2 does not suggest the omission of subtitles.

Chapter 18: The Vertical File and Other Special Collections.

AACR 2 makes a major change in the rule for describing microforms. Microform reproductions are to be described in terms of their present format, not the original publication. The place, publisher, and date of publication of the reproduction are given in the publication, distribution, etc., area; and a description such as "1 microfilm reel; 16 mm." is given in the physical description area. Notes relating to the original are given following the notes relating to the microform.

Glossary

AACR *Anglo-American Cataloging Rules,* a widely accepted set of rules for describing and establishing name headings for books and other library materials. The second edition (AACR 2) was published in 1978.

Accession number A number assigned to each book or other acquired item in order of its receipt by the library.

Acquisitions The area of technical services involved with the acquiring of books, periodicals and other materials by purchase, exchange, or gift.

Added entry Any entry in the catalog other than the main entry. Sometimes used to refer only to additional entries other than those for subjects. Also called a secondary entry.

Analytic A separate entry for one part of a work or one item in a set for which a comprehensive, or main, entry has already been made for the larger unit. Analytics may be made for authors, titles, or subjects, or the individual parts may receive full cataloging. Also called analytical entry.

Approval plan An agreement between a library and a vendor that all books of a publisher or all volumes fitting certain criteria will automatically be sent with the library having the option of returning uneeded volumes.

Archives The organized body of records pertaining to an organization, institution, or governmental unit.

Audiovisuals Materials that present information in audible and/or visible form. (In this book discussion of audiovisuals is limited to types of materials that require equipment for use.)

Author The person or corporate body chiefly responsible for the intellectual or artistic content of a work. (AACR 2 does not include corporate bodies in its definition.)

Author number The symbol used to distinguish a book from all other books with the same classification number. It usually consists of the first initial of the author's last name plus one or more numbers. Sometimes called a book number. A Cutter number is one type of author number.

Authority file A record of the correct headings to be used for names, subjects, or series. Its purpose is to provide consistency.

Blanket order An agreement to purchase one or more copies of all books issued by a publisher.

Body of the entry The part of the catalog entry that begins with the title and ends with the date of publication.

Book number *See* Author number.

CIP Cataloging in Publication. A partial cataloging record that appears on the reverse side of the title page in many books.

Call number A location symbol, usually a combination of letters and numbers, which indicates where a particular book is shelved. It includes both the classification number and the author number.

Catalog A systematic record of the materials in a library or group of libraries.

Cataloging The process by which books and other library materials are made accessible to intended users. It includes the operations concerned with maintaining a library catalog and a useful shelf arrangement of materials.

Cataloging copy The cataloging information for a book or other item as it appears in sources such as Cataloging in Publication, the *National Union Catalog*, data bases, or printed cards. When one library uses the cataloging prepared by another library, it is called cataloging with copy.

Claim A follow-up on an order or subscription to determine why a missing item has not arrived.

Classification number The number assigned to a book or other item to show its subject.

Collation That part of a catalog entry that describes the work by indicating paging, illustrations, size, and other elements of physical description.

COM Acronym for computer output microfilm COM catalogs for libraries may be either on microfiche or microfilm.

Copyright The exclusive right granted by a government to publish a work for a specified number of years.

Corporate body An organization or a group of people identified by a particular name and acting as a unit. Corporate bodies include associations, conferences, societies, institutions, business firms, religious bodies, and government agencies.

Cutter number A number from the Cutter or Cutter-Sanborn tables used as an author number.

Desuperimposition The reversal of a policy of superimposition. *See* Superimposition.

Dictionary catalog A catalog in which all entries (author, title, subject, series, etc.) are arranged in one alphabet.

Divided catalog A catalog separated into two or more parts. For example, author and title entries may be in one part and subject entries in another part.

Edition One of the successive forms in which a published work is issued. A new edition usually contains additions or changes.

Entry A record of a book or other item in a library catalog.

Heading The word, name, or phrase at the top of a catalog entry that provides the filing element, or access point, for the entry.

ISBD International Standard Bibliographic Description, an internationally accepted system for the recording of descriptive information.

ISBN International Standard Book Number, a distinctive and unique number assigned to a book. It is hoped that eventually the system will cover all of the publishers in the world.

ISSN International Standard Serial Number, a distinctive and unique number assigned to a serial.

Imprint The name of a publisher printed on the title page of a book, often with the address and date of publication.

In print Currently available from the publisher.

Indention Distance from the left-hand side of the catalog card at which typing or printing begins.

Jobber A wholesaler who stocks or supplies the books of many publishers for resale to bookstores and libraries.

LC The Library of Congress, the largest library in the United States.

Main entry A full catalog entry, usually the author entry, which gives complete information about a work, including a record of other entries made. The principal access point for an item that appears in several places in a catalog.

Manuscript A handwritten or typewritten work.

MARC Machine Readable Cataloging, a program of the Library of Congress in which machine-readable cataloging is distributed in LC format.

Media Plural of medium. Printed and audiovisual forms of communication, such as books, periodicals, films, records, and transparencies. When used to refer to library materials, the term may or may not include books.

OCLC, Inc. The nation's largest on-line bibliographic data base. It was founded as the Ohio College Library Center but is now an incorporated, nationwide, organization.

Open entry A catalog entry that provides for the addition of information as further volumes of a serial or set are received.

Out of print No longer available from the publisher.

Pamphlet A short paperbound printed work that is of interest chiefly for its subject content and is not likely to be requested by author or title.

Periodical A publication issued in successive parts at stated or regular intervals and intended to be continued indefinitely. Usually it has a distinctive title, each issue contains articles by different contributors, and there are two or more issues per year. Newspapers and society proceedings are generally not considered periodicals, but usage of the term varies from library to library. *See also* Serial.

Pseudonym A name used by an author to conceal his or her identity.

Recto The right-hand page of a book. *See also* Verso.

Secondary entry *See* Added entry.

Serial An inclusive term for publications issued in successive parts at regular or irregular intervals and intended to be continued indefinitely. Includes periodicals, newsletters, proceedings, reports, memoirs, annuals, and numbered series.

Shelf list A record of the works in a library arranged in the order in which they are arranged on the shelves.

Standing order An order for all works in a series, all volumes of a set, or all editions of a work.

Superimposition The policy of not revising headings already in a catalog in spite of rule changes. Refers in particular to the policy of the Library of Congress in regard to the 1967 *Anglo-American Cataloging Rules*.

Technical services. All library operations concerned with acquiring and organizing materials for future use.

Terminal set A work of two or more volumes that is or will someday be complete.

Thesaurus An authority of selected words or concepts that shows their relationship to each other. It is usually restricted to a more limited field of knowledge than a words authority file or subject heading list.

Title page A page near the beginning of a book containing the title, and usually the author or editor's name, and imprint.

Tracing The listing on a catalog entry of other entries made for the work.

Trade book A book considered to be of wide reader appeal, such as a novel or a book on a subject of general interest.

Uniform title The title chosen for cataloging purposes when a work has appeared under various titles.

Unit card A basic catalog card in the form of the main entry. Appropriate headings are typed at the top of the cards for the other entries.

Vanity press A publishing firm that requires authors to subsidize the publication of their books. Also called a subsidy press.

Verso The left-hand page of a book. The verso of the title page is its reverse side. *See also* Recto.

Vertical file A file in which folders containing pamphlets, pictures, clippings, and other similar materials are kept.

Weeding The process of removing books no longer needed from a library collection.

Bibliography

Basic bibliographical and cataloging tools are not included in this bibliography; references to them are listed in the index.

Akers, Susan Grey. *Akers' Simple Library Cataloging*. 6th ed. Completely revised and rewritten by Arthur Curley and Jana Varlejs. Metuchen, NJ, Scarecrow Press, 1977. Covers all aspects of cataloging with emphasis on the problems of small libraries. Includes many examples and illustrations.

Applebaum, Edmond L., ed. *Reader in Technical Services*. Washington, DC, NCR Microcard Editions, 1973. The material in this collection covers a wide variety of subjects such as on-approval order plans, book catalogs, subject headings, and MARC. Clara D. Brown's "57 Ways of Keeping a Serials Librarian Happy" is a very entertaining account of the difficulties of working with serials.

Bernhard, Genore H. *How to Organize and Operate a Small Library*. Rev. ed. Fort Atkinson, WI, Highsmith Co., 1975. A short and simple guide for the beginner.

Bidlack, Russell E. *Typewritten Catalog Cards: A Manual of Procedure and Form with 300 Sample Cards*. 2d ed. Revised and expanded by Constance Rinehart. Ann Arbor, MI, Campus Publishers, 1970.

Illustrates the form in which the information prescribed by the Anglo-American Cataloging Rules (1967) should be recorded on catalog cards. Because of the many types of examples included it would be useful even in a library that does not follow these rules.

Bloomberg, Marty, and Evans, G. Edward. *Introduction to Technical Services for Library Technicians*. 3d ed. Littleton, CO, Libraries Unlimited, 1976.
One of the few books covering all aspects of technical services work.

Broadus, Robert N. *Selecting Materials for Libraries*. New York, H. W. Wilson Co., 1973.
Covers general selection principles, selection of various types of print and nonprint materials, and selection by subject field.

Dowell, Arlene Taylor. *Cataloging with Copy: A Decision-Makers Handbook*. Littleton, CO, Libraries Unlimited, 1976.
Discusses the various types of problems encountered in integrating cataloging from outside sources into a local catalog. Of particular interest to libraries that use Library of Congress cataloging copy.

Dunkin, Paul S. *Cataloging U.S.A.* Chicago, American Library Association, 1969.
The purpose of this book is not to list facts and recommend procedures; instead it deals almost entirely with theory and principles. As the author states, it is a why-do-it book rather than a how-to-do-it book.

Ford, Stephen. *The Acquisition of Library Materials*. Rev. ed. Chicago, American Library Association, 1978.
Covers all areas of acquisition work. Stresses topics that are of concern to libraries of all sizes.

Grannis, Chandler B., ed. *What Happens in Book Publishing*. New York, Columbia University Press, 1967.
Specialists in the various departments of publishing contribute articles which taken together provide a well-rounded picture of American publishing.

Hicks, Warren B., and Tillin, Alma M. *Developing Multimedia Libraries*. New York, R. R. Bowker Co., 1970.
Contains practical advice on acquiring, cataloging, and physical processing of audiovisual materials. Well-illustrated. Some of the cataloging information is now out of date.

Institute on the Use of the Library of Congress Classification, New York, 1966. *The Use of the Library of Congress Classification: Proceedings*. Ed. by Richard H. Schimmelpfeng and C. Donald Cook. Chicago, American Library Association, 1968.
Reviews the development, structure, and use of the Library of Congress Classification and discusses special problems with particular classes.

Katz, Bill, and Gellatly, Peter. *Guide to Magazine and Serial Agents*. New York, R. R. Bowker Co., 1975.
The scope of this book is broader than suggested by the title. It includes much useful background information on serials and their management as well as information on agents and their services.

Miller, Shirley. *The Vertical File and Its Satellites: A Handbook of Acquisition, Processing, and Organization*. Littleton, CO, Libraries Unlimited, 1971.
A useful guide to the acquisition and organization of pamphlets, clippings, vocational material, local history, maps, pictorial material, and other special collections.

Osborn, Andrew D. *Serial Publications: Their Place and Treatment in Libraries*. 2d ed. Chicago, American Library Association, 1973.
An authoritative work of particular interest to libraries with large serial collections.

"Perspectives on Publishing," *Annals of the American Academy of Political and Social Science*. Vol. 421, Sept. 1975.
Includes articles on many aspects of publishing, such as textbook publishing, the role of editors, publishing history, and independent publishing. The emphasis of the volume is on scholarly publishing.

Piercy, Esther J. *Commonsense Cataloging: A Manual for the Organization of Books and Other Materials in School and Small Public Libraries*. 2d ed. Revised by Marian Sanner. New York, H. W. Wilson Co., 1974.
A practical manual for the beginning cataloger, trained or untrained.

Salmon, Stephen R. *Library Automation Systems*. New York, Marcel Dekker, 1975.
Discusses the background, problems, and prospects of library automation systems and describes actual operating systems for acquisitions, cataloging, serials, and circulation.

Tillin, Alma M., and Quinly, William J. *Standards for Cataloging Nonprint Materials*. 4th ed. Washington, DC, Association for Educational Communications and Technology, 1976.
Gives detailed rules for cataloging all types of audiovisual materials. Includes many sample cards.

Weihs, Jean Riddle; Lewis, Shirley; and MacDonald, Janet. *Nonbook Materials: The Organization of Integrated Collections*. Ottawa, Canadian Library Association, 1973. Gives general rules and directions for various types of media.

Wynar, Bohdan S. *Introduction to Cataloging and Classification*. 5th ed. Littleton, CO, Libraries Unlimited, 1976. Techniques of cataloging as practiced in American libraries and the theories underlying them are presented in this text designed for beginning cataloging courses.

MAGAZINE ARTICLES CITED IN THE TEXT

Dickinson, Elizabeth. "Of Catalogs, Computers, and Communication." *Wilson Library Bulletin*, Vol. 50, no. 6 (Feb. 1976), p. 463–470.

Malinconico, S. Michael. "The Library Catalog in a Computerized Environment." *Wilson Library Bulletin*, Vol. 51, no. 1 (Sept. 1976) p. 53–64.

Massonneau, Suzanne. "Bibliographic Control and Cataloging Cost Control: Interlocking Problems." *Library Journal*, Vol. 98, no. 12 (June 15, 1973), p. 1890–1893.

Ohmes, Frances, and Jones, J. F. "The Other Half of Cataloging." *Library Resources and Technical Services*, Vol. 17, no. 3 (Summer 1973), p. 320–329.

Rather, John C. "Filing Arrangement in the Library of Congress Catalogs." *Library Resources and Technical Services*, Vol. 16, no. 2 (Spring 1972), p. 240–261.

Wehmeyer, Lillian M. "Cataloging the School Media Center as a Specialized Collection." *Library Resources and Technical Services*, Vol. 20, no. 4 (Fall 1976), p. 315–325.

Index